# Social Evolutionism

# Studies in Social Discontinuity

*General Editor Charles Tilly, The New School for Social Research*

**Studies in Social Discontinuity** began in 1972 under the imprint of Academic Press. In its first 15 years, 53 titles were published in the series, including important volumes in the areas of historical sociology, political economy, and social history.

Revived in 1989 by Basil Blackwell, the series will continue to include volumes emphasizing social changes and non-Western historical experience as well as translations of major works.

Published:

**The Perilous Frontier**
Nomadic Empires and China
*Thomas J. Barfield*

**Regents and Rebels**
The Revolutionary World of an Eighteenth-Century Dutch City
*Wayne Ph. te Brake*

**Nascent Proletarians**
Class Formation in Post-Revolutionary France
*Michael P. Hanagan*

**Social Evolutionism**
A Critical History
*Stephen K. Sanderson*

**Coercion, Capital, and European States**
AD 990–1990
*Charles Tilly*

In preparation:

**Modern French Anti-Semitism**
A Political History
*Pierre Birnbaum*

**Coffee, Contention, and Change**
in the Making of Modern Brazil
*Mauricio Font*

**Rites of Revolt**
The War of the Demoiselles in Ariège, France (1829–1831)
*Peter Sahlins*

# Social Evolutionism

*A Critical History*

STEPHEN K. SANDERSON

Basil Blackwell

First published 1990

Basil Blackwell, Inc.
3 Cambridge Center
Cambridge, Massachusetts 02142, USA

Basil Blackwell Ltd
108 Cowley Road, Oxford, OX4 1JF, UK

*British Library Cataloguing in Publication Data*

A CIP catalogue record for this book is available
from the British Library.

*Library of Congress Cataloging in Publication Data*

Sanderson, Stephen K.
  Social evolutionism: a critical history/Stephen K. Sanderson.
    p. cm. — (Studies in social discontinuity)
  Includes bibliographical references.
  ISBN 1–55786–073–4
    1. Social evolution.  I. Title.  II. Series: Studies in social discontinuity (Basil Blackwell Publishers)
  GN360.S25  1990
  303.4—dc20                                        89–18385
                                                         CIP

Typeset in 10.5 on 12pt Ehrhardt
by Hope Services (Abingdon) Ltd.
Printed in Great Britain
by T. J. Press Ltd, Padstow, Cornwall

To my mother, Marjorie King Sanderson,
and to the memory of my father,
W. E. ("Wally") Sanderson

# Contents

# Editor's Preface

THIS SERIES

*Studies in Social Discontinuity* present historically grounded analyses of important social transformations, ruptures, conflicts, and contradictions. Although we of Basil Blackwell interpret that mission broadly, leave room for many points of view and absolve authors of any responsibility for propaganda on behalf of our intellectual program, the series as a whole demonstrates the relevance of well-crafted historical work for the understanding of contemporary social structures and processes. Books in the series pursue one or more of four varieties of historical analysis: (1) using evidence from past times and places systematically to identify regularities in processes and structures that transcend those particular times and places; (2) reconstructing critical episodes in the past for the light they shed on important eras, peoples, or social phenomena; (3) tracing the origins or previous phases of significant social processes that continue into our own time; (4) examining the ways that social action at a given point in time lays down residues that limit the possibilities of subsequent social action.

The fourth theme is at once the least familiar and the most general. Social analysts have trouble seeing that history matters precisely because social interaction takes place in well-defined times and places, and occurs within constraints offered by those times and places, producing social relations and artifacts that are themselves located in space–time and whose existence and distribution constrain subsequent social interaction. The construction of a city in a given place and time affects urban growth in adjacent areas and subsequent times. Where and when industrialization occurs affects how it occurs. Initial visions of victory announce a war's likely outcomes. A person's successive migrations have cumulative effects on his or her subsequent mobility through such simple matters as the presence or absence of information about new opportunities in different places and the presence or absence of social ties to possible destinations. A population's previous experience with wars, Baby Booms, and migrations haunts it in the form of bulging or empty cohorts and unequal numbers of the sexes. All these are profoundly historical matters, even when they occur in the present; time and place are of their essence. They form the essential subject matter of *Studies in Social Discontinuity*.

Edward Shorter, Stanley Holwitz, and I plotted the Studies in Social Discontinuity in 1970–1; our first book, William Christian's *Person and God in a Spanish Valley*, appeared in 1972. Over the years, Academic Press published more than 50 titles in the series. But during the early 1980s publication slowed, and then ceased. In 1988, happily Basil Blackwell agreed to revive the Studies under my editorship. Stephen Sanderson's *Social Evolutionism*, a work of criticism and synthesis, now joins the historical monographs with which the renewed series began.

### THIS BOOK

In the first course on computing I ever took, many years ago, the instructor began by showing us how a mechanical sorter reads the holes on a standard punched card. Step by step he explained the electronic computer's equivalent of that operation, taught us how to count and calculate in a binary system, helped us write instructions in machine language, and thus led us small step by small step to FORTRAN programming. At the time, the whole approach often seemed obsessive, redundant, and slow. But in later years I often cheered that instructor for having communicated the logic, if not the precise mechanics, of what went on when I wrote a computer program. Stephen Sanderson recalls that heroic instructor: patient, systematic, determined, lucid. He is not, however, slow.

In his recent *Macrosociology*, Sanderson took an evolutionary approach to sociological analysis as a whole. In his new book, he explicates and criticizes the varied evolutionary accounts of social change major thinkers of the last century and half – and not just sociologists – have proposed. Herbert Spencer, Karl Marx, Charles Darwin, V. Gordon Childe, Talcott Parsons, Marvin Harris, and many other well-known authors move across Sanderson's screen as he points out their peculiarities and assesses their strengths. A gifted expositor, Sanderson takes care to tell us what his authors said before he criticizes them. No dummies or caricatures for him! Having explicated, however, Sanderson does not hesitate to state his opinion. No reader of his book will miss the fact that he greatly prefers Marvin Harris's evolutionary ideas to those of Talcott Parsons, or the features of the two analyses that motivate his preference.

Sanderson makes clear that a disparate crowd of thinkers have paraded under the evolutionary banner. Instead of attempting to catalog and chronicle all of them, he paces out the space in which they have marched, identifies the various corners of that space, then locates exemplary authors in the appropriate corners. He builds especially on Stephen Toulmin's distinction between "evolutionary" and "evolutionist" models – the first treating changes as responses to the challenges of successive historical situations, the second treating them as outcomes of a master pattern in, or above, history. His critique of Parsons's evolutionist arguments constitutes one of the book's highlights. It also illustrates Sanderson's resolute rejection of functionalism, that frequent crutch of evolutionary analysis.

Sanderson provides more than explication and critique. He turns from social-scientific treatments of evolution to a thoughtful exploration of what evolutionary biology (as it actually exists) can contribute to social analysis, and then returns to answer standard grounds for rejecting evolutionary thinking in all its guises. He shows that the standard objections apply only to some sorts of evolutionary models, and leave others virtually untouched. Sanderson commends those unscathed others to the attention of everyone who cares about the study of long-term, large-scale social change.

CHARLES TILLY

# Preface

My serious interest in evolutionary theories in the social sciences was first kindled when I read, in late 1976, Marvin Harris's *The Rise of Anthropological Theory* (1968). I had never paid any particular attention to such theories before that, except for the kind of evolutionary model developed by Gerhard Lenski in *Power and Privilege* (1966) and *Human Societies* (1970). I was well aware that evolutionary theories had been severely criticized, but Lenski's work impressed me as an exemplary way of doing sociology. I was sufficiently impressed with it to contemplate using *Human Societies* as a textbook for one of my courses. When I read Harris's magisterial work, the affinities between his materialist evolutionary approach and Lenski's brand of evolutionism struck me. As a result, I began to study *Human Societies* more thoroughly and eventually started teaching from it.

About the same time (early 1977) the philosopher Maurice Mandelbaum of Johns Hopkins University invited me to study with him in a summer postdoctoral seminar. During that seminar I intensively pursued what I was then calling "evolutionary theory," which I thought was a relatively homogeneous and coherent approach to the study of social life. My work in the seminar concentrated mainly on the work of those anthropological evolutionists who, since the 1930s, had been insisting on the legitimacy and importance of an evolutionary approach: Gordon Childe, Leslie White, Julian Steward, Marshall Sahlins, Elman Service, Marvin Harris, Morton Fried, Robert Carneiro, Gerhard Lenski, and a few others. I paid no real attention to the classical evolutionists, to any contemporary Marxist evolutionists, or to the evolutionary approach developed by Talcott Parsons and others who followed his version of functionalism. For me, evolutionism was basically coterminous with the ideas promoted by the above-named thinkers.

Fortunately, I was soon to disabuse myself of this very naive notion. As I thought more about these issues after the seminar had ended, I began to recognize that evolutionism was a global term used to describe a vast array of theories that differed markedly. Indeed, it became obvious that some of these theories had almost nothing in common except for a commitment to identifying and explaining sequences of directional social change. And thus the idea of writing this book was born. Someone needed, I thought, to write a book surveying the variety of evolutionary theories in the social sciences and showing in detail that the word "evolutionism" was a vague omnibus term that meant very little unless it were specified much further.

My interest in writing such a book was also sparked by reading, during Mandelbaum's seminar, his *History, Man, and Reason* (1971). In this book Mandelbaum attacked evolutionary theories by arguing that they were based upon an illegitimate notion he termed a *directional law*: a law positing that sequences of historical change represented the unfolding of latent potentialities toward some endstate. Societies evolved because it was somehow inherent in their nature to do so, and the stages through which they evolved were essential to their reaching the goal for which they were striving. Mandelbaum thought that whatever directional sequences might be identified in history had to be explained in terms of *functional laws*, or laws relating specific variables at specific times and in specific places.

Mandelbaum concentrated his attack on the classical evolutionists of the second half of the nineteenth century, but it was obvious that he thought modern evolutionary theories suffered from the same defect. At the time I thought that he may well have been right for the classical evolutionists, but it seemed to me that he was quite wrong for many modern evolutionists. And thus I thought I had identified one of the major themes of the book: in the history of social evolutionism there had been a general abandonment of directional-law conceptions of social evolution and a shift toward the kinds of explanatory models of evolutionary change that Mandelbaum thought were epistemologically unobjectionable.

I would have started this book right away, but I had slightly earlier conceived the idea of writing an undergraduate sociology textbook that would be built along the lines of a materialist evolutionary approach. This textbook would draw extensively on the ideas of Lenski and Harris, but would modify them in certain ways and liberally throw in a number of related notions. That book was finally completed and published as *Macrosociology: An Introduction to Human Societies* in 1988. I am somewhat embarrassed to say that it took so long, but the reason is that my ideas underwent some major changes as I was writing. As I wrote I was gradually moving increasingly away from Lenski's brand of evolutionism without quite realizing it, and by the time a first draft was done I realized that the later chapters fit awkwardly with the early ones. The book was finished only after a substantial period of reconceptualization. It represents, in the considerably simplified form that textbooks require, what I think the broad outlines of an adequate evolutionary theory look like. It is a theory very different from Lenski's in many important respects. It looks much more like Harris's evolutionary model, but with the incorporation of many ideas from certain Marxian and Weberian versions of historical sociology.

Once this textbook was finished I began to write the present book, which might be regarded as a higher-level theoretical companion to the text. In the interim of many years since I first conceived this book, I have learned much more about all sorts of evolutionary theories, and my thinking has changed on some issues. For example, it is now clear to me that there are contemporary versions of evolutionary theory that are firmly rooted in a directional-law mode of explanation. In addition, I now recognize that the concept of adaptation is more problematic than I originally thought and thus requires a full-scale discussion of its uses and potential abuses. I have also become aware of the need to bring into focus the relation between theories of social evolution and theorizing in evolutionary biology.

My overall conception of the book, though, is essentially the same. Thus the book before you will survey the broad range of evolutionary theories in the social sciences, compare and contrast them to each other, and critically examine their logical and epistemological foundations. I originally intended that it would also set forth and defend a particular evolutionary model of societal change. But it is now apparent that this is a task much too large to be relegated to a chapter or two at the end. I am hopeful of eventually completing this task, but that will require another volume.

This book has benefitted from the critical commentary and advice of a number of people. Michael Armer, Christopher Chase-Dunn, John Hofley, Pierre van den Berghe, and Erik Olin Wright read the introduction and commented on the worthwhileness of the project as a whole. A critical reaction to one or more chapters was provided by Andrew Altman (chapter 4), Randall Breitwisch (chapter 8), Randall Collins (chapters 1 and 7), Robert Graber (chapters 2 and 7), and Michael Ruse (chapter 8). I am especially grateful for the comments of Breitwisch and Ruse on chapter 8 because, as an evolutionary biologist and a philosopher of evolutionary biology respectively, they have reassured me that I have not made a complete mess of my incursions into that field. Regarding that same chapter, I benefitted from being reminded by Steven Gaulin of the importance of George Williams's *Adaptation and Natural Selection* (1966) for many of the issues being discussed. It is essential to add that, had it not been for Pierre van den Berghe's reaction to the proposed project, there would have been no such chapter. I am confident that this has improved the manuscript significantly, even though I know that van den Berghe will strongly disagree with some of the conclusions reached in the chapter.

Charles Tilly and Robert Carneiro read the entire manuscript and offered numerous suggestions that I am certain have helped me produce a better book. I really owe a very special debt of gratitude to Carneiro for the enormous effort he put into his critical reading. He took a great deal of time out from his own work to produce a line-by-line analysis that resulted in literally hundreds of specific comments. He has saved me from some errors and dubious interpretations and made a variety of suggestions that I have found helpful. I feel compelled to point out that, although Bob and I agree on a great deal, he has some substantial objections to several of my conclusions. And obviously neither he, nor any of the above-named persons, bears any responsibility for the failings of this book. I alone am responsible, especially since I have been too stubborn to take a lot of the advice I was given.

I am extremely pleased that Peter Dougherty and Sean Magee agreed to have this book published by Basil Blackwell, and I am grateful to Romesh Vaitilingam of Blackwell for seeing it through to publication.

I thank the National Endowment for the Humanities for providing me with a summer seminar at Johns Hopkins University in 1977 that led to the initial conceptualization of this book. I also thank the Institute of Social Studies in The Hague, The Netherlands, with which I was associated as a visiting lecturer during the first four months of 1988. This gave me an opportunity to present a series of lectures based on initial drafts of several chapters of the book, as well as to have time to work on other chapters. This Dutch interlude was made possible by a sabbatical leave granted by my own university, Indiana University of Pennsylvania, for which I am appreciative.

Finally, I am grateful to my wife, Ruth, for her usual support of my intellectual endeavors, and to my children, Derek and Sarah, for providing delightful diversions from the tensions that inevitably accompany book-length projects.

*Stephen K. Sanderson*
*Indiana, Pennsylvania*

# 1

# The Nature of Social Evolutionism

This is a book about evolutionary theories in the social sciences over the past century and a half: their history, their diversity, their underlying intellectual assumptions, and their adequacy as modes of explaining social life. Social scientists have long had a love–hate relationship with these sorts of theories. The disciplines of sociology and anthropology were virtually born evolutionary, for most of the leading founders of these fields embraced evolutionism of one type or another, some of them strongly so. The person who is usually credited with being the "father" of sociology, Auguste Comte, had a thoroughly evolutionary conception of the development of modern industrial society, one that was based on a view of the expansion of the powers of the human mind. Emile Durkheim carried on some of Comte's basic evolutionary ideas. Although he did so in modified form, and although his evolutionary ideas are generally regarded as less significant than many of his other notions, he had an evolutionary perspective nonetheless. Even markedly different thinkers like Karl Marx and Herbert Spencer were very much evolutionists. Marx's theory of history makes no real sense except as a type of evolutionism, and Spencer was so much an evolutionist that he attempted to formulate a law of evolutionary change that applied not only to societies but to the totality of phenomena in the universe. Although the evolutionary doctrines of Marx and Spencer were fundamentally different, both rested on similar intellectual assumptions implicit in nineteenth-century thought. To a large extent, these assumptions, which were actually heritages of the Enlightenment, were shared as well by both Comte and Durkheim.

In anthropology, the story is much the same. The individual whom anthropologists generally regard as the "father" of their discipline, Edward Burnett Tylor, was famous for his evolutionary outlook. Tylor's American contemporary, Lewis Henry Morgan, was even more thoroughly imbued with evolutionism. His greatest work was a massive attempt to trace the major outlines of cultural evolution from simplest prehistoric times to the present. But Morgan and Tylor were only the most prominent of a range of evolutionary thinkers in the second half of the nineteenth century whom modern anthropologists regard as their intellectual ancestors.

The heyday of evolutionism was the second half of the nineteenth century, for it was then that the doctrines of Morgan, Tylor, Spencer, Marx, and others were being produced. This "golden age" of evolutionary social science came rather suddenly to an end shortly after the turn of the century, however, and the first few decades of the twentieth century represented a sort of "dark age" for evolutionism. During this time evolutionism was severely criticized and came to be regarded as an outmoded approach that self-respecting scholars should no longer take seriously. Evolutionary theories did not die out completely, but they were seldom seen, and even the word "evolution" came to be uttered at serious risk to one's intellectual reputation. Antievolutionism, rather than evolutionism, was the watchword of the day.

Yet the reign of antievolutionism was itself to last no longer than had the evolutionism that preceded it. By the 1930s some scholars were beginning to take evolutionism seriously again, and by the 1940s an "evolutionary revival" was well under way. By the 1960s an evolutionary perspective was advocated by many anthropologists. The anthropology of the 1960s and 1970s was not dominated by evolutionism as was the anthropology of a century earlier, but a whole new generation of evolutionary thinkers built their formulations on the new foundations that had been established in the 1940s and 1950s. This revival of evolutionism was more an anthropological than a sociological phenomenon, but sociologists were significantly involved nevertheless. Sociology's best-known theorist, Talcott Parsons, extended his own thinking along distinctly evolutionary lines, and the sociologist Gerhard Lenski was developing a different sort of evolutionary theory at almost exactly the same time.

It turns out, though, that contemporary social science has its own antievolutionists. In the late 1960s Robert Nisbet published a major attack against evolutionary theories of all types, both classical and contemporary. That Nisbet's book was very well received indicated that many sociologists were still skeptical about evolutionary interpretations, or that the new wave of sociological interest in evolutionism had already begun to turn sour. About the same time Maurice Mandelbaum, a philosopher well acquainted with the social sciences, published a critique of evolutionary theories that replicated many of Nisbet's objections. The latest all-out attack on social evolutionism has been made by the British sociologist Anthony Giddens, who declares that evolutionary theories are so multiply deficient that social theory must rid itself of them entirely. Giddens makes some of the same criticisms that preoccupied Nisbet and Mandelbaum, but he has added quite a few others as well.

Unfortunately, what has been obscured in this thumbnail sketch of the fate of evolutionary theories in the history of social science is an extremely important fact: the terms "evolutionary theory" or "evolutionism" are extraordinarily general ones for characterizing a range of ideas that do share certain basic assumptions but that otherwise are often radically different. The employment of such terms without further specification as to the particular type of evolutionary theory that is intended results in extremely misleading and, quite frequently, useless talk. Along these lines the philosopher Stephen Toulmin has suggested that social scientists have created enormous confusion for themselves by persistently failing to distinguish between *evolutionist* and *evolutionary* formulations. Toulmin argues that this conflation was especially characteristic of the nineteenth century, but that these separate notions have not been completely disentangled even in contemporary social science. For Toulmin, evolutionist formulations are those that account for long-term societal changes "in some mysterious way, as the 'conclusions' of a Cosmic Argument, which unfolds 'logical implications' operative throughout the whole History of Society" (Toulmin, 1972:329). Evolutionary formulations, on the other hand, are those that, like Darwin's account of biological evolution, attempt to explain changes as responses to the particular requirements imbedded in specific-historical situations.

This conflation of evolutionist and evolutionary theories is perhaps the most serious problem currently facing intelligent critical discussion of theories of social evolution. But other serious difficulties arise as well from the casual use of terminology, for theories that have been labeled evolutionist or evolutionary have differed in several other major respects. For example, although the terminology of evolution in one way or another has been used to characterize the theories of the sociologist Talcott Parsons and the anthropologist Marvin Harris, these theories actually have very little in common. Parsons's more evolutionist account (in Toulmin's sense of evolutionist) is a version of cultural idealism that sets forth entirely different mechanisms from those proposed in Harris's materialist and evolutionary (again, in Toulmin's sense) account. About all Harris and Parsons agree on is that history reveals important patterns of change and that it is important to formulate a general theory to explain those patterns.

Nevertheless, the fact that the common label "evolutionary" (in the loose sense) or its equivalent persistently attaches to such theories in spite of their differences suggests that there is a basic core of elements that they share. What, then, do evolutionary theories have in common even when all their differences are ignored? What would be a set of minimal criteria for identifying such theories? Anthony Giddens (1984) has proposed several basic characteristics by which we can recognize any sort of evolutionary account of social life. He suggests that many evolutionary theories are based on an endogenous or "unfolding" model of change. That is, they assume that social changes occur as the result of the internal development of the latent potentialities originally built into a society. As he notes, the word evolution itself was originally derived from the Latin *evolutia*, meaning an "unrolling," and that it was first used to speak about the unrolling of parchments (cf. Service, 1971b).

In addition to this criterion, which he apparently believes is not a foolproof identifying mark of an evolutionary theory, Giddens lists four traits that he believes are such marks. First, there must be at least some conceptual continuity with biological evolution: "To use the term 'evolution' in the social sciences is rather gratuitous if it does not have at least some connections with the conceptual vocabulary which has become established in biology" (1984:231). An evolutionary theory must also postulate a sequence of stages through which some phenomenon progresses from "lower" to "higher" forms, and the criteria for this progression must be identified independently of a notion of "moral progress" (although Giddens adds that evolutionary theories are prone to conflate progression and progress). In addition, a genuinely evolutionary theory must also specify a mechanism or set of mechanisms that will explain the postulated sequence of stages, and it must show how the explanatory mechanism produces the displacement of one stage by another. Finally, Giddens claims that evolutionary theories presume that the entire spectrum of changes in human history can be accounted for in terms of the adaptive character of these changes. Indeed, "the notion of adaptation is so important in evolutionary theories that without it they lose most of their cogency" (1984:233).

Giddens's delineation of the basic features of evolutionary theories is not without its merits, but it does contain certain errors and overstatements. In the first place, he greatly overestimates the extent to which evolutionary theories rely on endogenous and unfolding models. It is true that evolutionary theories do tend to give pride of place to internal factors in societal change, but even the most endogenous of them never fail to take external factors (e.g., diffusion, war) into account at some point, and in many evolutionary theories external factors play a substantial role. As for the notion that unfolding models are typical of evolutionary theories, this is simply untrue. The nineteenth-century evolutionists were most prone toward this kind of model, but it has been gradually abandoned in the development of evolutionary theories in the twentieth century, with the exception of Parsonian evolutionism and other forms of evolutionism that draw upon Parsons. Rather than explaining historical changes in terms of the grand unfolding of latent potentialities toward some endpoint, most contemporary evolutionary theories explain them "as responses to the particular requirements imbedded in specific historical situations."

Giddens's suggestions that evolutionary theories must specify a progression of stages and a mechanism designed to explain the sequence are well argued, and he is correct to note that there is often a tendency for evolutionary thinkers to convert progression into "progress." However, there is no inherent connection between an evolutionary theory and a belief in steady human progress. We can have one without the other. Indeed, as we shall see, certain contemporary evolutionary thinkers have explicitly argued against equating evolution with progress, even to the point of tracing out the actual *regressive* aspects of social evolution.

Giddens's other two criteria are open to serious objection. A number of social evolutionary theorists have stressed a conceptual concordance between their theories and bioevolutionary theories, some even attempting to build theories of social evolution along Darwinian lines. But this feature is a secondary aspect of many theories, and in any event social evolutionary theories can be formulated and judged on their own terms. Contrary to Giddens, the terms "evolution" and "evolutionary" have meaning quite apart from their usage in evolutionary biology.

Giddens's claim that the concept of adaptation is vital to evolutionary theories is entirely correct. However, he fails to appreciate that this concept is a complex and subtle one that has several different dimensions, and thus it can be put to quite varied uses. Giddens thinks that the concept implies a transhistorical human drive for "mastery," and that it is closely linked to a conception of progress – that evolutionary theories postulate improved adaptation with social evolution. It must be admitted that such a conception of adaptation has been characteristic of a number of different evolutionary theories. However, the concept of adaptation is often used in a quite different way. In the evolutionism of Marvin Harris, for example, the concept implies neither a basic human tendency toward "mastery" nor a belief that adaptation is somehow a quality that increases throughout social evolution. For Harris, adaptation is a concept that principally relates to how individuals make choices under particular kinds of material constraints. Thus, while the concept of adaptation may be basic to most evolutionary theories, it is so in a more complicated and problematic way than Giddens recognizes.

Erik Olin Wright (1983) has offered a very different set of criteria for identifying an evolutionary theory, being prompted to develop them because of his own dissatisfaction with Giddens's criteria. He suggests that for a theory to be considered evolutionary it must have three features:

1　It must propose a typology of social forms with potential directionality.
2　It must order these social forms in the way it does on the assumption that the

probability of remaining at the same stage in the typology is greater than the
probability of regressing.
3   It must assert a probability of transition from one stage of the typology to another.

It therefore claims the existence of a tendency toward directionality, no
matter how weak, in social change. It is also clear that Wright demands the
presence of a mechanism that would explain such a directional tendency,
for he goes on to say that his definition of an evolutionary theory does not
imply a universal mechanism that would explain every single evolutionary
transition, but recognizes that "the actual mechanisms which might explain
movement between adjacent forms on the typology need not be the same at
every stage of the typology" (Wright, 1983:26–7).

Wright's characterization of an evolutionary theory is admirably free of
the kinds of dubious and gratuitous assumptions that plague Giddens's
definitional effort. As Wright is at pains to point out, his way of identifying
an evolutionary theory makes no claim that the typology of social forms
represents a teleological unfolding of latent potentialities, nor does it claim
that such a typology represents a rigid sequence of stages through which all
societies must move. Wright does not even assume that all (or even most)
societies necessarily evolve. Regression is entirely permitted, and it is fully
acknowledged that in most societies "long-term steady states may be more
likely than any systematic tendency for movement" (Wright, 1983:26).

Wright thus seems much closer than Giddens to pinpointing the
genuinely irreducible elements of evolutionary theories in the social
sciences. Indeed, he sets forth perhaps the best characterization of an
evolutionary theory available. Accordingly, I shall adopt his formulation as a
rough guide for selecting the theories to be included in this book.[1]

That brings us, then, to the aims of the book, which are basically twofold.
In the first instance, the book attempts a systematic survey of the historical
ebb and flow of evolutionary theories in the social sciences from the middle
of the nineteenth century to the present. More importantly, it attempts a
detailed critical analysis of the theories presented, with special attention
being given to the explanatory logic underlying the evolutionary formulations they promote. Especially close attention will be paid to whether or not
a particular theory is evolutionist or evolutionary (in Toulmin's sense)[2] in
character, but other crucial aspects of the structure of evolutionary theories
will also be explored. These include, but are by no means limited to, such
things as the scope of their application, the particular conception of
adaptation upon which they rest, whatever tendency they might have to
merge progression with progress, the extent to which they admit of
exogenous influences on societal change, and their implicit or explicit
conceptual linkage with bioevolutionary theories.

It is crucial that it be understood what this book is *not*. Despite a concern with the historical fate of evolutionary theories, the book's aims are more properly characterized as analytical and critical than as historical (the book is a *critical* history, not a critical *history*). Moreover, even as history it makes no pretense to being an exhaustive account of all the theories that have at one time or another been called evolutionary. No account is given, for example, of those theories of the late eighteenth and, early nineteenth centuries that have often been thought of as evolutionary – the theories emanating from the Scottish and French Enlightenments, or those of Saint–Simon and Comte. And for the late nineteenth century, only the three most important thinkers of that period are treated, many others being ignored altogether.

The entire social and cultural context of the theories treated is also ignored. The book therefore makes no claim to be an exercise in the sociology of knowledge: an account of the social and cultural conditions that have helped shaped the reception of evolutionary theories by social scientists. This is not because I deem such an exercise to be unworthy. On the contrary, a book written along such lines is badly needed, and one that was judiciously done would constitute a major contribution to social theory and sociological analysis more generally. But this is not such a book, and the reader expecting such will only be disappointed.

The plan of the book is essentially as follows. Chapter 2 discusses the three most important of the nineteenth-century evolutionists: Herbert Spencer, Lewis Henry Morgan, and Edward Burnett Tylor. It explores several aspects of the theories of these thinkers, but its most important contribution is its argument that the classical evolutionists indiscriminately merged evolutionist and evolutionary conceptions, with the former being dominant.

Chapter 3 takes a look at the sharp reaction against evolutionary theories that began toward the end of the nineteenth century and lasted until the 1950s. It delineates the major criticisms made during this time against evolutionary theories and attempts to show that these criticisms were largely misdirected.

Chapter 4 examines the evolutionary foundations of classical Marxism, emphasis being placed on the epistemological character of the works of both Marx and Engels. It is claimed that Marx did not have a teleological or unfolding model of historical change and, more contentiously, that Engels very likely did not either. The chapter also explores several other concerns pertinent to the social evolutionism of Marx and Engels, such as the intellectual relationship between Marx, Engels, and Morgan, and Marx's admiration for Darwin.

Chapter 5 pursues the revival of evolutionary theories in the 1930s and 1940s in the works of V. Gordon Childe, Leslie White, and Julian Steward. Although careful scrutiny of the ideas of these thinkers reveals a number of serious difficulties, it is argued that they made many significant intellectual gains over earlier evolutionary theorists and laid the foundations for a solid materialist theory of social evolution.

Chapter 6 discusses a very different kind of evolutionary theory: the functionalist evolutionism of Talcott Parsons and his followers. The principal argument of the chapter is that Parsons's extension of his functionalist model to a theory of social evolution produced a particularly extreme version of evolutionism highly vulnerable to the leading criticisms of the antievolutionists.

Chapter 7 looks at those contemporary anthropological evolutionists whose ideas have been formulated since 1960. The theories of Marshall Sahlins, Elman Service, Robert Carneiro, Gerhard Lenski, and Marvin Harris are the focus of attention. Some of these theories embody many of the functionalist claims of the Parsonians. Others are strongly materialist and are built around a conflict rather than a functionalist model of social life. Yet others overlap into both camps. It is argued that the theories of Marvin Harris constitute the most promising of these, and even of all existing, evolutionary theories.

Chapter 8 explores various dimensions of the relationship between evolutionary biology and theories of social evolution. Of particular concern are natural selection models of social evolution, as well as so-called coevolutionary theories. The chapter also takes up a detailed analysis of certain key evolutionary concepts – those of adaptation, differentiation, and progress – that have been of central concern to both biological and social evolutionists. It attempts to clarify the meaning (or meanings) of these concepts and indicate the extent to which they can be fruitfully employed by social evolutionists. The chapter concludes with some observations on the appropriateness of evolutionary biology as a reference point for the development of theories of social evolution.

Chapter 9 recapitulates the major objections to evolutionary theories raised by Mandelbaum, Nisbet, and Giddens that were touched on in earlier chapters, and it explores some additional criticisms as well. The main argument of the chapter is that, because these critics fail to distinguish among markedly different versions of evolutionary theory, their criticisms apply only to some theories and have little or no relevance to others. Certain evolutionary theories are therefore vigorously defended against these critical attacks.

Chapter 10 concludes the book by suggesting the lines along which a comprehensive evolutionary theory of world history should be constructed. It also points to some of the most important historical phenomena that such a theory must be able to address.

NOTES

1 Most of the thinkers and theories discussed in the book meet Wright's criteria quite well; a few, though, are perhaps a bit marginal, being evolutionary in a somewhat weaker and more limited way. If one wanted to reduce Wright's definition to an even simpler form, it might be said that the absolutely vital defining characteristic of an evolutionary theory is the provision of a general mechanism or set of mechanisms to account for what are presumed to be at least some general directional sequences of societal change. All of the thinkers discussed in this book meet this weaker criterion.

2 In chapter 2 different terms will be suggested for this distinction, and after this point the terms evolutionist and evolutionary will be used simply as general descriptive terms having no reference to the technical meanings assigned them by Toulmin.

# 2

# Classical Evolutionism

The systematic emergence of evolutionary theories of human society began essentially with the Enlightenment, especially with the works of the Scottish thinkers Millar and Ferguson and the French philosophers Condorcet and Turgot (cf. Harris, 1968). Rather different sorts of evolutionary theories were also quite popular during the early nineteenth-century reaction against much of Enlightenment thought, as the works of Saint-Simon and Comte demonstrate. But, as was pointed out in the preceding chapter, the heyday of evolutionary thought – its "golden age" – came in the second half of the nineteenth century. After 1850, and especially after the 1860s, evolutionary theories of human social life dominated the social sciences. Such thinkers as Spencer, Morgan, Tylor, Bachofen, Westermarck, Maine, Lubbock, and numerous others wrote tomes, often multivolumed ones, in which elaborate evolutionary schemes were set forth and accompanied by massive compilations of data designed to support them. This chapter examines the theories of those three thinkers generally regarded as the most significant of the nineteenth-century evolutionists: Herbert Spencer, Lewis Henry Morgan, and Edward Burnett Tylor. It overviews their leading evolutionary doctrines and endeavors to explicate their views in regard to four major themes: their underlying epistemological assumptions, their notions of the basic causes of evolutionary transitions, their relation to Darwinism, and their views regarding human progress.

## HERBERT SPENCER

Spencer's commitment to an evolutionary interpretation of social life is readily apparent when one considers his view of history as a discipline. As

J. D. Y. Peel (1971:158) has noted, "Spencer's attitude to history was mostly dismissive and to historians nearly always dismissive and contemptuous." Spencer objected to traditional historical investigation because of its emphasis on the uniqueness of historical events and the causal role it gave to individuals. Spencer thought that traditional historical study had to be replaced by, or at least supplemented with, a kind of comparative sociology that could organize the facts of history so as to allow "for the subsequent determination of the ultimate laws to which social phenomena conform" (Spencer, 1972:89).

Spencer formulated a general law of evolutionary change in his famous essay, "Progress: its law and cause," originally published in 1857. This law asserted a tendency for all phenomena to change from a state of incoherent homogeneity to one of coherent heterogeneity. The law applied to all features of the universe: to the earth, to life on the earth, and to the character of human society. It thus had the status of a universal, indeed cosmological, principle. The evolution of human social life was merely one manifestation of a generic process inherent in nature itself.

This great universal tendency toward increasing differentiation was exemplified in the social realm particularly by societies' political and religious institutions and by the development of social stratification. As Spencer puts it (1972[1857]:42–4):

As we see in existing barbarous tribes, society in its first and lowest form is a homogeneous aggregation of individuals having like powers and like functions: the only marked difference of function being that which accompanies difference of sex. Every man is a warrior, hunter, fisherman, tool-maker, builder; every woman performs the same drudgeries; every family is self-sufficing, and save for purposes of aggression and defence, might as well live apart from the rest. Very early, however, in the process of social evolution, we find an incipient differentiation between the governing and the governed. Some kind of chieftainship seems coeval with the first advance from the state of separate wandering families to that of a nomadic tribe. . . .

At the same time there has been arising a co-ordinate species of government – that of Religion. For a long time these connate forms of government – civil and religious – continue closely associated. For many generations the king continues to be the chief priest, and the priesthood to be members of the royal race. . . .

[N]o sooner does the originally homogeneous social mass differentiate into the governed and the governing parts, then this last exhibits an incipient differentiation into religious and secular – Church and State. . . .

Simultaneously, there has been going on a second differentiation of a more familiar kind; that, namely, by which the mass of the community has been segregated into distinct classes and orders of workers.

Closely associated with his general law of evolution was Spencer's classification of societies into four levels of differentiation, which he referred to as simple, compound, doubly compound, and trebly compound.

Simple societies are politically headless or have only rudimentary forms of headship. Compound societies have achieved a form of differentiation in which their various political heads are subordinated under one general head. Compound societies that have acquired a completely settled residential pattern are characterized as well by a clear division in social ranks, well-developed ecclesiastical organizations, an advancing division of labor, and relatively permanent buildings. Doubly compound societies involve a recompounding of the groups found in compound societies. They are characterized by a still higher government and thus greater political integration, a developed ecclesiastical hierarchy, a complex division of labor, a system of laws, towns and roads, and substantial progress in knowledge and technology. The trebly compound level is that of the great civilized nations. Spencer's examples of this stage of social evolution include, *inter alia*, ancient Mexico, the Egyptian Empire, the Roman Empire, Great Britain, and France.

Spencer also developed a distinctly different typology of societies that he was never able to integrate completely with his typology based on the level of social differentiation. This was his dichotomy of militancy and industrialism. Military societies are those that are highly characterized by warfare and the preparation for warfare. The crucial feature of the military society, though, is the fact that the individual is highly subordinated to the social whole and compelled to obey its dictates. Coercion rather than individual freedom is the hallmark of everyday social life. The industrial society, by contrast, is one in which military organization and warfare are much less significant, and thus individuals are less restrained by the social whole. This type of society is characterized by a dominance of agricultural, commercial, or industrial activities over military ones, and by the voluntary cooperation of individuals in the maintenance of the larger society.

Although Spencer recognized that simpler societies were sometimes characterized more by the industrial type, and that complex societies were sometimes highly militant in character, he perceived a general evolution from the one to the other. He noted that (1972[1876]:159), "From the primitive predatory conditions under which the master maintains slaves to work for him, there is a transition through stages of increasing freedom to a condition like our own, in which all who work and employ, buy and sell, are entirely independent."

### LEWIS HENRY MORGAN

Perhaps the most significant and controversial of the classical evolutionists was Lewis Henry Morgan, whose contributions to evolutionary theory were set forth primarily in his book *Ancient Society* (1974[1877]). In the opening chapters of *Ancient Society* Morgan develops his general evolutionary scheme, which is an effort to trace the development of several "ethnical periods" in human prehistory. Each of these periods represents a particular type of society arranged in an evolutionary sequence and identified primarily by its level of technological development. Morgan considers three major ethnical periods, the first two of which are subdivided into three subperiods. The oldest stage of human society is *savagery*. The *Lower Status* of savagery marks the very beginnings of human social life, and little is known of it. It ends with the development of a fish subsistence and the acquisition of an understanding of the use of fire. The *Middle Status* of savagery runs from the acquisition of fish subsistence and use of fire to the invention of the bow and arrow. The *Upper Status* of savagery begins with the bow and arrow and ends with the development of pottery-making, at which point the *Lower Status* of *barbarism* begins. The *Middle Status* of barbarism begins in the Eastern hemisphere with the domestication of animals and in the Western hemisphere with the development of irrigation and the architectural use of adobe-brick and stone. This level ends with the development of iron, and the *Upper Status* of barbarism lasts from this point until the invention of the phonetic alphabet and writing. The emergence of these last inventions marks the transition to the final ethnical period, that of *civilization*.

The remainder of *Ancient Society* is taken up wlth a discussion of the evolution of government, the family, and of property, or, as Morgan puts it, of "the idea of government," "the idea of the family," and "the idea of property." Roughly two-thirds of the book focuses on the development of governmental institutions. According to Morgan, human societies evidence two main plans of government. The earliest is based on the existence of gentes, phratries, and tribes. This stage of political evolution, to which Morgan gave the name *societas*, is one in which kinship is the central organizing principle of social life and in which social relations are relatively egalitarian and democratic. The other main type of government, *civitas*, rests upon the principles of property and territory as organizing devices. Here civilization and the state have evolved and the gens has greatly declined in importance. Inequalities based upon differential property ownership have emerged, and the democracy of earlier times has decayed in favor of various types of despotism.

The basic social and political unit at the level of *societas* is the *gens*, that kinship unit that anthropologists today call the clan or sib. Morgan spends several hundred pages tracing the worldwide existence of the gens and its ultimate breakdown as the basic principle of political organization. Most of his discussion focuses on the gens among the Iroquois and in ancient Greece and Rome. In all three societies Morgan notes that gentes combined together to form higher forms of government. Several gentes would combine into a phratry, and several phratries joined together constituted a tribe. These higher organizational forms are viewed as natural evolutionary growths out of the gentes themselves.

As already noted, the emergence of political society or *civitas* undermined the equality and democracy of the gentes and substituted the rule of property and governments whose main purpose was the protection of property. As Morgan says in regard to the transition to political society in ancient Rome (1974[1877]:348):

The Romans were now carried fairly out of gentile society into and under the second great plan of government, founded upon territory and upon property. They had left gentilism and barbarism behind them, and entered upon a new career of civilization. Henceforth the creation and protection of property became the primary objects of government, with a superadded career of conquest for domination over distant tribes and nations.

In his treatment of the family, Morgan distinguishes five major stages in its evolution, each of which is essentially a form of marriage. The oldest form of the family is the *consanguine*, which involved the union of all brothers and sisters in a kind of group marriage. This existed in the lowest stage of savagery and is no longer found among remaining savages. Next there occurred the *punaluan* family. This also was a type of group marriage, but it added a prohibition on incestuous unions. It was widespread in savagery and occasionally found in the Lower Status of barbarism. This form of the family was followed by the *syndyasmian* or *pairing* family, a widespread feature of barbarism. In the syndyasmian family monogamous marriage is practiced, but in the context of larger kinship groups (gentes) to which the marital pair is subordinated. Another form of the family is the *patriarchal*, which Morgan thinks of as a highly specialized type limited mainly to the Semitic tribes and the Romans. In this form of the family, several persons, both free and unfree, were bound into a family unit under the control of a strong patriarch. Finally, the *monogamian* family emerged with the transition to civilization. It involved the marriage of single pairs who exclusively cohabited.

In the final two chapters of *Ancient Society* Morgan discusses the evolution of property or systems of inheritance. During the stage of savagery the idea of property was little developed, and little emotion was attached to it. In the Lower Status of barbarism communal ownership still prevailed, but with some movement in the direction of a possessory right by the individual. By the Middle Status of barbarism there had occurred a substantial increase in personal property, yet ownership of land by the whole tribe was still the dominant principle. By the end of the Upper Status of barbarism communal ownership of land had been strongly undermined, and with the transition to civilization land came to be owned primarily by private individuals or by the state. It is clear, then, that for Morgan there is an overall evolution toward increasingly private forms of property ownership.

## EDWARD BURNETT TYLOR

Even a superficial familiarity with Tylor's evolutionism, especially as it is represented in his major work *Primitive Culture* (1924 [first edition, 1871]), will show that it is strikingly different from Spencer's and Morgan's. Indeed, as Robert Carneiro (1973a:61) has suggested, "Tylor showed himself to be a good deal more of a cultural historian than an evolutionist. His concern was largely with tracing the history of myths, riddles, customs, games, rituals, artifacts, and the like, rather than with laying bare the general process or stages in the evolution of culture as a whole." Nonetheless, Tylor's commitment to a general evolutionary perspective is apparent. In *Primitive Culture* (1924, I:33) he says, "That the tendency of culture has been similar throughout the existence of human society, and that we may fairly judge from its known historic course what its prehistoric course may have been, is a theory clearly entitled to precedence as a fundamental principle of ethnographic research." Moreover, in his general textbook of anthropology his commitment to a general evolutionism is stated even more explicitly (1916:20 [first edition, 1881]):

On the whole it appears that wherever there are found elaborate arts, abstruse knowledge, complex institutions, these are results of gradual development from an earlier, simpler, and ruder state of life. No stage of civilization comes into existence spontaneously, but grows or is developed out of the stage before it. This is the great principle which every scholar must lay firm hold of, if he intends to understand either the world he lives in or the history of the past.

Tylor is also famous for his use of the concept of *survivals* as a means of demonstrating evolutionary sequences. These he defined as items of culture that had been carried by the force of custom into stages of social development beyond the one in which they originated. For Tylor they proved that presently observed states of culture had evolved from older ones.

In the second chapter of *Primitive Culture* Tylor engages in much discussion of the well-known nineteenth-century theory of degeneration: the view that more primitive and simpler cultures were vestiges of older elaborate civilizations. He actually grants considerable credence to this theory, admitting that a number of elements of culture have to be explained by it. Yet he thought of degeneration as clearly a secondary phenomenon to evolution.

Like Morgan and earlier thinkers, Tylor divided the prehistory of human societies into three great stages, those of savagery, barbarism, and civilization. In savagery humans subsisted by hunting and gathering and had an extremely limited technology. The stage of barbarism was reached when agriculture became available. This development led to settled villages and town life and great improvements in knowledge, manners, and government. Civilization began with the development of writing. Although this scheme is less elaborate than Morgan's, it is basically the same.

The evolution of technology, though, was not an overriding concern for Tylor, and his evolutionism was applied mainly to the development of language, myth, and religion, especially to the last of these. Indeed, virtually the entire second volume of *Primitive Culture*, and part of the first as well, is taken up with a discussion of the evolution of *animism* through its various stages. Here the contrast with Morgan is striking, for Morgan thought that religion was especially unsuitable for evolutionary treatment because of the "grotesque" and "unintelligible" character of primitive religion. For Tylor, though, primitive religion had a certain rationality about it, given the conditions that primitive peoples faced, and the evolution of religion demonstrated an increasingly rational understanding of the world. In general, this evolution was from a belief in souls to that of spirits, then on to a polytheistic pantheon of gods, and then finally to monotheism.

THE EPISTEMOLOGIES OF THE CLASSICAL EVOLUTIONISTS

These bare sketches of the classical evolutionists can scarcely begin to do justice to the complexity and elaborateness of their ideas, and they are intended only to give something of the flavor of their most basic notions. The really interesting and most theoretically germane aspects of their thinking are yet to be considered. Let us begin with their epistemological conceptions – with the assumptions they made about the basic character of social evolution and of the "laws" that could be formulated to explain it.

In recent years much attention has been given to the epistemological character of evolutionary theories, classical evolutionism in particular. In chapter 1 we noted Toulmin's distinction between evolutionist and evolutionary models of historical change, a distinction between those models that explain history as the logical unfolding of a preordained plan and those that explain it as a series of specific responses to particular conditions and requirements. A very similar distinction has been drawn by Maurice Mandelbaum (1971).

Mandelbaum has attempted to situate the early evolutionists within the pervasive nineteenth-century doctrine that he has termed *historicism*. As Mandelbaum defines this much-used term, historicism refers to *"the belief that an adequate understanding of the nature of any phenomenon and an adequate assessment of its value are to be gained through considering it in terms of the place which it occupied and the role which it played within a process of development"* (1971:42; emphasis Mandelbaum's). According to Mandelbaum, the doctrine of historicism usually implies an epistemological conception that he calls a *directional law*. A directional law assumes that historical change is to be represented as a process of natural development or unfolding, one in which the historical transformation of an entity occurs as the result of the actualization of the potentialities inherent in that entity from the very beginning. Mandelbaum contrasts directional laws with *functional laws*, which he assumes to be the classic type of law in scientific formulations. Functional laws postulate no inherent scheme of unfolding, no actualization of inherent potentialities, but rather attempt to explain historical changes as the result of particular factors operating in particular ways within the context of a particular set of constraints.[1]

Mandelbaum holds that directional laws are epistemologically illegitimate constructions that have no place in historical explanation, and that any presumed directional tendency can be explained only by reducing it to a complex set of functional relationships. Mandelbaum does not deny that there may be orderly sequences of historical change, but he insists that such sequences have to be understood as the cumulative effect of a whole series of functional relationships operating over time. He illustrates explanation in terms of a directional law and the functional law alternative to it as follows (1971:121, 126):

If there were a directional law defining a sequence of stages in the forms of marriage, then, in order to explain the existence of a particular form of marriage, one would relate that form to its necessary antecedents, and one would know what subsequent form of marriage might be expected to replace it: one would not account for these changes in terms of specific historical conditions, appealing to the ways in which (under these specific conditions) changes were brought about through the operation of psychological, ecological, or functional factors, or by the effects of external contacts. An explanation by means of a law of developmental stages would be analogous to an explanation of why a particular planet follows a particular trajectory over one section of its course through appealing directly to the fact that this trajectory constitutes a segment of the planet's elliptical orbit. . . .

We have seen, however, that in order to understand an actual pattern of development, we cannot view it as a single process formed in accordance with a directional law; if we are to explain it by means of a reference to laws, we must do so by showing how particular functional relationships, operating on specific initial conditions, shape each of the successive steps of change. Once completed, these successive steps may be regarded as having defined some definite pattern, but that pattern would be a consequence of other forces, and would not itself represent a directional tendency. Thus, insofar as we wish to use models of explanation which are derived from scientifically acceptable modes of explanation, we shall *not* seek to explain any phenomenon by placing it within the context of a developmental series: we shall, on the contrary, explain every phenomenon in terms of the specific conditions and the functional laws which, at each moment in time, was [sic] responsible for its being precisely what it was.

Mandelbaum believes that the basic explanatory logic of the nineteenth-century evolutionists involved the historicist's employment of directional laws. He gives little credence to the possibility that they formulated functional-law explanations of evolutionary sequences. A very similar view of the epistemological grounding of the classical evolutionists has been offered by Robert Nisbet in his highly influential book *Social Change and History* (1969). Nisbet has claimed that the classical evolutionists rooted their understanding of evolution in the notions that change is natural, directional, immanent, continuous, and necessary. Nisbet regards the idea of immanent change as the very essence of classical evolutionism, and it is this idea that closely parallels Mandelbaum's emphasis on the explanatory logic of directional laws.

As is well known, Nisbet has been a major critic of evolutionary theories of all sorts, and his view that they rest upon an inadmissible conception of immanent change has been perhaps the strongest basis of his rejection of them. I agree with Nisbet's rejection of immanence, and as well with Mandelbaum's denouncement of directional laws, as an appropriate grounding for a theory of societal change.[2] But the overriding question at the moment is whether Mandelbaum and Nisbet are correct to claim that classical evolutionism was epistemologically of this sort. Indeed, Robert Carneiro (1973a), a well-known contemporary student of the classical evolutionists (actually a leading expert on Spencer) and a contemporary evolutionist himself, has challenged this argument. He believes that the notion of evolutionary change as an unfolding of immanences is a very old idea that had been largely abandoned by the time the classical evolutionists began to produce their works. He alleges that the nineteenth-century evolutionists basically espoused a model of functional-law causation, and he goes on to suggest many candidates as causes of evolutionary change registered by Spencer, Morgan, and Tylor.

I want to claim that Mandelbaum and Nisbet are closer to the truth, but that Carneiro certainly has an important point to make. To a very large extent, the classical evolutionists had a confused and philosophically weak understanding of causation, one that led them to formulate intellectual systems that were rather unwieldy mixtures of developmentalist and ordinary causal explanation.[3] Let me develop the evidence to support this claim by first attempting to show the extent to which a developmentalist model was fundamental to the classical evolutionists, and then considering the kinds of ordinary causes that these thinkers advanced to account for some aspects of social evolution.

Spencer is a good place to begin, since he was the most explicit about his evolutionary propositions. Paul Hirst (1976) has asserted that Spencer's conception of evolution was a fundamentally developmentalist one, and that although he identified proximate causes of evolution, his system rested on the postulation of one big ultimate cause: the tendency toward differentiation inherent in the cosmos. Thus Hirst argues that the sociological Spencer was dependent upon the philosophical one. There is every reason to believe that Hirst is correct. In "Progress: its law and cause" Spencer sets forth nearly as developmentalist a conception of evolution as one can find. It is in this essay, of course, that he states his general cosmological law of the tendency of all things toward increasing differentiation (1972[1857]:40):

This law of organic progress is the law of all progress. Whether it be in the development of the Earth, in the development of Life upon its surface, in the development of Society, of Government, of Manufactures, of Commerce, of Language, Literature, Science, Art, this same evolution of the simple into the complex, through successive differentiations, holds throughout. From the earliest traceable cosmical changes down to the latest results of civilization, we shall find that the transformation of the homogeneous into the heterogeneous, is that in which Progress essentially consists.

The developmentalism implied by this law of evolution is even more obvious when we realize that Spencer regarded the process of differentiation as an *inherent tendency* of all things, and as implying a fundamental necessity.

Valerie Haines (1988) and Carneiro (1981b) have challenged this interpretation of Spencer. Haines claims that Spencer's abstract developmentalist statements were intended only as *descriptions* of the course of evolution, not as actual explanations of it. He explained evolution, she claims, by invoking the notion of adaptation to environmental conditions. Carneiro claims that, although Spencer may have started out as a developmentalist, he eventually abandoned such a doctrine in favor of a conception of ordinary causal explanation. Against the developmentalist interpretation, Carneiro produces a seemingly damaging quote from the sixth edition of Spencer's *First Principles* (Spencer, 1937; cf. Carneiro, 1981b: 159–60). Here Spencer denies that social evolution is inevitable or that it implies some sort of intrinsic tendency toward the development of higher forms. It is not a necessary process, Spencer says, but "depends on conditions."

I do not find these arguments compelling. Spencer's writings are filled with inconsistent statements, so one denial that evolution is an immanent and inevitable process really means little. The fact remains that throughout his life Spencer continued to revise his *First Principles* (first published in 1862), an extremely abstract metaphysical work that formed the foundation for the remainder of his work. The developmentalism of the early essay, "Progress: its law and cause," is retained and greatly elaborated in *First Principles* and is never abandoned. As Hirst has suggested, it seems that the developmentalism of this work is the ultimate mode of explanation on which Spencer depends, and thus the basis for his ordinary causal explanations.

Upon turning to Morgan, we also find a strong commitment to developmentalism, *Ancient Society* being filled with statements that are grist for the mill of Mandelbaum and Nisbet. Here is an especially pregnant passage (1974[1877]:4):

As we re-ascend along the several lines of progress toward the primitive ages of mankind, and eliminate one after the other, in the order in which they appeared, inventions and discoveries on the one hand, and institutions on the other, we are enabled to perceive that the former stand to each other in progressive, and the latter in unfolding relations. While the former class have had a connection, more or less direct, the latter have been developed from a few primary germs of thought. Modern institutions plant their roots in the period of barbarism, into which their germs were transmitted from the previous period of savagery. They have had a lineal descent through the ages, with the streams of the blood, as well as a logical development.

There are three striking earmarks of developmentalism in this passage: the notion that social institutions exist in "unfolding relations"; the idea that these institutions evolved from "a few germs"; and the view that the whole sequence of evolution is a process of "logical development." Another passage from *Ancient Society* is even more revealing. In speaking of the sequence of evolutionary development constituted by the family, Morgan says that it (1974[1877]:515) "affords both a rational and a satisfactory explanation of the facts of human experience, so far as they are known, and of the course of human progress." In other words, an evolutionary sequence requires no particular explanation, but *is its own explanation*. One would be hard pressed to find a more exemplary passage in any of the writings of the classical evolutionists of Mandelbaum's notion of explanation in terms of a directional law. A sequence of changes can constitute its own explanation only to the extent that these changes are assumed to have unfolded as the result of the potentialities inherent in the entity from the very beginning of its existence.

Mandelbaum does not cite the passages quoted above in support of his argument, but he easily could have. Moreover, although these passages are especially revealing ones, the idea they express is stated repeatedly throughout *Ancient Society*. Morgan again and again refers to the "germs of thought" from which later institutions have been developed, and this notion seems to be the guiding philosophical basis of the entire work.

Although Tylor's work is more resistant to clear interpretation on this issue, it seems that even here historicism, if not developmentalism, is a guiding theme, as the following passage from *Primitive Culture* suggests (1924, I:37):

> The principle of development in culture has become so ingrained in our philosophy that ethnologists, of whatever school, hardly doubt but that, whether by progress or degradation, savagery and civilization are connected as lower and higher stages of one formation.

Yet despite Tylor's apparent commitment to historicism, his evolutionism is really of a different sort than Spencer's and Morgan's, for it does not appear that his historicism was actually accompanied by a developmentalism. Passages clearly denoting a commitment to an epistemology of directional laws are difficult, if not impossible, to locate in Tylor's work. In fact, Mandelbaum excludes Tylor from an identification with such an epistemology, claiming that (1971:107):

> Tylor did not assume that the general laws which could presumably explain cultural change were laws regulating or governing the successive steps in the processes to which they applied. . . . [I]n most cases in which Tylor made concrete suggestions concerning the types of laws which explain cultural phenomena, these did not define and summarize a necessary direction in which change proceeded; instead, he attempted to show how facts concerning language, myth, magic, and the like, depend upon general principles governing the processes of human thought.

This interpretation of Tylor closely corresponds to that of Carneiro (1973a), who has claimed that Tylor's preoccupation with cultural minutiae prevented him from developing a broad theoretical conception of evolutionary change.

ORDINARY CAUSAL EXPLANATION IN THE CLASSICAL EVOLUTIONISTS

Despite their historicism, and in the case of Spencer and Morgan their developmentalism, each of the classical evolutionists advanced ordinary causes to explain specific aspects of evolutionary change. As suggested earlier, the classical evolutionists did not have a carefully worked out understanding of the need for a model of causation that could be philosophically defended, and therefore they saw no difficulty in relying on two fundamentally different models of evolutionary causation. One might be more charitable, as Paul Hirst (1976) has been in the case of Spencer, and regard their ordinary causes as *proximate* causes and their developmentalist formulations as *ultimate* causes. Yet to do so would seem to stretch the general meaning of these terms too far and give the nineteenth-century evolutionists more credit than they deserve.[4]

In any event, what kinds of ordinary causes did they propose? Let us begin in this case with Morgan and first recount the huge debate that has centered around whether he was a materialist or an idealist. Until recently, the overwhelming tendency was to see Morgan as a materialist. This interpretation has been especially closely associated with the Marxist tradition, and Marx and Engels regarded Morgan as having independently discovered the materialist conception of history. Later thinkers in the Marxist tradition, such as Eleanor Burke Leacock, the French anthropologist Emmanuel Terray, and, more loosely, Leslie White, are perhaps the most prominent defenders of a materialist Morgan.

In her introduction to the republication of *Ancient Society*, Leacock maintains that Morgan's (1963, Ivi) "materialistic theory of history so closely paralleled that of Marx and Engels that *Ancient Society* was used as the foundation for Engels' *The Origin of the Family, Private Property and the State.*" Leacock's interpretation stresses Morgan's emphasis on the determining role of technology and property. Terray (1972) has declared that the concepts that are the essence of Morgan's theoretical system are the concepts of Marxism. Moreover, he has claimed that what earned Morgan the admiration of Marx and Engels was his view that "the determinant sphere is that of the arts of subsistence" (1972:52). For Terray, "Morgan's arts of subsistence are, in fact, no different from Marx's productive forces; the ethnic period is the mode of production together with the juridicial and political superstructures it has called forth. Both Morgan and Marx see the economy as determinant in the final analysis" (1972:66).

Leslie White (1948, 1949a) has done as much as anyone to champion the materialist interpretation of Morgan. He believes that for Morgan the principal determinants of social evolution were technology and systems of property. Actually, White holds that Morgan had both a materialist and an idealist theory of social evolution, but that the former was clearly dominant. He concedes that Morgan regularly referred to the development of social institutions out of a few germs of thought, but maintains that Morgan held the growth of these ideas to be dependent on prior changes in material conditions.

Idealist interpretations of Morgan have been advanced by, *inter alia*, Morris Opler (1965), Fred Voget (1975), and, to some extent, Elman

Service (1981). Opler's idealist Morgan is perhaps the most celebrated. Opler argues for an idealist interpretation along a number of lines, two of which are most prominent. First, he plays down the fact that Morgan's classification of evolutionary stages rests on technology, denying that by such a classification system Morgan wished to give any particular causal significance to technology (cf. Ingold, 1986:62). He says that (1965:89) "Morgan does not say that human progress *has* been due to increased subsistence; he says it has been 'identified' with it. In fact Morgan takes pains to disassociate himself from those who have used technology too exclusively as a criterion of progress." Second, Opler places considerable emphasis on Morgan's frequent references to the importance of the "germs of thought" and to the mind or brain in the development of culture, and he is able to quote copiously from Morgan in this regard. As Opler notes (1965:90), "Time and again Morgan subordinates both the institutional and the technological to intellect."

Some scholars have held that Morgan advocated an eclectic combination of materialism and idealism. Carneiro (1973a) has suggested that Morgan was an especially good example of a thinker in whom both idealism and materialism were unselfconsciously intertwined. He also believes that during his career Morgan moved increasingly in the direction of emphasizing material factors. Harris (1968) has suggested that Morgan was philosophically and theoretically an eclectic who failed to develop a consistent theory of the causes of cultural evolution.

Of these three positions, the first is clearly the weakest. To regard Morgan as a consistent and unadulterated materialist requires an extra-ordinary ability to ignore the much larger context in which Morgan's statements about technology and property are made. There are just too many remarks about the importance of germs of thought, the logic of the human brain or mind, or the development of intelligence to be ignored. And these statements clearly outweigh the number of references made to the importance of material conditions. One can go through *Ancient Society* and extract numerous references to ideas and their causal role in social evolution. Here is a sampling:

An attempt will be made in the following pages to bring forward additional evidence of the rudeness of the early condition of mankind, of the gradual evolution of their mental and moral powers through experience, and of their protracted struggle with opposing obstacles while winning their way to civilization (1974[1877]:3).

The principal institutions of mankind have been developed from a few primary germs of thought; and . . . the course and manner of their development was predetermined, as well as restricted within narrow limits of divergence, by the natural logic of the human mind and the necessary limitations of its powers (1974[1877]:18).

The work of society in its totality, by means of which all progress occurs, is ascribed far too much to individual men, and far too little to the public intelligence. It will be recognized generally that the substance of human history is bound up in the growth of ideas, which are wrought out by the people and expressed in their institutions, usages, inventions and discoveries (1974[1877]:311).

The obvious importance given to ideas by Morgan lends considerable credence to the idealist position. The fact that Morgan also made statements of an apparently materialist sort might be reconciled by arguing that, within the realm of his limited ordinary causal epistemology, Morgan regarded material conditions as proximate causes that are themselves brought into existence by deeper ultimate causes, and that these ultimate causes are always ideas. But although I believe this is an interpretation that can be supported by most of the text of *Ancient Society*, there are some passages that appear to ride roughshod over it. Here are two that may be especially brought to light:

Around the simple ideas relating to marriage and the family, to subsistence and to government, the earliest social organizations were formed; and with them an exposition of the structure and principle of ancient society must commence. Adopting the theory of a progressive development of mankind through the experience of the ages, the insulation of the inhabitants of Oceania, their limited local areas, and their restricted means of subsistence predetermined a slow rate of progress (1974[1877]:387).

When field agriculture had demonstrated that the whole surface of the earth could be made the subject of property owned by individuals in severalty, and it was found that the head of the family became the natural center of accumulation, the new property career of mankind was inaugurated. It was fully done before the close of the Later Period of barbarism. A little reflection must convince any one of the powerful influence property would now begin to exercise upon the human mind, and of the great awakening of new elements of character it was calculated to produce (1974[1877]:553–4).

These two passages refer to the direct causal influence of certain material conditions upon the human mind itself. In the first instance geographical isolation is said to hold back the progress of the mind, while in the second changes in human thinking are held to derive from new property systems. We hardly have here, then, a situation in which material factors are proximate and ideas ultimate.

It is passages like these that cause exegetes to climb the walls and that make a definitive interpretation of Morgan's conception of ordinary causal explanation impossible. Although there is really no basis for considering Morgan a consistent materialist, it is also difficult to regard him as a consistent idealist. Those who have seen his position as a rather muddled eclectic one are therefore on safest ground. It should not be especially surprising that Morgan was vague and seemingly inconsistent in regard to the identification of ordinary causes, for his more fundamental notion of causation was a developmentalist one in which evolutionary change is essentially its own explanation. Yet when his probable eclecticism in regard to ordinary causation is combined with a strong reliance on a developmentalism, the result is causal confusion on a grand scale. It is clear, then, that Morgan's epistemology was an especially messy one that would scarcely be tolerated by modern philosophical standards.

A similar debate about materialism versus idealism has also been carried out with respect to Tylor, with the exception that there have been fewer advocates for Tylor the materialist. Leslie White (1949a), though, has taken up this position. White sees Tylor in the same light as Morgan: as proposing a basically technological interpretation of the causes of social evolution. He argues that Tylor distinguished his evolutionary stages in terms of control over the food supply, that he saw changes in political organization as closely following technological changes, and that he even interpreted some intellectual features of culture as expressions of material conditions.

White's perspective, however, is curiously one-sided, and most scholars have opted either for an idealist Tylor, or for an eclectic one with the idealist elements dominant. Mandelbaum (1971) suggests that Tylor's work was primarily devoted to understanding how the various features of culture are rooted in basic principles governing the nature of human thinking. Opler (1964) is one of the most vigorous proponents of an idealist foundation to Tylor's evolutionism, suggesting that his work was dominated by intellectual development – particularly the development of increasingly rational thought – as the key to social evolution. As he does in the case of Morgan, Opler extracts numerous passages from various of Tylor's works to support his case. Voget's Tylor is also an idealist one (1975:289):

When in the nineteenth century Tylor . . . sagely advised that development in the material arts provided an excellent guide for charting the rise from a savage mental state to that of civilized man, he simply echoed a common view of Developmentalists generally. The study of technology was always approached with the idea that the tool was the expression of an idea.

Just as they propose an eclectic Morgan, Carneiro and Harris advocate an eclectic Tylor. Harris (1968) claims that Tylor had no consistent theory of the causes of culture, but he believes that he leaned more in the idealist direction. Despite a high regard for the importance of material conditions in social evolution, Harris suggests, Tylor was a fervent embracer of the Enlightenment's idealist heritage, never really questioning the preeminence of mind in guiding the evolution of material culture.

Settling the score with respect to Tylor is much easier than it is in regard to Morgan. Tylor makes reference again and again to the human mind, to the mental state of savages or of civilized men, and to the intellect; and he does so without making any really countervailing statements that suggest the subordination of intellectual conditions to material advances. As Opler and others have done, one can select numerous passages from almost any of his works to support an idealist interpretation. Here are just two of the strongest, since they depict material changes as rooted in the human mind:

Lastly, *civilized* life may be taken as beginning with the art of writing, which by recording history, law, knowledge, and religion for the service of ages to come, binds together the past and the future in an unbroken chain of intellectual and moral progress (1916:24).

In the various branches of the problem which will henceforth occupy our attention, that of determining the relation of the mental condition of savages to that of civilized men, it is an excellent guide and safeguard to keep before our minds the theory of development in the material arts. Throughout all the manifestations of the human intellect, facts will be found to fall into their places on the same general lines of evolution. . . .

The study of savage and civilized life alike avail us to trace in the early history of the human intellect, not gifts of transcendental wisdom, but rude shrewd sense taking up the facts of common life and shaping from them schemes of primitive philosophy. It will be seen again and again, that savage opinion is in a more or less rudimentary state, while the civilized mind still bears vestiges, neither few nor slight, of a past condition from which savages represent the least, and civilized men the greatest advance (1924, I:68–9).

When it is additionally recognized that most of Tylor's work focused on the evolution of religion, and that his conception of religion was itself a rather narrowly cognitive one, then his idealism appears paramount. If for Marx and Engels humans were basically tool makers and productive manipulators of their environment, for Tylor they were essentially philosophers thinking their way toward increasingly rational understandings.

Let us turn now to Spencer, whose thinking falls largely outside the context of the materialism/idealism debate. It is somewhat ironic that he, perhaps the most explicitly developmentalist of all the classical evolutionists with his grandiose Law of Evolution, stated numerous ordinary causes of social evolution in a remarkably modern way. The main ordinary causes Spencer consistently evoked were population pressure, the environment, economics, and warfare, the first of which he seemed to regard as the most important (cf. Hirst, 1976). As he claimed in an early essay (1972[1852]:37):

The excess of fertility has itself rendered the process of civilization inevitable. From the beginning, pressure of population has been the proximate cause of progress. It produced the original diffusion of the race. It compelled men to abandon predatory habits and take to agriculture. It led to the clearing of the earth's surface. It forced men into the social state; made social organization inevitable; and has developed the social sentiments. It has stimulated to progressive improvements in production, and to increased skill and intelligence.

Carneiro (1973a) has shown how Spencer regarded environment, economics, and warfare as important causes of social evolution. Spencer regarded the environment as an important determinant in a manner analogous to modern cultural ecologists. Carneiro suggests that the importance Spencer attached to economic determinants can be clearly seen in his analysis of the role of commerce and industry in helping prepare the way for the development of Greek democracy. Spencer also gave considerable importance to warfare, as the following passage demonstrates (1899:280; cited in Carneiro, 1973a:110):

In the struggle for existence among societies, the survival of the fittest is the survival of those in which the power of military cooperation is the greatest; and military cooperation is that primary kind of cooperation which prepares the way for other kinds. So that this formation of larger societies by the union of smaller ones in war, and this destruction or absorption of the smaller un-united societies by the united larger ones, is an inevitable process which the varieties of men most adapted for social life, supplant the less adapted varieties.

As Carneiro has pointed out, Spencer's emphasis on warfare and inter-societal conflict was a major manifestation of his "social Darwinism," his view that social struggle leading to the "survival of the fittest" played a crucial role in the evolution of society.

Although there has been no serious materialist/idealist debate centering around Spencer, and even though Spencer took the trouble to denounce a materialist perspective, it is clear that he was very much a materialist nonetheless (cf. Carneiro, 1973a). His unambiguous emphasis on demo-graphic, environmental, and economic factors as important determinants of social evolution not only places him substantially in the materialist camp, but it does so in a very modern sense. This is particularly the case in regard to the role he gave to population pressure. Spencer has here anticipated a leading modern theory of social evolution (see chapter 7). We thus return to the irony noted earlier: Despite some of his quaintness, and despite the profound developmentalism of his overblown Law of Evolution, there is a side to Spencer that is strikingly modern and scientific. Like that of most of the other classical evolutionists, as well as that of many other nineteenth-century social thinkers, Spencer's thought was a curious epistemological and theoretical mélange.

THE CLASSICAL EVOLUTIONISTS AND DARWINISM

The classical theories of social evolution historically coincided with the rise to prominence of Darwinian bioevolutionary theory. This was clearly no accident, and theories of evolution in both the biological and social realms were related. The specific nature of this relationship has been the subject of much discussion.

Most of the attention has focused on Spencer's evolutionism. Since Spencer was perhaps the leading advocate of the doctrine of social Darwinism, it has been widely believed that his evolutionary doctrines were largely a transferral of Darwinian theory to the sociocultural realm, a direct application of the Darwinian concepts of "struggle for survival" and "natural selection" to social life. In the last quarter-century, though, the mythical character of this belief has been exposed by numerous scholars, most particularly by J. D. Y. Peel (1971) and Marvin Harris (1968). Peel has suggested that, despite their superficial resemblances, the theories of Darwin and Spencer were actually quite different. For instance, he points out that Darwin's theory was much more modest and that it altogether lacked the developmentalism and necessitarianism of Spencer's.[5] Harris pursues a somewhat different course and makes a much bolder set of claims. He argues that the doctrine of "the struggle for survival" found in both Darwin and Spencer was independently derived by each from Malthus, and he also claims a certain priority for Spencer in the development of evolutionary concepts.[6] It was Spencer rather than Darwin, Harris claims, who popularized the term "evolution" itself.[7] Moreover, Spencer's term "survival of the fittest" was originally developed by him and actually borrowed by Darwin as a preferred synonym for his own term "natural selection" in the fifth edition of *Origin of Species*. Harris also shows that Spencer had already established his key evolutionary doctrines well before Darwin's ideas appeared in print. Harris actually goes so far as to suggest that the label "social Darwinism" is a complete misnomer, and that, in view of the priority of Spencer and the esteem in which Darwin held him, "the term 'Biological Spencerism' would be an appropriate label for that period of the history of biological theory in which Darwin's ideas gained their ascendancy" (1968:129).[8]

Yet in the final analysis it is not really a claim for the causal influence of Spencer on Darwin that Harris is arguing for. Rather, it is the view that both Darwin's and Spencer's evolutionary theories were largely independent outcomes of the same cultural and intellectual milieu. As Harris puts it (1968:129):

It was not a matter of one discipline aping another, but rather a parallel response by both disciplines to similar ideological needs. The biologization of sociocultural theory arose from the need for countering the politically subversive environmentalism of the eighteenth century. The conversion of biological theory to evolutionism was an outgrowth of the social scientists' interest in progress and perfectibility, while the concept of natural selection arose from an interest in racial, national, and class forms of war and conflict.

While one can have strong reservations about this exceptionally bold claim, that need not invalidate Harris's more general point about the proper relation between Spencer and Darwin. The point is that Spencer's ideas were his own rather than a simple imitation of Darwin's.

As for the relation of Tylor and Morgan to Darwinism, some scholars have attempted to portray both as self-consciously using Darwinian concepts to explain social evolution. Opler (1964, 1965), for example, suggests that Tylor was an explicit "cultural Darwinist," and he cites no fewer than eight passages from Tylor's various works as evidence for his case. The following is an example (Tylor, 1871, I:68-9; cited in Opler, 1964:133-4; emphasis Opler's):

It will be seen again and again, by examining such topics as language, mythology, custom, religion, that savage opinion is in a more or less rudimentary state, while the civilized mind still bears vestiges, neither few nor slight, of a past condition from which savages represent the least, and civilized men the greatest advance. Throughout the whole vast range of the history of human thought and habit, while civilization has to contend not only with survival from lower levels, but also with degeneration within its own borders, it yet proves capable of overcoming both and taking its own course. History within its proper field, and ethnography over a wider range, combine *to show that the institutions which can best hold their own in the world gradually supersede the less fit ones, and that this incessant conflict determines the general resultant course of culture.*

In the other passages cited by Opler, we find Tylor using phrases like "unless when superseded by some better device" or "which form in any age their fittest representatives," or at least more indirectly suggesting the operation of a process of natural selection in social life.

Carneiro's view of Tylor is much the same as Opler's, and in fact Carneiro's preferred evidentiary passages overlap with Opler's, including the one cited immediately above. Carneiro also proposes Tylor's famed discussion of exogamy rules, in which he remarks that "primitive tribes must have had plainly before their minds the simple practical alternative between marrying-out and being killed out" (Tylor, 1889:267), as an exemplification of Tylor's reliance on a kind of natural selection theory.

Opler and Carneiro propose the same basic interpretation for Morgan. Although Opler believes that Morgan relied less frequently on a Darwinian kind of social evolutionism than Tylor did, he views Morgan as embracing a kind of Darwinism nonetheless, and he notes that Morgan explicitly used the term "natural selection" at several points in *Ancient Society*. Both Opler and Carneiro regard Morgan's discussion of the evolution of social organization and the family as based on a principle of natural selection. A passage they both cite states that "the organization into classes upon sex, and the subsequent higher organization into gentes upon kin, must be regarded as the results of great social movements worked out unconsciously through natural selection" (Morgan, 1974[1877]:48).

White has strongly denied any influence of Darwinism on either Tylor or Morgan, and with respect to Tylor he claims that Tylor himself explicitly proclaims his independence of Darwin. White quotes from Tylor's preface to the second edition of *Primitive Culture* to the following effect: "The present work [is] arranged on its own lines, coming scarcely into contact of detail with the previous works of these eminent philosophers [Darwin and Spencer]." Opler counters White's claim with the argument that if this quoted fragment is placed in its larger context, then Tylor can only be reasonably interpreted to mean that he is borrowing generally from Darwinian and Spencerian ideas but makes few specific references to them because his own data are neither biological nor philosophical in character.

There is little doubt but that Opler has the better interpretation of Tylor's meaning here. Certainly one could not use Tylor's comments in his preface to prove that Tylor is denying any Darwinian influence, for the possibility that he is actually endorsing a general sort of debt to Darwin is clearly there. And it also seems to be the case that Tylor, and Morgan as well, did have a loose sort of natural-selection conception of evolutionary change running through their works. This is not particularly surprising inasmuch as their works were published a decade or two after Darwin's, and by that time Darwinian ideas were well known and of substantial influence. But whether they were self-consciously copying Darwin is doubtful, given the popularity of Darwinian natural-selection and Spencerian survival-of-the-fittest ideas by the 1870s. It is even more doubtful that these ideas were fundamental to their thinking in the sense that they were for Spencer. Thus a loose kind of natural-selection conception seems to be part of Tylor's and Morgan's evolutionary thinking, but it does not identify, let alone overpower, that thinking. As we have seen, other ideas are more basic to the evolutionism of Tylor and Morgan.

CLASSICAL EVOLUTIONISM AND THE DOCTRINE OF PROGRESS

The doctrine of progress – the idea that with the evolution of society there is a steady improvement in such aspects of the human condition as intelligence, morality, and happiness – has roots which are firmly planted well before the late nineteenth century. Indeed, this doctrine was virtually the cornerstone of Enlightenment social thought. The nineteenth-century evolutionists inherited this doctrine and perpetuated it, though, as we shall see, they did not accept it without reservation.

Spencer's conception of progress was a feature of his social Darwinism. Through various forms of conflict and struggle new social forms emerged from older ones through a kind of survival of the fittest, and these more fit social arrangements led to an enhanced social adaptation and hence an improvement in the human condition. Spencer's cosmic evolutionary law is also closely related to this view. Increasingly differentiated social arrangements produce more advanced levels of cooperation and integration, and these social arrangements are thus more adaptive.

Spencer's conception of progress is nowhere more evident, however, than in his discussion of the evolution from militant to industrial society. As noted earlier, Spencer conceptualized a movement away from a type of society based upon the pervasiveness of military organization and the domination of individuals by society as a whole, and toward a type of society depending little upon military organization and resting on the voluntary cooperation of free individuals. Individual freedom was the key to industrial society, and the increasing movement toward freedom was viewed by Spencer in extremely favorable terms, as is quite evident from the following passage (Spencer, 1972[1876]:159–60):

[With industrial society] there go sentiments and ideas concerning the relation between the citizen and the State, opposite to those accompanying the militant type. In place of the doctrine that the duty of obedience to the governing agent is unqualified, there arises the doctrine that the will of the citizens is supreme and the governing agent exists merely to carry out their will. Thus subordinated in authority, the regulating power is also restricted in range. Instead of having an authority extending over actions of all kinds, it is shut out from large classes of actions. Its control over ways of living in respect to food, clothing, amusements, is repudiated; it is not allowed to dictate modes of production nor to regulate trade.

Nor is this all. It becomes a duty to resist irresponsible government, and also to resist the excesses of responsible government. There arises a tendency in minorities to disobey even the legislature deputed by the majority, when it interferes in certain ways; and their oppositions to laws they condemn as inequitable, from time to time cause abolition of them. With which changes of political theory and accompanying sentiment, is joined a belief, implied or avowed, that the combined actions of the social aggregate have for their end to maintain the conditions under which individual lives may be satisfactorily carried on; in place of the old belief that individual lives have for their end the maintenance of this aggregate's combined actions.

The received wisdom on Spencer's political and moral views is that he was an extremely vigorous defender of modern laissez-faire capitalism and imperialism. Such a view, for instance, is strongly advocated by Marvin Harris (1968). Yet this conventional viewpoint is something of an exaggeration. Carneiro (1967) has suggested that Spencer had important reservations about some of Britain's colonial policies, and that on more than one occasion he reported feeling ashamed of his country. Peel (1971) has been even more emphatic in his effort to counter the conventional wisdom on Spencer. He claims that Spencer was a peace lover vehemently opposed to the colonial wars of the late nineteenth century, that he was hardly the apologist for capitalism that he has been made out to be, and that some of his writings reveal serious misgivings about modern industrial capitalism. Peel remarks that (1971:216):

After comparing the life of a factory operative with that of a cottager, [Spencer] admitted "that this industrial development has proved extremely detrimental to the operative." His work-life is monotonous, his faculties are either overused or disused, and he is not really free to contract at will: "this liberty amounts in practice to little more than the ability to exchange one slavery for another, since, fit only for his particular occupation, he rarely has an opportunity of doing anything more than decide in what mill he will pass the greater part of his dreary days". . . . He observes that "in the course of social progress parts . . . are sacrificed for the benefits of the society as a whole"; whereas in earlier days men were killed in war, now there was a "mortality entailed by the commercial struggle," and "in either case men are used up for the benefit of posterity; and so long as they go on multiplying in excess of the means of subsistence, there appears no remedy."

Tylor and Morgan also generally believed that social evolution could be equated with human progress. The very names they used for their evolutionary stages – savagery, barbarism, civilization – indisputably reveal this. Moreover, their writings are liberally sprinkled with statements attesting to the "rude conditions" of savages and their gradual improvement in barbarism, and, especially, in civilization, and they continually use words like "higher" and "lower" in reference to societies at different evolutionary stages. They are also quite explicit about their commitment to a view of progressive improvement in the human condition. Tylor says for example (1924, I:27): "From an ideal point of view, civilization may be looked upon as the general improvement of mankind by higher organization of the individual and society, to the end of promoting at once man's goodness, power, and happiness." And Morgan refers to "the inferiority of savage man in the mental and moral scale, undeveloped, inexperienced, and held down by his low animal appetites and passions" (1974[1877]:41). Numerous other passages from the works of both Tylor and Morgan could easily be cited to demonstrate their ethnocentrism and their belief in progress.

But it is also clear that, like Spencer, Tylor and Morgan scarcely held an unqualified view of progress. Tylor, in fact, is at pains to point to the important qualifications that have to be made with respect to equating evolution with progress (Tylor, 1924, I:27–9):

But even those students who hold most strongly that the general course of civilization, as measured along the scale of races from savages to ourselves, is progress towards the benefit of mankind, must admit of many and manifold exceptions. Industrial and intellectual culture by no means advances uniformly in all its branches, and in fact excellence in various of its details is often obtained under conditions which keep back culture as a whole. . . . Thus, even in comparing mental and artistic culture among several peoples, the balance of good and ill is not quite easy to strike.

If not only knowledge and art, but at the same time moral and political excellence, be taken into consideration, it becomes yet harder to reckon on an ideal scale the advance or decline from stage to stage of culture. . . . Whether in high ranges or in low of human life, it may be seen that advance of culture seldom results at once in unmixed good. . . . The white invader or colonist, though representing on the whole a higher moral standard than the savage he improves or destroys, often represents his standard very ill, and at best can hardly claim to substitute a life stronger, nobler, and purer at every point than that which he supersedes.

As for Morgan, he had constant praise for the democracy and equality of the gens and on several occasions alluded to the ill effects of property and social inequality. The now famous closing words of *Ancient Society* were remarked upon by Marx and Engels and have been quoted many times since, but they still bear repeating (1974[1877]:561–2):

Property and office were the foundations upon which aristocracy planted itself.

Whether this principle shall live or die has been one of the great problems with which modern society has been engaged through the intervening periods. . . . Although several thousand years have passed away without the overthrow of privileged classes, excepting in the United States [!], their burdensome character upon society has been demonstrated. . . .

A mere property career is not the final destiny of mankind, if progress is to be the law of the future as it has been of the past. . . . Democracy in government, brotherhood in society, equality in rights and privileges, and universal education, foreshadow the next higher plane of society to which experience, intelligence and knowledge are steadily tending. It will be a revival, in a higher form, of the liberty, equality and fraternity of the ancient gentes.

NOTES

1  Mandelbaum's notion of functional laws should not be confused with what is usually called functionalist explanation, or with the sociological school of thought known as functionalism. Mandelbaum might have less misleadingly called these laws *causal* laws.

2  A number of other scholars have developed similar conceptions to characterize and criticize the nineteenth-century evolutionists. Karl Popper's famous book *The Poverty of Historicism* (1957) developed the concept of historicism along much the same lines that Mandelbaum did a decade and a half later. Mandelbaum's directional law/functional law dichotomy is virtually repeated in Leon Goldstein's (1967) contrast between developmental and causal laws, although Goldstein applies this distinction to recent rather than classical thinkers. In chapter 1 we referred to Anthony Giddens's (1981, 1984) notion that most evolutionary accounts rest on unfolding models. For the sake of terminological simplicity, I shall henceforth use the term *developmentalism* to characterize epistemological conceptions of social evolution that are historicist and that rest on directional or developmental laws or unfolding models.

   This discussion obviously suggests the question of the relation between developmentalist and *teleological* conceptions of historical change. Conceptually, teleological and developmentalist views of change cannot be strictly equated. The former assume the existence of a specific purpose or set of purposes whose realization drives history forward, and the latter do not necessarily do so. Yet in practice all teleological conceptions of history will be developmentalist, and most developmentalist ones will no doubt end up being teleological. Whether the formulations of the classical evolutionists were teleological in addition to being developmentalist is perhaps something of an open question, but it is likely that they were (cf. Hirst [1976] for a discussion of Spencer and Morgan on this point).

   An interesting attempt to defend a type of developmentalism has been made by Olding (1978). It is noteworthy, though, that Olding's examples involve things like stellar evolution and the sprouting of apple trees from apple seeds, and he says nothing of the history of societies. Even with respect to the kinds of physical and biological phenomena he addresses, however, his arguments seem dubious, because one can still reply that these highly law-like patterns of change can be explained by reducing them to certain functional laws.

3  The meaning of the term "developmentalist" is explained in note 2. The phrase "ordinary causal explanation" refers to what Mandelbaum means by explanation in terms of functional laws. I shall use this phrase (or the phrases "ordinary causation" or "ordinary causes") from this point on in order to avoid the reader's confusing this form of explanation with functionalist modes of analysis.

4  Actually, Hirst is probably right in the case of Spencer. Spencer often used the words "proximate" and "ultimate" in his explanatory statements, and thus he may well have consciously understood that he was employing two very different models of explanation (and, if so, he would obviously not have seen them as incompatible).

5  The same point has been made numerous times in recent years, and it is clear that Darwin's model of causation adhered to Mandelbaum's conception of explanation in terms of a functional law (cf. Toulmin, 1972).

6  Much the same argument is made by Burrow (1966). Young (1969) and Freeman (1974) are also important contributions to the discussion about the theories of Malthus, Spencer, and Darwin and the relations among them, although they have other concerns of their own as well. Freeman's article places great emphasis on the differences between Darwin's and Spencer's theories to the detriment of Spencer. Although Freeman is probably correct, he exaggerates the differences and paints an

unduly negative picture of Spencer, regarding him as little more than a speculative metaphysician in comparison with Darwin the rigorous scientist.

7 Toulmin (1972:330–1) notes that Darwin generally resisted the word "evolution" because he rejected what he took to be its developmentalist implications. He did not use this word at all until the sixth edition of *Origin*, and then did so only sparingly.

8 Harris's interpretation of Spencer on these counts closely corresponds to that of Carneiro (1967), from which, in fact, it is substantially derived.

# 3

# The Antievolutionary Reaction

Social evolutionism's golden age came crashing to a halt soon after the beginning of the twentieth century, the decline actually starting in the last decade of the nineteenth. The increasing disfavor that evolutionism was beginning to encounter can be seen in a number of ways. For one thing, Spencer's reputation sharply declined in the waning years of his life. Spencer was widely known to the general public and had a very favorable image among intellectuals, but in his last years his ideas came increasingly under attack and he was forced to modify them in order to keep others interested in them at all. In addition, the works of Morgan and Tylor were systematically attacked in American anthropology under the leadership of Franz Boas. Boas taught his students that evolutionism contained serious logical and theoretical errors, and during the first half of the twentieth century the antievolutionism that he and his followers espoused clearly prevailed over evolutionism.

The objections of the Boasians against evolutionism were essentially fourfold. They thought that it was logically flawed in its employment of the comparative method as a basis for reconstructing evolutionary sequences; that it employed rigid unilinear evolutionary schemes; that it gave insufficient attention to the influence of diffusion, the widespread existence of which undermined evolutionary arguments; and that it proposed an illegitimate doctrine of progress, thereby denigrating cultures to the extent that they were less culturally developed. This chapter explores the first three of these criticisms. (It more or less concedes the last of them, which was discussed in the previous chapter.) The argument will be that the Boasians were either incorrect, or that they grossly exaggerated and oversimplified matters, on all three counts.

CLASSICAL EVOLUTIONISM AND THE COMPARATIVE METHOD

The comparative method was widely employed by the classical evolutionists in the construction of evolutionary sequences. Although they did not ignore archaeological data and used it whenever possible (Harris, 1968), its paucity at this time meant that it could not form the primary basis for their theoretical notions. The comparative method therefore of necessity constituted their major methodological tool. It was a procedure well known in their day and had been employed to a considerable extent by their eighteenth-century predecessors. The procedure was actually a quite simple one. It involved collecting information about known cultures that differed markedly among themselves and then arranging these cultures in a manner presumed to represent an actual historical sequence, a sequence through which such cultures could be said to have passed. In other words, contemporary cultures of a certain type were presumed to closely resemble historical cultures as they would have looked in their own time. Arranging known cultures in a particular manner according to certain specified criteria allowed one to infer historical change and to assume that the synchronic data represented an actual evolutionary sequence.

Spencer was perhaps the most avid employer of the comparative method. In his monumental work *Descriptive Sociology* (1873-1934) he compiled highly detailed descriptions of individual cultures. These descriptions formed the basis for the actual comparisons and theoretical generalizations he made in the three volumes of his *The Principles of Sociology*. The first volume of *Descriptive Sociology* was published in 1873 and by the time of his death eight volumes had appeared. These dealt with such diverse groups as the English, ancient Mexicans and Peruvians, Malayo–Polynesian cultures, African cultures, various Asian groups, North and South American Indians, Hebrews and Phoenicians, and the French. Some of Spencer's followers continued to turn out new volumes after his death, and by 1934 another seven had appeared. These dealt with the Chinese, the Hellenic and Hellenistic Greeks, ancient Egypt, ancient Mesopotamia, ancient Rome, and additional African groups.

Tylor and Morgan also made extensive use of the comparative method. Tylor claimed that "by comparing the various stages of civilization among races known to history, with the aid of archaeological inference from the remains of prehistoric tribes, it seems possible to judge in a rough way of an early general condition of man" (1924, I:21). Notice that in this passage Tylor indicates that the comparative method is to be used in conjunction with archaeological evidence, and that he claims no more than that contemporary cultures "approximate" earlier ones.

One major way in which Tylor used the comparative method was through his concept of survivals, the existence of which, he thought, provided a reasonable foundation for inferences about evolutionary changes. As he put it, survivals "are processes, customs, opinions, and so forth, which have been carried on by force of habit into a new state of society different from that in which they had their original home, and they thus remain as proofs and examples of an older condition of culture out of which a newer has been evolved" (Tylor, 1924, I:16).

In *Ancient Society* Morgan claimed that (1974[1877]:506–7), "Like the successive geological formations, the tribes of mankind may be arranged, according to their relative conditions, into successive strata. When thus arranged, they reveal with some degree of certainty the entire range of human progress from savagery to civilization." Morgan made great use in *Ancient Society* of ethnographic materials from the Iroquois and the ancient Greeks and Romans, but he also drew upon information regarding numerous other preliterate and literate societies.

This method was widely decried by Boas and many of his disciples and pupils. Boas himself identified it as logically flawed, saying that "if anthropology desires to establish laws governing the growth of culture it must not confine itself to comparing the *results* of the growth alone, but whenever such is feasible is must compare the *processes* of growth" (Boas, 1940a[1896]:280; emphasis added). Boas's point was essentially that the comparative method rested on a process of mere inference that was much too insecure a foundation for establishing fundamental theoretical principles. The alternative to the comparative method was therefore the historical method, a method that actually observed the historical changes that had taken place in a particular society.

A similar objection was made by one of Boas's most prominent students, Alexander Goldenweiser, except Goldenweiser went further and charged that the comparative method rested upon the fallacy of circular reasoning. In his famous textbook *Anthropology* he asked (1937:508):

What right has the evolutionist to arrange instances of cultural facts or processes gathered from different tribes into a successive series, and then claim it as historical, claim, that is, that it has actually occurred in this form, that the different instances were comprised in a concrete historic series of stages at some particular place and time, or in all places and times, whenever the particular institution has developed in history? . . . The only answer the evolutionist could give here would be that according to the general principles of evolution such were the stages, and that now they were concretely illustrated; therefore the evolutionary hypothesis was correct. This reply cannot be accepted as valid. The instances may be factual and accurate enough as instances, but the ordering of them into a series of temporal succession, never as such observed nor deducible from the facts, could only be validated by the assumption of uniformity in development which is one of the tenets of evolution, the very hypothesis, that is, the procedure was intended to prove. The argument is therefore circular: something that is to be proved, or an inherent part of that something, is assumed in order to make the proof valid.

As we shall see in later chapters, the comparative method is still a major tool of modern evolutionists, and the criticisms made against it by the Boasians are still widely endorsed today by numerous antievolutionary sociologists and anthropologists. Are these criticisms valid? Indeed, they are not, and defenses of the legitimate employment of the comparative method have been made by numerous scholars. Robert Carneiro (1973a) has noted that the comparative method was already a well-known tool by the time the classical evolutionists began their work. Use of it was so well established that it was implicit in their work and they therefore hardly felt a need to defend its use. Of course, the fact that it was time-honored is hardly a suitable defense of it, but Carneiro suggests that the classical evolutionists actually had some clearly worked out principles whereby they could defend the comparative method's employment. All of them used cultural complexity as a criterion for classifying cultures. This was, for example, Spencer's main basis for his classifications. Similarly, Tylor proposed that (1871, I:28; quoted in Carneiro, 1973a:69):

the principal criteria of classification are the absence or presence, high or low development, of the industrial arts, especially metal-working, manufacture of implements and vessels, agriculture, &c., the extent of scientific knowledge, the definiteness of moral principles, the condition of religious belief and ceremony, the degree of social and political organization, and so forth.

Marvin Harris (1968) has insisted that the use of the comparative method by the classical evolutionists was *in principle* sound, and that a distinction must be drawn between its appropriate employment and some of the abuses of it that were perpetrated by the nineteenth-century evolutionists. Harris points out that the classical evolutionists tended to underestimate the degree of diversity in both contemporary and ancient societies. This led them to make a number of serious errors, such as assuming that the lack of metallurgy implied the absence of social stratification, or assuming a universal matrilineal stage of family organization preceding a universal patrilineal one. But, Harris argues, the comparative method is without doubt a legitimate, and actually a crucial, tool if properly employed. Are there such things as surviving stone-age cultures, he asks? Indeed, the assumption that there are is a perfectly valid one in precisely the same sense as the assumption widely employed by evolutionary biologists that contemporary species are survivals from the past (and that there are morphological similarities between surviving species and extinct ones).

Along the same lines Elman Service puts it exceptionally well when he asks (1971a:7; emphasis added):

If the aboriginal culture of the Arunta of Australia is not a form of adaptation to a particular kind of (total) environment made long, long ago and preserved into modern times because of its isolation, *then what is it?* Does a people have whatever kind of culture it might dream up at any given time? Obviously not. Do the Arunta have a rudimentary technology and simple social life because that is as far as their mental powers would take them? No. . . . What else can explain such a culture, then, but that there have been survivals into the present of ancient cultural forms which because of relative isolation have maintained a relatively stable adaptation.

This defense of the comparative method is actually associated with a profound irony, and that is that the antievolutionists themselves sometimes recognized the value of the comparative method and made their own use of it. Carneiro (1973a) has pointed out that Boas himself would occasionally equate contemporary primitives with ancient societal forms, and he quotes him as saying that "we find in modern times isolated tribes living in a way that may very well be paralleled with early conditions" (Boas, 1932:608; cited in Carneiro, 1973a:74). Moreover, Goldenweiser was a promoter of the comparative method in spite of himself. What else could have provided the basis for the following remarks (Goldenweiser, 1937:520–1)?

Take, for example, chieftainship. It is probable that one or another kind of leadership has existed in human society from the beginning, but certainly not hereditary leadership. Before succession in office was established or could have been thought of, there must have been leaders or officials whose office was not hereditary. Similarly, leadership must have developed in relatively small groups; the presence of a chieftain wielding power over a populous tribe or group of tribes, could not possibly be regarded as a primary or truly primitive state of affairs. . . . [I]n the domain of religion and magic . . . the data indicate that the more primitive forms of supernatural creatures and magical devices are associated with single or at any rate simple purposes and functions. A primal magical rite is for fertility, protection, success in hunting or in love; a primitive spirit is of sickness or famine, of craftsmanship or of valour. The more comprehensive forms of magical power, the more versatile deities encountered among the more advanced primitives as well as in historic times, came into being through a process of syncretism – powers and functions originally connected with separate things, acts, or supernatural beings, now became concentrated in a single carrier. We cannot very well conceive of this process as reversed, except under very special conditions, without going both in the face of known facts and of theoretical probability.

Or take the field of economics. Once more, some sort of vague proprietary sense may, perhaps, be regarded as having belonged to man from the beginning. Do we not see incipient elements of it already among animals? But here also the idea of inheritance of property must have appeared later. This theoretically feasible conception is fully vindicated by a survey of primitive tribes; the cruder ones either manage without the notion of property inheritance or have no very definite regulations in this connexion. The exchange of goods or commodities, again, may be very old indeed, but before a medium of exchange developed there was exchange in kind, and it is out of the perplexities and inconveniences of the latter that the stimulus arose first to regard certain goods as a medium of exchange, then to devise a separate medium which no longer had much or any value except as a medium.

Their formal protestations notwithstanding, it would definitely appear that at least some of the Boasians unconsciously knew a good thing when they saw it.[1]

## WERE THE CLASSICAL EVOLUTIONISTS UNILINEARISTS?

One of the strongest objections made by the Boasians against the nineteenth-century evolutionists was that they proposed rigid evolutionary schemes in which they interpreted all cultural development as occurring along uniform lines – that they were unilinear evolutionists. The Boasians differed somewhat among themselves in terms of how severely they chastised the classical evolutionists for this alleged characteristic, but they were all generally agreed that it constituted a serious flaw in their works. Boas was willing to admit the existence of certain parallels in cultural development in different parts of the globe, but he thought them insufficient to establish a hypothesis of "a single general line of development" (Boas, 1940b[1920]; cf. Harris, 1968). Other Boasians, like Goldenweiser and Robert Lowie, were perhaps willing to admit greater parallelism than Boas was, but they too would admit only "limited parallels." In general, the Boasians preferred to emphasize the unique historical development of every society.

Were the Boasians correct in their judgment that the nineteenth-century evolutionists were unilinearists? Although there are still many contemporary social scientists who believe that they were (more commonly sociologists rather than anthropologists, I suspect; cf. Appelbaum, 1970), a number have attempted to expose this view as little more than a myth (Hirst, 1976; Kaplan and Manners, 1972; Harris, 1968; Carneiro, 1973a). Two of the most vigorous advocates of the inaccuracy of the Boasian claim are Harris and Carneiro. Harris has emphasized that the classical evolutionists introduced numerous qualifications into their statements about a general line of cultural development and thus scarcely promoted a rigid, lockstep view of evolutionary change. He points out that the classical evolutionists thought the general similarities in cultural development more interesting and more worth pursuing because their express aim was to develop a "science of universal history." This could hardly have been achieved by dwelling on diversity and the unique features of cultural change.

Carneiro exempts all of the classical evolutionists from the charge of rigid unilinearism. Like Harris, he notes that they introduced numerous qualifying statements into their generalizations. He has been especially eager to exempt Spencer from the unilinearist charge and cites a prominent passage from Spencer to suggest that he "was not only not a unilinear evolutionist, he was not even a linear evolutionist" (Carneiro, 1967:xlii). The passage in question is a particularly famous one in which Spencer says, "Social progress is not linear but divergent and re-divergent. . . . [M]ultiplying groups have tended ever to acquire differences, now major and now minor: there have arisen genera and species of societies" (1900:331). This passage is also cited by Harris and by numerous other exegetes of Spencer's evolutionism.

Both Harris and Carneiro are able to cite numerous passages from the works of the classical evolutionists to support their arguments, and there can be little doubt about the validity of their interpretation of these passages. It would not be difficult to adduce further passages to the same effect. Yet there is a sense in which both thinkers engage in overstatement and oversimplification. The issue really turns on what is meant by unilinearism. For his part, Harris seems to take it to mean the view that all cultures inexorably evolve through the same stages, with no stage-skipping, stagnation, or regression being permitted. If this is what unilinearism means, then it is child's play to show that the classical evolutionists were not unilinearists. In fact, it would be difficult to imagine anyone's ever holding such a view.

It is possible, however, to define unilinearism in a somewhat looser way. Unilinearism can be defined as the view that cultural development *generally* moves along *broadly similar* (but not rigidly uniform) lines.[2] Let us call the type of unilinearism focused on by Harris *strong unilinearism*, while identifying the type defined in the preceding sentence as *weak unilinearism*. This allows us to say with relative ease that, although the classical evolutionists were scarcely strong unilinearists, they certainly were weak unilinearists.[3] Indeed, weak unilinearism is the hallmark of their analyses, and statements to this effect are easy to locate in their writings. Spencer's qualification that evolution is not linear but divergent and redivergent aside, how else could we interpret his famous Law of Evolution but as a type of weak unilinearism? Consider also Spencer's claim that there is a generalized movement from militant to industrial society. Even more significant is his classification of societies along the dimension of societal complexity. In speaking of societies in the context of this scheme, he says, "The stages of compounding and re-compounding have to be passed through in succession. . . . In this order has social evolution gone on, and only in this order does it appear to be possible" (1972[1876]:147–8). And consider the following passages from the writings of Morgan and Tylor that can be sensibly interpreted only as manifestations of a weak unilinearism:

The tendency of culture has been similar throughout the existence of human society, and . . . we may fairly judge from its known historic course what its prehistoric course may have been (Tylor, 1924, I:33).

It may be remarked finally that the experience of mankind has run in nearly uniform channels; that human necessities in similar conditions have been substantially the same; and that the operations of the mental principle have been uniform in virtue of the specific identity of the brain of all the races of mankind (Morgan, 1974[1877]:8).[4]

The course and manner of [societal] development was predetermined, as well as restricted within narrow limits of divergence, by the natural logic of the human mind and the necessary limitations of its powers. Progress has been found to be substantially the same in kind in tribes and nations inhabiting different and even disconnected continents, while in the same status, with deviations from uniformity in particular instances produced by special causes (Morgan, 1974[1877]:18).

Mankind were able to produce in similar conditions the same implements and utensils, the same inventions, and to develop similar institutions from the same original germs of thought (Morgan, 1974[1877]:562).

In support of the claim that the classical evolutionists did indeed favor a type of unilinearism, let us also not overlook a key argument of the previous chapter: that nineteenth-century evolutionism was substantially based on a doctrine of developmentalism. A conception of evolutionary transformation as a predetermined unfolding of immanences automatically presupposes a unilinear conception of change, and in such a view divergence can only be regarded as a deviation from a typical path (witness the usage of this very word by Morgan in the third passage quoted above, and notice how he claims that such divergence must be explained by "special causes"). The developmentalism of the classical evolutionists presents, in fact, the strongest case for their unilinearism.[5]

### CLASSICAL EVOLUTIONISM AND DIFFUSION

A third major challenge to the classical evolutionists involved the role that external factors were thought to play in the formation of the particular characteristics of any given society. By and large, the Boasians opposed "independent evolution" to "diffusion" and declared diffusion the winner. The classical evolutionists were said to be unaware, or at least insufficiently aware, of the facts about the role of diffusion, and this was deemed another nail in their coffin.

Although this idea is often held even today (cf. Mandelbaum, 1971), the Boasians committed an especially egregious error in this regard, and thus it has been extraordinarily easy for modern scholars to refute it. In all fairness, it must be pointed out that some of the Boasians recognized that the classical evolutionists were aware of the facts about diffusion. Yet they thought that the evolutionists either did not realize the implications these facts had for evolutionary theories, or that they produced unacceptable defenses of their theories in light of them (cf. Goldenweiser, 1937:517; Lowie, 1937:74-81). Lowie, for instance, cites numerous instances of Tylor's high regard for the facts of diffusion, and notes that he "remains one of the few scholars whose championship of independent evolution is not a sterile, however unwarranted, denial of diffusion" (Lowie, 1937:81). Lowie also mentions Morgan's awareness of diffusionary influences (Lowie, 1937:59).

The facts of the matter, though, suggest that even Lowie grossly underestimated the appreciation the classical evolutionists had for diffusion. Although Tylor did show it an extraordinary regard, sometimes even to the point of favoring diffusionary explanations over those emphasizing independent evolution, he was alone only in the extent of his regard. As Harris (1968) has pointed out, Morgan not only knew about diffusion, but considered it to be an important factor in bringing about many of the uniformities of cultural evolution. Thus (Morgan, 1974[1877]:39; modified from citation in Harris, 1968:177):

Whenever a continental connection existed, all the tribes must have shared in some measure in each other's progress. All great inventions and discoveries propagate themselves; but the inferior tribes must have appreciated their value before they could appropriate them. In the continental areas certain tribes would lead; but the leadership would be apt to shift a number of times in the course of an ethnical period.

Along similar lines, Carneiro shows that in explaining the widespread occurrence of clans Morgan actually favored a diffusionary theory over one stressing independent invention.

Harris and Carneiro make an outstanding case not only for the keen awareness by the classical evolutionists[6] of the facts of diffusion, but for their integration of these facts into their evolutionary formulations.[7] Here is another passage from Tylor not cited by either Harris or Carneiro, but that further buttresses this point (Tylor, 1924, I:39):

In striking a balance between the effects of forward and backward movement in civilization, it must be borne in mind how powerfully the diffusion of culture acts in preserving the results of progress from the attacks of degeneration. A progressive movement in culture spreads, and becomes independent of the fate of its originators.

And here is another passage from Morgan to the same effect (Morgan, 1974[1877]:16):

Some tribes and families have been left in geographical isolation to work out the problems of progress by original mental effort; and have, consequently, retained their arts and institutions pure and homogeneous; while those of other tribes and nations have been adulterated through external influence.

We see, then, that at least some of the classical evolutionists knew all about diffusion and saw no difficulty at all in integrating it into their evolutionary schemes. This makes it all the more curious that Lowie should have uttered his famous statement that "diffusion plays havoc with any universal law of sequence" (1937:60). That statement can only make sense to someone who sees cultural evolution as a purely endogenous process and who thus regards evolution and diffusion as diametrically opposed. But such a viewpoint was never held by the classical evolutionists. They seemed to have understood the point that Ingold has made so elegantly: that "diffusion is merely discovery at second hand" (1986:40). In other words, they realized that diffusion is not an automatic process, but occurs in a highly selective manner. People do not simply borrow from others indiscriminately, but take those things that fit into their culture and for which a need is perceived. Likewise, many elements of other cultures are rejected because of their incompatibility or their inability to satisfy particular needs and wants. Once we conceptualize the human rationale behind diffusion in this more sophisticated and subtle way, we need no longer oppose it to an evolutionary scheme, even a weakly unilinear one.[8]

### THE CONTRIBUTIONS OF THE CLASSICAL EVOLUTIONISTS

During the first few decades of the twentieth century evolution was a dirty word in Western social science. Evolutionism as a theoretical approach was held in contempt by many and viewed with great skepticism by most of the rest of the social–scientific world. It did not completely die out, and some prominent evolutionary works appeared during this period, two of the most notable of which were Hobhouse, Wheeler, and Ginsberg's *The Material*

*Culture and Social Institutions of the Simpler Peoples* (1965[1915]) and A. G. Keller's *Societal Evolution* (1915; cf. Sumner and Keller, 1927) (Keller was a disciple of William Graham Sumner, who, of course, was greatly influenced by Spencer). But it was a way of thinking about the nature of society that was practiced or endorsed only at risk to one's intellectual career.

What filled the breach? In the United States it was the approach of Boas himself, an approach often identified by contemporary scholars as *historical particularism*. Boas always recommended detailed study of the history of individual societies as being highly preferable to the comparative method. Early in his career he was willing to admit that general laws of societal development existed, and that it was appropriate for social scientists to search for them. Thus in his famous 1896 essay, "The limitations of the comparative method of anthropology," he says, "By comparing histories of growth general laws may be found" (1940a[1896]:279). Moreover, at one point he was willing to admit certain basic parallels in cultural evolution in diverse regions of the world. But later in his career he had abandoned even this limited nomothetic viewpoint, declaring that "cultural phenomena are of such complexity that it seems to me doubtful whether valid cultural laws can be found. The causal conditions of cultural happenings lie always in the interaction between individual and society, and no classificatory study of societies will solve this problem" (1940c[1932]:257). He had settled upon the notion that the study of each society's unique historical trajectory was the proper aim of social science, and this notion was widely perpetuated by his students and disciples, who dominated American anthropology during this time.[9]

The Boasians were an exceptionally cautious and skeptical lot whose epistemology dictated that social–scientific research required faithful attention to the precise details of cultural life. When the Boasians looked at various societies and cultures, it was the differences rather than the similarities that struck them and that they found more worthy of attention. It is against this underlying conception of the nature of social science that the contributions of the classical evolutionists must be judged. Of course many of their more specific notions must be rejected outright. They had a philosophically inappropriate epistemology that curiously mixed together ordinary causal and developmentalist modes of explanation, and even when they focused on specific causes of particular transformations they tended toward a kind of confused eclecticism. They held a powerful ethnocentrism, and for the most part illegitimately equated evolution with progress. They clearly tended to overestimate the amount of uniformity in historical change despite their recognition of divergence and diversity. Their empirical errors were legion. Witness, for example, Morgan's theory that a universal stage of matriliny preceded a universal stage of patriliny.

This list of their general flaws and specific errors could be extended considerably, but it would be pointless to do so. The classical evolutionists should not be evaluated in terms of the specificity of their contributions, but should be judged according to their underlying aims and the extent to which they provided a model for future generations in the better execution of those aims. As Harris has emphasized, the classical evolutionists were attempting to construct a "science of universal history," an intellectual aim that had roots sunk back into the eighteenth century. The nineteenth-century evolutionists wanted as parsimonious an understanding of the historical development of human culture as possible, and this is what led them to focus on broad similarities, even at the expense of overstressing them. In this regard the classical evolutionists hewed much closer to the character of science as it has been practiced for hundreds of years in Western civilization, for the principle of parsimony – the idea that one seeks to explain the most with the least – has been a hallowed principle of scientific work for all that time.[10] There is a fundamental irony in the Boasian conception of science. Although it was rigorously scientific in its deep respect for empirical documentation of assertions, it was profoundly antiscientific in its focus on the particular rather than the general. To their immense credit, the classical evolutionists achieved a much greater balance of these scientific aims.

### NOTES

1 In a later chapter I shall say more about contemporary use of the comparative method and its vindication by the findings of modern archaeology.

2 In another article, Carneiro (1973b) takes essentially the same view as proposed here.

3 Carneiro has pointed to yet another version of unilinearism in the works of the nineteenth-century evolutionists. He suggests that Morgan held the view that any society currently at Stage B must have passed through Stage A, although he never held that any society in Stage A must eventually evolve to Stage B. He offers the following passage from Morgan to substantiate his claim: "It can now be asserted upon convincing evidence that savagery preceded barbarism in all tribes of mankind, as barbarism is known to have preceded civilization" (Morgan, 1974[1877]:5; cited in Carneiro, 1973a:80). Carneiro regards this as a reasonable form of unilinearism and one that has never been refuted by the Boasians or any other antievolutionist.

It seems most appropriate to inquire into the type of unilinearism the Boasians charged the classical evolutionists with promoting. Carneiro (1973b) has suggested that the Boasians meant their usage of the word unilinearism in the strong sense. Boas himself apparently did, for he says the "evolutionary point of view presupposes that the course of historical changes in the cultural life of mankind follows *definite laws which are applicable everywhere*, and which bring it about that cultural development is, in its main lines, *the same among all races and all peoples*" (Boas, 1940b[1920]:281; emphasis added). It is clear, though, that at least some of the

Boasians understood it in a weaker sense. Lowie, for instance, recognized that the classical evolutionists clearly qualified their generalizations (cf. Lowie, 1937: 59).

To the extent that Harris is arguing that the classical evolutionists were not strong unilinearists, he is of course correct in speaking of a "myth of unilinear evolution." But there is no myth with respect to a weak unilinearism. I suspect Harris intends his argument to apply only to the strong version.

4 Harris (1968:171) cites the same passage in support of his argument against strong unilinearism, but italicizes the words "nearly" and "substantially."

5 That they saw themselves as tracing the development of Culture rather than specific cultures, itself really part and parcel of their developmentalism, also clearly demonstrates a commitment to unilinearism (cf. Ingold, 1986:39).

6 At least Morgan and Tylor were keenly aware of these facts. I have been unable to uncover any passages from Spencer's writings that refer to the influence of diffusion. It is likely, however, that Spencer wrote such statements. He did not conceive of social evolution as a strictly endogenous process, for he was well aware of such external influences on societies as war.

7 Doubtless no one has done more than Leslie White (1945a) to show the attention the classical evolutionists gave to diffusion. White has been able to extract no fewer than 15 passages from the writings of Morgan and Tylor that stress the importance of diffusion. Several of these passages clearly show how these thinkers integrated evolutionary and diffusionist concerns. White suggests three reasons for the Boasian misunderstanding on this score. First, he argues that their strong antievolutionism biased their reading of the classical evolutionists from the start. Second, he wonders with what care the Boasians actually read the works of the nineteenth-century evolutionists. Finally, he asserts that the Boasians consistently confused the evolution of culture as a whole with the evolution of specific tribes or nations. Since the classical evolutionists were principally concerned with the evolution of culture in an overall sense, the facts of diffusion could easily be acknowledged in a way consistent with evolutionism. But the Boasians failed to recognize this and misunderstood the classical evolutionists as trying to explain the historical development of particular cultures.

8 For further discussion of this point see Collins (1986:5n) and Harris (1968, 1988:128–30). It is interesting to note that Goldenweiser recognized the defense the classical evolutionists made of their position when confronted with the facts of diffusion by their critics. Goldenweiser says that (1937:517):

> the evolutionists attempted to defend their position on the ground that of the cultural features entering a group from the outside only those would prove acceptable and, therefore, assimilable, which fitted into the pre-existing culture of the recipient group. If they did not so fit they would be rejected or at best remain unassimilated, loosely afloat, as it were, in a hostile or uncongenial cultural medium. If, on the other hand, the extraneous features did fit and as a consequence were accepted and assimilated, then this very fact would bear evidence to the preparedness of the recipient group to accept such features and, if so, it should also be credited with the capacity or readiness to evolve them independently, had it not chanced to receive them from without. At first blush this argument sounds convincing enough.

It does indeed sound convincing enough, and it is precisely the same argument used by contemporary evolutionists. Goldenweiser's objection to the argument seems to be, first, that a culture's failure to absorb an item from another culture does not constitute proof of its inability or unwillingness to do so, and second, that in fact most items can be appropriated by one culture from another. The first point is obviously true but stands as a good example of the rather unrealistic caution employed by the Boasians. The second point is patently false, and any modern anthropologist or comparative sociologist can construct a long list of items that would be extremely unlikely to diffuse from one culture to another. (Think, for example, of contemporary Western capitalists borrowing hunter-gatherer reciprocity as a new guiding ideal for operating their businesses, or contemporary hunter-gatherers adopting bureaucratic techniques employed by modern governments.) The great selectivity of diffusion is today well established.

9 The widespread modern consensus that Boas and his followers were antievolutionists has been challenged by Harris, for whom it is another myth in the history of social theory. Harris can say this only because of his conception of social evolution as any qualitative transformation in a sociocultural system, and thus his implicit conception of an evolutionist as one who attempts to describe and explain these transformations (cf. Harris, 1968:259–60, 348–51, 641–53). Harris's notion of an evolutionary theory is much too loose. As argued in chapter 1, such a theory is one that assumes at least some broad directional trends in history and at least some general causes of these trends. Although Boas's admission early in his career of limited parallels might have qualified him as a type of evolutionist, by the end of his career he warned against the search for general trends and laws by which to explain them. This kind of historical particularism is still the dominant mode of thinking among historians today, and it is subscribed to by many anthropologists and some sociologists as well. No major scholar that I know of other than Harris regards this emphasis on the historically unique as legimately belonging within the province of evolutionism, and modern historical particularists are generally at pains to emphasize their opposition to evolutionary interpretations (cf. Mann, 1986).

Harris's published statements on this matter are disconcerting given his lifelong stress on the prominence of general directional trends in history and the crucial need for nomothetic explanation of those trends. Harris's views are taken up once again in chapter 7 where I will try to show that he has slipped into a very simple confusion, the recognition of which turns his entire argument into a tempest in a teapot.

It was apparently Leslie White who popularized the term "antievolutionism" (he actually referred to the Boasians as "reactionary antievolutionists"). White claims that he appropriated the term from Goldenweiser, who used it to characterize the general Boasian outlook. White provides a convincing justification for his continued use of Goldenweiser's term (cf. White, 1947a).

10 For further discussion of the importance of the principle of parsimony in science, see Sanderson (1987). For its historical prominence see Maxwell (1974a,b).

# 4

# Marxism as Evolutionism

Historical materialism has long been regarded by many Marxists and interpreters of Marx as a form of evolutionism. Yet the specific character of the evolutionism of the originators of historical materialism has remained very much in doubt and debate continues to rage over many questions, especially whether Marx was at heart a basically teleological thinker whose theory of history was ultimately developmentalist. This long-standing question has become a central one once again with the recent assertion of G. A. Cohen (1978) that Marx was a technological determinist and a resolutely teleological and developmentalist thinker. Cohen does not address himself to Engels, but the character of Engels's evolutionism, and especially of the extent to which it is consistent with Marx's, has been another of the unsettled exegetical questions surrounding historical materialism.

It is these questions that are the leading concerns of this chapter, which attempts a systematic analytical assessment of the nature of Marxism as an evolutionary theory. Because of the tremendous attention paid in recent years to Cohen's intepretation of Marx, that interpretation is used as a point of departure. Did Marx, as Cohen asserts, give causal primacy to the productive forces, and did he link this causal conception to a deeply developmentalist conception of historical change? As we will see, the prevailing viewpoint has been against Cohen's position. My own conclusions will be the same. Moreover, I will argue that even positions similar to Cohen's – those that argue for a developmentalist Marx in a more general and less technologically determinist way – are wrong. Marx, in short, attempted to explain social transformations in ordinary causal terms.

And what then of Engels? The prevailing tendency has been to separate him sharply from Marx and to suggest that he was a crudely developmentalist and teleological thinker in a way that Marx never was. I will suggest, however, that this view is incorrect and that the evolutionisms of

Marx and Engels were not markedly different in tone and character. One central aspect of the relation between the evolutionary theories of Marx and Engels was the high regard both thinkers had for Morgan's *Ancient Society*, and thus the nature of the relationship between Marxism and Morganism will need to be explored. I will also consider the relation between Marxism and Darwinism because, as in the case of Marx's and Engels's attitude toward Morgan, understanding the appreciation they had for Darwin's work contributes much to understanding the character of their evolutionary theories.

## COHEN'S INTERPRETATION OF MARX

Cohen's *Karl Marx's Theory of History: A Defence* (1978) is perhaps the most important book on Marx's historical materialism to appear in recent years. The interpretation of Marx that Cohen advances in this book can be broken down into two essential theses. What Cohen calls the *primacy thesis* holds that, for Marx, the productive forces determine the basic character of the relations of production. Since for Cohen Marx's notion of productive forces reduces largely to technology, the primacy thesis essentially means that Marx attributed causal priority to technology and technological change in historical transformation. The *development thesis* is the notion that there is an inherent tendency for the productive forces to develop throughout history. Human beings are constituted so as continually to attempt to advance their level of technology to higher and higher levels; they are highly rational beings who desire to advance their technology as a means of overcoming scarcity.

Cohen combines these theses and adds an interesting theoretical wrinkle to them to produce his unique interpretation of Marx. The wrinkle that Cohen adds is the notion that the relationship between the productive forces and the relations of production is a functional one: the productive forces determine the relations of production in the sense that the relations of production are functionally adapted to the productive forces, that is, these relations are as they are because they are best suited at a particular time to advance the productive forces to the maximum extent. This leads Cohen to a specific viewpoint on Marx's explanation of both social stability and social transformation. Social stability prevails when the existing relations of production continue to promote the development of the productive forces. Yet at some point in any mode of production the relations of production exhaust themselves, as it were, and turn into barriers ("fetters") against any further development of the forces. At this point an upheaval in the relations of production occurs. The old relations are stripped away and replaced by new relations that can once again promote the development of the forces. Social stability is then regained, but only to be lost again when the new relations of production eventually turn into fetters on the productive forces, and so on throughout history until the stage of communism is reached.

Cohen thus holds that Marx was both a technological determinist and a teleological thinker. In this view, Marx saw history as being guided by an ultimate purpose, which was the existence of a socialist society in which people are free and in which their basic material needs are easily satisfied. This ultimate endpoint of history can only be achieved through a historical process of the unfolding of successive stages in the development of the forces and relations of production. Cohen's Marx is a deeply historicist one who views historical change as being explained in terms of a directional law, which in this case is the inherent tendency for humans to want to advance the development of the productive forces. At one point Cohen does admit that Marx frequently offers specific causal factors as explanations for historical changes, factors that especially involve aspects of class struggle. But Cohen asserts that, for Marx, such explanations are not his *fundamental* explanations. His fundamental explanations are developmentalist ones that appeal to the need for productive relations to change in order to continue advances in the productive forces.

Most of the textual evidence for Cohen's exegesis derives from Marx's famous 1859 Preface, where Marx produces an extremely abstract summary of his basic theoretical position. The part of the Preface that Cohen pays closest attention to states that:

In the social production of their life, men enter into definite relations that are indispensable and independent of their will, relations of production which correspond to a definite stage of development of their material productive forces. The sum total of these relations of production constitutes the economic structure of society, the real basis, on which rises a legal and political superstructure, and to which correspond definite forms of social consciousness. The mode of production of material life conditions the social, political, and intellectual life process in general. It is not the consciousness of men that determines their being, but, on the contrary, their social being that determines their consciousness. At a certain stage of their development, the material productive forces of society come in conflict with the existing relations of production, or – what is but a legal expression of the same thing – with the property relations within which they have been at work hitherto. From forms of development of the productive forces these relations turn into their fetters. Then begins an epoch of social revolution. . . . No social formation ever perishes before all the productive forces for which there is room in it have developed; and new, higher relations of production never appear before the material conditions of their existence have matured in the womb of the old society itself . . . the productive forces developing in the womb of bourgeois society create the material conditions for the solution of that antagonism.

Cohen has also located numerous statements outside the Preface that he believes support the primacy thesis. The quotes he produces – from *The German Ideology*, *The Poverty of Philosophy*, *The Communist Manifesto*, *Wage Labour and Capital*, *Capital–I*, *Capital–III*, and the *Grundrisse* – are indeed extremely similar to some of the most fundamental statements of the Preface. Cohen is therefore able to claim that a wide range of texts that Marx wrote over many years offer statements that are strongly consistent with the technological determinist and developmentalist interpretation. However, Marx also makes many other statements, and engages in numerous historical analyses, that are either not especially supportive of Cohen's interpretation or that strongly contradict it. For these reasons Cohen has had no dearth of critics, and it is the arguments of some of them that we now need to consider.

## WAS MARX A TECHNOLOGICAL DETERMINIST?

In Cohen's interpretation the primacy and the development theses are actually inextricably intertwined, and thus Cohen's interpretation only makes sense when these theses are considered as part of a single argument. This means that if the primacy thesis is rejected the development thesis must fall with it. With this in mind, let us consider some of the main objections that have been made against the primacy thesis.

Jon Elster (1985) agrees that Marx's abstract statements clearly appear to support the primacy thesis, but he notes that some of Marx's most important historical analyses deviate sharply from the abstract theory. Elster asserts that Marx's analyses of the dynamics of precapitalist societies do not assert the development of the productive forces to be the engine of change, but rather concentrate on the role of population growth. Elster also suggests that Marx's analysis of the transition from feudalism to capitalism at the end of *Capital–I* departs markedly from the abstract theory. Elster concludes that historical materialism as formulated and practiced by Marx is a vague and often markedly inconsistent doctrine.

Richard Miller (1981) does not reach the dramatic conclusion that Marx was vague and inconsistent, nor does he believe that there is a fundamental rift between his abstract statements and his concrete analyses of historical transformations. But he does suggest that even modest attention to Marx's practices as a social historian will serve to bring Cohen's interpretation strongly into question. Like Elster, Miller pays close attention to Marx's famous analysis of the transition from feudalism to capitalism. Miller believes that in this analysis Marx gives clear priority to economic and political processes, not to technology. Miller says that in Marx's discussion (1981:99–100):

the old nobility is "devoured by the great feudal wars," and replaced by a new nobility of mercantile supporters of the competing dynasties. . . . With this new nobility taking the lead, large landowners respond to Continental demand for wool by expropriating their tenants, converting peasant holdings to sheep pastures. . . . This change does not occur because it makes farming more efficient. Quite traditional methods of sheep-herding have simply become more lucrative for landowners. . . .

Rich merchants use their new financial resources to set up manufacturing enterprises, often employing desperate refugees from the rise of capitalism in the countryside. Their large financial resources are crucial to the rise of manufacturing, for non-technological reasons. . . .

The rise of capitalism eventually includes substantial increases in productivity . . . but the crucial shifts in productive forces are not autonomous. In explaining this paradigmatic change in the level of productive forces, commercial and political processes are as important as the general desire to overcome material scarcity through technological improvement. . . .

Marx's one extensive discussion of technological change in a relatively narrow sense of "technological" is his account of the new reliance on machinery in the Industrial Revolution. There Marx gives approximately equal emphasis to the greater efficiency of machine production and to its social advantage to the capitalist, as a means of reducing wages, extending the work day, and instilling labor discipline by destroying bargaining advantages of skilled craftsmen.

Miller also shows that there is a strong clash between Cohen's interpretation and Marx's analyses of slavery and feudalism. In Marx's analyses of these modes of production he emphasizes that the relations of production characteristic of them prevailed because of the social power of an economically dominant class, not because such relations promoted technological development. Indeed, Marx points to the strongly fettering role of the relations of production during the stable phases of slavery and feudalism. In short, Marx's analyses of these earlier modes of production are in one sense the very opposite of what Cohen is suggesting.

## WAS MARX A DEVELOPMENTALIST?

The evidence against Cohen's primacy thesis is strong, and the general weight of scholarly opinion has indeed been solidly against it. The objections of Elster and Miller are merely representative of views held by many of Cohen's readers. Therefore the claim that Marx was a technological determinist must be rejected. And if Marx was not a technological determinist, then he could not have been a developmentalist in the sense that Cohen paints him. If Marx gives numerous arguments against the notion that technological change has been the principal cause of historical changes in the relations of production, then he could hardly have thought that there is a transcendent human tendency to advance the forces of production, a tendency that actually impels the movement of history toward some goal. It is still possible, however, that Marx could have been a developmentalist in some more general sense.

One of the most vigorous contemporary defenders of such a Marx is Jon Elster (1985), himself, as just noted, a strong opponent of the primacy thesis. Elster has "little doubt that Marx was indeed guided by a teleological view of history" (1985:107). He claims that Marx actually had two fundamentally different ways of accounting for historical change: a speculative teleological philosophy of history in which history unfolds in a largely predetermined manner toward socialism, and an empirical theory of history that attempted to explain the transition from one mode of production to another in terms of the operation of particular causal processes. Moreover, he claims that Marx's simultaneous reliance on developmentalist and ordinary causal explanatory models presented no problem for him, for "it is part and parcel of the teleological tradition that all events can be explained twice over, causally as well as teleologically" (1985:115).

Elster acknowledges that in some of his writings Marx appears to take a strong stand against teleology, but he declares nonetheless that the bulk of Marx's writings reveal its presence. The key passage in a quotation Elster takes from one of Marx's articles for the *New York Daily Tribune* ("The British rule in India") declares (quoted by Elster, 1985:111):

The question is, can mankind fulfil its destiny without a fundamental revolution in the social state of Asia? If not, whatever may have been the crimes of England she was the unconscious tool of history in bringing about that revolution.

Elster also finds passages in the 1861–63 *Critique* and the *Grundrisse* that he believes are clear indications of a firm commitment to teleology. To concentrate only on the most salient statements that Elster doubtless has in mind, we may list the following:

But obviously this process of inversion is a merely *historical* necessity, a necessity for the development of the forces of production solely from a specific historic point of departure, or basis, but in no way an *absolute* necessity of production; rather, a vanishing one, and the result and the inherent purpose of this process is to suspend this basis itself, together with the form of the process (quoted in Elster, 1985:112).

This surplus labour is, on the one hand, the basis of a society's free time, and, on the other, it provides the material basis for the entire development of society and of culture in general. By forcing the great mass of society to carry out this work which goes beyond its immediate needs, the coercive power of capital creates culture: it fulfils an historical and social function (quoted in Elster, 1985:114–15).

The higher development of the individual is thus only achieved by a historical process during which individuals are sacrificed, for the interests of the species, as in the animal and plant kingdoms, always assert themselves at the cost of the interests of individuals (quoted in Elster, 1985:115).

It is not at all obvious how these are clear indications of a teleological attitude on Marx's part. All of these statements can admittedly be interpreted in a teleological vein, but it seems more likely that Marx was identifying certain necessary conditions and causal relationships, often with a rather dramatic linguistic flair (for which he had, of course, a well-known penchant). For example, when, in the first passage above, Marx speaks of mankind fulfilling its destiny and of England as the unconscious tool of history, I think it extremely unlikely that he meant such statements in a literal teleological sense. These are just dramatic ways of stating likely outcomes of certain processes. This interpretation seems highly preferable to Elster's when we recognize the very explicit statements that Marx does make against teleology in various of his writings, a matter to be explored more carefully in a moment.

Mandelbaum (1971) reaches conclusions on this matter that are sharply at variance with Elster's. He freely admits that many of Marx's statements appear strongly to endorse a thoroughly developmentalist conception of historical change. He believes, though, that the appearance of developmentalism in Marx is highly illusory, and that Marx actually followed the explanatory logic of ordinary causal laws. Mandelbaum believes that Marx's analysis of the transition to capitalism found in the latter chapters of *Capital–I* cannot be rendered sensible unless it is viewed in this light.

Since I have already indicated my skepticism of Elster's imputation of teleology to Marx, it is obvious that I think that Mandelbaum's conclusion is more sensible. Apart from the highly equivocal nature of the quotations on which Elster relies, there are some excellent additional reasons for thinking that Marx's view of history was not a developmentalist and teleological one. One piece of evidence not to be taken lightly concerns Marx's opinion of Darwin. It is well known that Marx was a fervent admirer of Darwin, but it is perhaps less well understood that one of the major reasons for this admiration was Darwin's antiteleological conception of nature. Shortly after *Origin of Species* first appeared, Marx wrote to Lassalle about it, saying (Letter to Lassalle, Jan. 16, 1860; quoted in Heyer, 1982:15):

Darwin's book is very important and serves me as a basis in natural science for the class struggle in history. . . . [N]ot only is the death blow dealt here for the first time to "teleology" in the natural sciences but their rational meaning is empirically explained.

Of course, Marx was precisely correct: Darwin did develop a theory that abolished teleology from nature and explained biological transformations in terms of the operation of simple causal mechanisms. And it seems almost inconceivable that, if Marx was himself so antagonistic to teleological explanations in nature, he could have endorsed them for society and history. Note also Marx's reference to "class struggle" in his letter to Lassalle, and how he believed this paralleled Darwin's usage of the notion of struggle in nature. This also strongly suggests that specific causal mechanisms are the proper basis for explaining historical change. That is hardly an endorsement of an irreducible directional law as the basis of explanation.

Consider also the following famous passage from *The German Ideology* (1964[1845–6]:59; cited in Elster, 1985:110; emphasis added):

History is nothing but the succession of the separate generations, each of which uses the materials, the capital funds, the productive forces handed down to it by all the preceding generations, and thus, on the one hand, continues the traditional activity in completely changed circumstances, and, on the other, modifies the old circumstances with a completely changed activity. *This can be speculatively distorted so that later history is made the goal of earlier history, i.e. the goal ascribed to the discovery of America is to further the eruption of the French Revolution.*

This is an extraordinarily explicit statement against a teleological conception of history and a strong endorsement of explaining the flow of history in terms of the operation of specific causal forces at particular times. "History does nothing," Marx says. That can only mean that history is no abstraction with a goal and a purpose beyond the concrete goals and purposes of men and women struggling with and against one another for the fulfillment of *their* basic aims and desires. Ironically, the very passage above is quoted by Elster but dismissed in the most cavalier manner as starkly in contrast to Marx's other writings and as inexplicable except perhaps for some particular influence of Engels. In regard to such a dismissal, it must be noted that the contrast is not nearly as stark as Elster seems to think, since there are numerous other instances in which Marx rather explicitly rejects a teleological attitude. Moreover, it seems more than just a little odd that Elster relies on very ambiguous and highly equivocal statements and ignores a passage that is a model of clarity.

A third piece of evidence involves a particular commentary that Engels makes on Marx's theory of history that needs to be properly understood and appreciated. At one Point in *Anti-Duhring* Engels is concerned to defend Marxian dialectics against the attack of Herr Duhring. To do this, and to explain their concrete meaning, Engels cites a long passage from *Capital–I* in which Marx is discussing certain changes within the capitalist system that relate to the concentration and centralization of capital, the growing polarization of capitalists and workers, and the increasing unity and organization of the working class. Then Engels makes the following statement (1939[1894]:146–7; emphasis added):

And now I ask the reader: where are the dialectical frills and mazes and intellectual arabesques; where the mixed and misconceived ideas as a result of which everything is all one in the end; where the dialectical miracles for his faithful followers; where the mysterious dialectical rubbish and the contortions based on the Hegelian Logos doctrine . . . ? *Marx merely shows from history* . . . that just as the former petty industry necessarily, through its own development, created the conditions of its annihilation, i.e., of the expropriation of the small proprietors, so now the capitalist mode of production has likewise itself created the material conditions which will annihilate it. The process is a historical one, and if it is at the same time a dialectical process, this is not Marx's fault, however annoying it may be for Herr Duhring. . . .

In characterising the process as the negation of the negation, therefore, *Marx does not dream of attempting to prove by this that the process was historically necessary.* On the contrary: after he has proved from history that in fact the process has already occurred, and partially must occur in the future, he then also characterises it as *a process which develops in accordance with a definite dialectical law. That is all. It is therefore once again a pure distortion of the facts by Herr Duhring, when he declares that the negation of the negation has to serve as the midwife to deliver the future from the womb of the past.*

I interpret Engels to be saying that Marx has made a concrete study of history, identified certain trends from this study, and projected these trends into the future in terms of likely outcomes. Moreover, Engels suggests, it also happens to be the case that when these concrete processes and trends are closely examined it will be seen that they can be described as corresponding to a dialectical law known as the Law of the Negation of the Negation. Engels says that this historical process develops *in accordance with* a dialectical law. He does not say that there is an abstract law that actually determines or guides the process. I believe that the same rejection of a developmentalism is also apparent in Engels's statement that it is a distortion to view a dialectical law operating as a midwife.

None of the pieces of evidence I have submitted amount to anything like a definitive proof that Marx was a causal theorist who rejected all developmentalist and teleological modes of reasoning. Yet I do believe that they make a persuasive case. But even if the precise nature of Marx's theory of history must remain in some doubt, I still think that certain firm conclusions can be drawn. In the first place, even if we were to fall back on a position such as Elster's – that Marx had a speculative philosophy of history in addition to an empirical theory of history – I do not believe, as Elster seems to, that this developmentalist philosophy of history dominates his empirical theory of history. Nor do I believe that Marx could ever be characterized epistemologically in the way that I have characterized the classical evolutionists, especially Spencer and Morgan. In the writings of these thinkers, developmentalist and ordinary causal theories are both present, but the developmentalist aspects seem to swamp the ordinary causal ones. This is patently not the case for Marx. Even if we would grant that those statements of Marx's that sound developmentalist could be taken at face value, the ratio of ordinary causal analyses to developmentalist statements is very high, whereas for Spencer and Morgan the reverse is the case. Marx was an evolutionist, but his evolutionism is distinctly different from that of Spencer, Morgan, and Tylor.

It should not be overlooked that, like the classical evolutionists and other nineteenth-century thinkers, Marx *did* have a belief in historical progress. Slavery constitutes an improvement over primitive communism at least in the sense that it helps humankind to overcome the limitations of its meager technological apparatus. Capitalism, moreover, is progressive in numerous ways over feudalism: it abolishes the "idiocy" of rural life; it introduces democratic forms of government that, despite their substantial limitations, are preferable to absolutism; and, most importantly, it establishes certain conditions that help to pave the way for socialism. Socialism, of course, is superior to capitalism on many economic, political, and social counts. But none of this belief in progress necessarily reduces to a belief that there is some transcendent historical process that moves itself along toward some preordained end. One can see certain improvements resulting from major historical transformations without explaining those transformations as occurring *in order to* generate such improvements.

## AN ALTERNATIVE CONCEPTION OF MARX'S THEORY OF HISTORY

If Marx was neither a technological determinist nor any sort of developmentalist, then what *was* his theory of history? Perhaps the most powerful answer to this question has been given by Richard Miller (1981, 1984). Miller not only implicitly rejects a developmentalist Marx but, in contrast to Elster and a number of other Marxian exegetes, he refuses to believe that Marx was being fundamentally inconsistent or contradictory.[1] He does believe, though, that Marx had essentially two historical theories. One of these was his explicit general theory, and this was the theory that guided him in his more abstract pronouncements. The other theory was a broader and more flexible version of the general theory, and this was the one that he usually depended on when he engaged in specific historical analyses.

Miller presents what he calls a *mode of production interpretation* of historical materialism (hereafter called MPI). Marx's problem in historical materialism was, as we know, to account for both social stability and major social transformations. Cohen's interpretation is that Marx explained stability as resulting from the ability of a set of productive relations to promote technological development. Miller's MPI, of course, rejects this argument and instead claims that Marx explained social stability as resulting from the social power of an economically dominant class. A given set of productive relations prevails because it is in the interest of the dominant class that they continue and because that class has the power to make them continue, not because it has some particular capacity for promoting technological development at that point in history. Indeed, it may well be the case that such a class impedes technological progress, as in the historical cases of ancient slavery and feudalism.

With respect to social transformation, the MPI claims that Marx meant what he said when he referred in many of his abstract pronouncements to the fettering of the productive forces by the productive relations, and thus when he made the productive forces basic to explaining social change. But Miller argues that where Cohen goes wrong is in adopting much too narrow a reading of the productive forces, one that makes them essentially equivalent to technology. Miller argues that Marx had a much broader meaning in mind, and that he included among the productive forces not only technology but such things as modes of social cooperation and work relations. The advance of productive forces in this broader sense, and the emergence of constraints on these by the existing relations of production, create possibilities for generating numerous forms of internal change that can ultimately radically transform a mode of production. For example, "it may be that the new productive forces would be so much more productive in a new economic structure that a class that would dominate the new structure can organize successful revolution against the ruling class, based on a widespread hope for greater well-being" (Miller, 1984:207). Miller believes that it is just this kind of process that Marx emphasizes in his account of the rise of the bourgeoisie from feudalism. Or it might be that new productive forces in the form of new work relations would be so constituted that they provide opportunities for a subordinate class to organize against the dominant class. An illustration of this process would be Marx's prediction about how the spread of advanced capitalist work relations would provide greater opportunities for workers to organize themselves into highly disciplined movements in order to oppose capitalists.

Miller believes that the MPI fits Marx's abstract theoretical statements and many of his concrete historical analyses, but that there are some historical analyses that remain outside the scope of such a theory. He therefore suggests that Marx adopted in practice an even broader view of history, one positing that contradictions within an economic structure itself (and not just between the forces and relations of production) may also be crucial in generating major social transformations. Miller believes that this emphasis on internal economic contradictions can be found in various of Marx's writings, for example in *The Communist Manifesto* in which Marx "traces the rise of capitalism to ultimately self-destructive conflicts inherent in the feudal economic structure" (Miller, 1981:114); in the *Grundrisse* in which he emphasizes the transformative importance of class divisions in ancient Rome; and in *Capital–I* in which he emphasizes how chronic warfare among the feudal nobility was a major factor contributing to the dissolution of feudalism.

Miller concludes that there was always a fundamental tension between the narrower and broader versions of the MPI In Marx's writings, and that Marx himself was never really able to resolve this tension. Yet while the narrower MPI was the theory he followed when he made most of his explicit abstract statements, Miller believes that the broader version of the MPI was the theory he more commonly adopted as a practicing historian. This conclusion dovetails well with the arguments of Marxian exegetes who oppose technological determinism that Marx made class struggle central to his theory of history. But at the same time it is clear that Miller's interpretation of Marx is a more precise and painstaking one, for it attempts to come to grips with the real meaning (or meanings) of Marx's most abstract theoretical pronouncements and unite them with as much of his historical practice as possible. This is why I suggested earlier that Miller's exegetical contribution has a very special importance.[2]

### MARX'S PERIODIZATION OF HISTORY

Like most evolutionists, Marx offered a set of general stages for characterizing the evolution of human societies. Unfortunately, he is less clear about his stages than is any other major evolutionist, classical or modern. There are not only major ambiguities about just what he means by particular stages, but he offered more than one evolutionary scheme.

In *The German Ideology* we find Marx's first serious attempt at an evolutionary scheme. Here he lists four major stages from earliest times to the modern world, each of which is based on a characteristic mode of ownership of the productive forces: tribal, ancient, feudal, and capitalist modes of production. Marx identifies the tribal stage as one in which people live by hunting and fishing, by animal husbandry, or in some cases by rudimentary forms of agriculture. The division of labor at this stage is very simple, being little more than an extension of the division of labor found within the family. In the ancient stage, both communal and private property exist side by side. The division of labor is more extensive, and there emerges an antagonism between town and country. In the highest form of this stage, represented by ancient Rome, there is the complete development of a class division between citizens and slaves. Feudalism emerges with the downfall of Rome and its overrunning by the Germanic tribes. The principal subordinated class is a peasantry rather than a class of slaves, and therefore the main form of property is landed property with serf labor attached to it. The first stirrings of capitalism are felt in the sixteenth century, but as a mode of production proper it does not exist until after the middle of the eighteenth century. It is characterized by a class division between a bourgeoisie and an industrial proletariat and by the accumulation of capital as the driving force of economic life.

In the 1859 Preface Marx proposes a slightly different evolutionary scheme, speaking of Asiatic, ancient, feudal and bourgeois stages. In the *Grundrisse* (and especially in the section on the *Formen*, or forms of production preceding capitalist production), written in 1857–8, these stages are discussed to one extent or another, and two further stages are added, a Slavonic and a Germanic. These latter stages are apparently regarded as minor stages, but this is never made explicit, nor is there any definite account of how they relate to the other stages. Most of the discussion in the *Grundrisse* is difficult to follow and ambiguous in the extreme.

Eric Hobsbawm (1964) suggests that the most important innovation in the discussion of evolutionary stages in the *Grundrisse* concerns the Asiatic stage. It appears that Marx has now subsumed under the Asiatic type what he formerly called the tribal stage. In Asiatic society economic life centers around the clan and property is held communally. This primitive community is apparently a self-sustaining unit. It does not exist in isolation, however, because members of the community must pay tribute to a "despotic regime hovering over the little communes" (Marx, 1973(1857–8]:474). Marx gives as his principal examples of the Asiatic stage ancient Mexico and Peru, the Celts, and parts of India. He describes this stage in the following manner (1973(1857–8]:473):

Amidst oriental despotism and the propertylessness which seems legally to exist there, this clan or communal property exists in fact as the foundation, created mostly by a combination of manufactures and agriculture within the small commune, which thus becomes altogether self-sustaining, and contains all the conditions of reproduction and surplus production within itself. A part of their surplus labour and surplus production belongs to the higher community, which exists ultimately as a *person*, and this surplus labour takes the form of tribute etc., as well as of common labour for the exaltation of the unity, partly of the real despot, partly of the imagined clan-being, the god.

In the waning years of his life Marx began to concern himself intensively with the works of some of the classical evolutionists, especially Morgan, and he took a detailed series of notes on *Ancient Society* (these and Marx's notes on other nineteenth-century evolutionists have been compiled by Lawrence Krader under the title *The Ethnological Notebooks of Karl Marx* [Marx, 1972/1879–82]). But Marx never wrote anything for publication based on these notes and, although his understanding of primitive society had clearly been substantially augmented, this new knowledge was never incorporated into any new evolutionary scheme. It remained for Engels to develop the possibilities latent in Morgan and in Marx's notes on him, a subject to which we shall turn in the next section.

There has always been much thought given to the question of whether or not Marx was a unilinear evolutionist. Again, the tremendous ambiguities presented by Marx's evolutionary schemes make it difficult to provide a definitive answer to this question, but the weight of scholarly opinion seems solidly against identifying him as a unilinearist, at least in the strong sense of that term (Harris, 1968; Hobsbawm, 1964; Elster, 1985). He did, of course, believe that history revealed human progress in a general sort of way, and in the 1859 Preface he does say that the "Asiatic, ancient, feudal, and modern bourgeois modes of production can be designated as progressive epochs in the economic formation of society." Yet he never does say that these stages must follow one another in a strict sequence and that they are worldwide in scope. His discussion of the Asiatic stage, for example, seemed to emphasize that it contained a peculiar tendency toward stagnation rather than transformation. And his correspondence with Vera Zasulich shows that he apparently believed that Russia was capable of a direct transition to socialism, that is, that it did not have to go through a full development of capitalism. In view of these and other considerations, Hobsbawm has concluded that (1964:37–8):

It would seem . . . that [Marx's] analysis fits into a schema of the historical stages in the following way. The oriental (and Slavonic) forms are historically closest to man's origins, since they conserve the functioning (village) community in the midst of the more elaborate social superstructure, and have an insufficiently developed class system. . . . The ancient and Germanic systems, though also primary – i.e., not *derived* from the oriental – represent a somewhat more articulated form of evolution out of primitive communalism; but the "Germanic system" as such does not form a special socio-economic formation. It forms the socio-economic formation of feudalism in conjunction with the medieval town. . . . This combination then, which emerges during the Middle Ages, forms the third phase. Bourgeois society, emerging out of feudalism, forms the fourth. The statement that the Asiatic, ancient, feudal, and bourgeois formations are "progressive" does not therefore imply any simple unilinear view of history, not a simple view that all history is progress. It merely states that each of these systems is in crucial respects further removed from the primitive state of man.

In addition to suggesting why Marx was not a strong unilinearist, though, Hobsbawm's statement at the same time indicates that Marx clearly was a weak unilinearist. History has a general overall movement, and this movement can be roughly identified by a general classification scheme. Historical change is closely associated with the development of the productive forces and with the movement away from the social and economic conditions of the most primitive human communities. In this respect Marx was a weak unilinearist in much the same sense that the other classical evolutionists were. Yet for all defects of the evolutionary schemes of the other nineteenth-century evolutionists, in comparison to Marx's they had one overriding virtue: that of extraordinary clarity. Marx's schemes, however they may be interpreted, are a very poor foundation on which to build modern evolutionary theories. Despite their overly simple and obviously ethnocentric character, schemes like that of Morgan have proved a much better guide for modern evolutionists.

#### ENGELS'S EVOLUTIONISM

It is very well known that Frederick Engels made major contributions of his own to an evolutionary theory of society. In 1878 he published the famous *Anti-Duhring*, a savage polemic against a certain Herr Duhring, a rather minor German philosophical contemporary of Marx and Engels. This work contains Engels's most explicit abstract theoretical statements. In 1884 he published *The Origin of the Family, Private Property and the State*, a work that rehashes and extends Morgan's *Ancient Society*.

It has always been recognized that Engels's evolutionary formulations have had a distinctiveness about them, and no one has ever suggested that they could simply be assimilated to Marx's. Yet there has remained much controversy over whether or not Engels's ideas constituted a marked *departure* from Marx's thinking. In recent decades the predominant tendency in Western scholarship has been to suggest that they did in fact constitute such a departure, and to the detriment of Engels. Indeed, the belittling of Engels has become something of a favorite sport. It is far beyond the scope of the present book to attempt anything approaching a full-scale exegetical settling of this matter, but I would like to suggest some reasons why the attempt radically to separate the evolutionary thinking of Marx and Engels is misplaced.

To my mind the most pressing question concerning the evolutionisms of Marx and Engels concerns whether or not Engels's evolutionism qualifies as a form of developmentalism. Mandelbaum's view on this issue is a common one. Although he has exempted Marx from adherence to this doctrine, he claims that Engels was actually very closely associated with it.

Mandelbaum believes that Engels's development of a general dialectical conception of nature and of history is a classic instance of explanation in terms of a directional law. To assess Mandelbaum's argument, let us examine Engels's most abstract theoretical formulations with a special eye to those that Mandelbaum relies on most heavily in his interpretation.

In *Anti-Duhring* (1939[1894]) Engels develops an extremely abstract conception of all of nature and of human history and social life. This conception is based on the formulation of two dialectical laws, which Engels calls the Law of the Transformation of Quantity into Quality, and the Law of the Negation of the Negation. It is the second of these laws that Engels identifies as most fundamental to his dialectical philosophy, and it is developed in terms highly reminiscent of Spencer's Law of Evolution. According to Engels, this law is the basic law of all change everywhere in the universe. He applies it to such diverse phenomena as the sprouting of barley seeds, the development of rock formations, mathematical formulations, and human history. To get a proper feel for how Engels applies this law, I quote from him *in extenso* (1939[1894]:148–52):

Let us take a grain of barley. Millions of such grains of barley are milled, boiled and brewed and then consumed. But if such a grain of barley meets with conditions which for it are normal, if it falls on suitable soil, then under the influence of heat and moisture a specific change takes place, it germinates; the grain as such ceases to exist, it is negated, and in its place appears the plant which has arisen from it, the negation of the grain. But what is the normal life-process of this plant? It grows, flowers, is fertilised and finally once more produces grains of barley, and as soon as these have ripened the stalk dies, is in its turn negated. As a result of this negation of the negation we have once again the original grain of barley, but not as a single unit, but ten, twenty or thirty fold. . . .

[T]he whole of geology is a series of negated negations, a series arising from the successive shattering of old and the depositing of new rock formations. . . . In the course of millions of centuries, ever new strata are formed and in turn are for the most part destroyed, ever anew serving as material for the formation of new strata. But the result of this process has been a very positive one: the creation, out of the most varied chemical elements, of a mixed and mechanically pulverised soil which makes possible the most abundant and diverse vegetation.

It is the same in mathematics. Let us take any algebraic magnitude whatever: for example, *a*. If this is negated, we get $-a$ (minus *a*). If we negate that negation, by multiplying $-a$ by $-a$, we get $+a^2$, i.e., the original positive magnitude, but at a higher degree, raised to its second power. . . .

It is the same, too, in history. All civilised peoples begin with the common ownership of land. With all peoples who have passed a certain primitive stage, in the course of the development of agriculture this common ownership becomes a fetter on production. It is abolished, negated, and after a long or shorter series of intermediate stages is transformed into private property. But at a higher stage of agricultural development, brought about by private property in land itself, private property in turn becomes a fetter on production as is the case today, both with small and large landownership. The demand that it also should be negated, that it should once again be transformed into common property, necessarily arises. But this demand does not mean the restoration of the old original common ownership, but the institution of a far higher and more developed form of possession in common which, far from being a hindrance to production, on the contrary for the first time frees production from all fetters and gives it the possibility of making full use of modern chemical discoveries and mechanical inventions.

It can readily be seen that, so applied, the Law of the Negation of the Negation is just as vacuous a theoretical device as Spencer's Law of Evolution. With respect to human history, if Engels really means that invoking such a law can actually serve to explain historical change, then there is little reason to take such an argument seriously. But does Engels really mean this, or is this an illusion that masks another mode of explanation that is actually at work?

Mandelbaum obviously believes that Engels must be taken literally. He puts in evidence numerous statements of Engels that indisputably have a developmentalist ring to them, among them Engels's famous eulogy of Marx at his funeral that declared, "Just as Darwin discovered the law of development of organic nature, so Marx discovered the law of development of human history," as well as the following (1935[1888]:22; cited in Mandelbaum, 1971:76):

All successive historical situations are only transitory stages in the endless course of development of human society from the lower to the higher. Each stage is necessary, and therefore justified for the time and conditions to which it owes its origin. But in the newer and higher conditions which gradually develop in its own bosom, each loses its validity and justification.

There are also several passages in *Anti-Duhring* that have a strong developmentalist flavor, as when Engels makes ancient slavery necessary to the development of modern socialism, or when he makes class divisions essential for the development of the productive forces (cf. in particular Engels, 1939[1894]:199–201).

Still, I think a good case can be made that, even though Engels clearly seemed to fall back on developmentalist modes of presentation, he was not really a developmentalist at heart and that his explanations depended more on an ordinary causal conception of historical change, much as Marx's did. Consider first of all a statement quoted earlier that Engels had made about Marx. In polemicizing against Herr Duhring, Engels is at pains to show that there is nothing at all intellectually mysterious about dialectics, and he does so by quoting a long passage from near the end of *Capital–I* in which Marx is obviously describing changes within capitalism in terms of ordinary causal relationships. Engels then goes on to say that Marx is merely characterizing this process as one that develops *in accordance with* a dialectical law. Engels also vigorously denies that Marx was speaking of any sort of historical necessity, and asserts that he was not giving the negation of the negation the role of "historical midwife." As I noted in the earlier discussion, I think the simplest interpretation of this passage is that Engels is suggesting (explicitly for Marx, but undoubtedly for himself as well) that the actual mode of explanation Marxism follows is one based upon causal reconstructions of historical connections. Perhaps the crucial clue in this passage is Engels's phrase "in accordance with." It would seem that Engels uses such a phrase in order to deny any claim that Marx or he might be making to the effect that the Law of the Negation of the Negation actually *guides* or *determines* historical changes. On the contrary, Engels is asserting that the causal connections revealed by history add up in the end to *characterization* or *manifestation* in terms of the Law of the Negation of the Negation. If this interpretation is correct, then Engels does not believe in directional laws that are *irreducible,* the criterion that for Mandelbaum is crucial.

As a second piece of evidence in support of this interpretation I offer *The Origin of the Family, Private Property and the State* (1970[1884]). As noted earlier, this work is largely a rehash of Morgan's *Ancient Society* based on Marx's notes and Engels's own reading of Morgan, although Engels does extend some of Morgan's ideas and add a few of his own. Two things about *Origin* are especially relevant to the issue currently at hand. For one thing, it is clear that Engels engages in a good deal of ordinary causal explanation. For example, he traces the major historical decline in the status of women to growth of private property and social stratification. In addition, we find a famous causal analysis of the origin of the state in which this form of political society is seen as arising as a mechanism for protecting a society's ruling class against the threats to its position from subordinate classes.

In addition, despite the tremendous extent to which *Origin* relies on *Ancient Society,* the degree to which the developmentalism of Morgan has not been directly taken over by Engels is extremely noteworthy. One is hard pressed, for instance, to find Engels retaining Morgan's constant references to the "germs" contained in early social forms that are said to be the basis for the development of later social forms. Engels was a tremendous admirer of Morgan, and *Origin* takes over many of his ideas unchanged. It would seem that if Engels had really been philosophically committed to a developmentalist doctrine, then he would have taken that over from Morgan too, although perhaps in modified form. Thus the absence of developmentalist statements in *Origin,* Engels's major application of his evolutionary theories, seems to suggest much.

What I am really arguing is that Engels, like Marx, should be judged more by his practice of historical explanation than by his abstract theoretical statements in regard to history. It is true that Engels's abstract statements sound more blatantly developmentalist than Marx's, and the possibility remains that Engels may indeed have had one foot in this philosophical camp. But certainly there is a major difference between Engels and, say, Hegel, for whom there really was an abstract historical process that dragged concrete history along with it. There also seems to be a major difference between Engels and classical evolutionists like Spencer and Morgan. Although Engels's Law of the Negation of the Negation closely resembles in structure Spencer's Law of Evolution, I think the similarity is more apparent than real. Spencer's law is intended more literally and its application is less counterbalanced by other considerations than is the case with Engels's.[3]

MARX, ENGELS, AND MORGAN

The admiration of both Marx and Engels for Morgan's *Ancient Society* has already been made apparent, and indeed their view of Morgan has been well known to serious students of all three scholars. Marvin Harris has actually gone so far as to claim that (1968:246):

*Ancient Society* was a work of supreme importance to Marx and Engels because it opened their eyes to the complexity of primitive cultures and to the inadequacies of their own dabbling in this area. . . . As far as primitive culture is concerned, Marx and Engels bought Morgan lock, stock, and barrel. Morgan's scheme, its tri-part periodization, its evolution from sexual communism to monogamy, from gens to state, from matrilineality to patrilineality, became the standard source of ethnological enlightenment for Marxists and comunists throughout the world.

Although guilty of some overstatement, Harris is not far off the mark, at least with respect to Engels. In his preface to *Origin*, Engels refers to *Ancient Society* as "one of the few epoch-making works of our time" (1970[1884]:72). More significantly, he claims that "Morgan in his own way had discovered afresh in America the materialistic conception of history discovered by Marx forty years ago, and in his comparison of barbarism and civilization it led him, in the main points, to the same conclusions as Marx" (1970[1884]:71). *Ancient Society* also had apparently compelled Engels to modify some of his own thinking. Presumably as a result of Morgan's extensive analyses of kinship systems, Engels became convinced of their causal importance in social life, and so much so as to declare that (1970[1884]:71–2; emphasis added):

According to the materialistic conception, the determining factor in history is, in the final instance, the *production* and *reproduction* of immediate life. . . . The social organization under which the people of a particular historical epoch and a particular country live is determined by both kinds of production: by the state of development of *labor* on the one hand and of the *family* on the other.

Engels clearly regarded Morgan's thinking as Marxian in its theoretical and political essentials. Not only did he claim that Morgan had independently rediscovered the materialistic conception of history, but he also saw Morgan as a fellow socialist. Engels closes *Origin* with a long quote from *Ancient Society* in which Morgan criticizes the effects of private property and predicts the emergence of a new stage of social life that "*will be a revival, in a higher form, of the liberty, equality and fraternity of the ancient gentes* (Morgan, 1974[1877]:562; cited in Engels, 1970(1884]:237; emphasis Engels's).

Engels was obviously wrong in assuming that Morgan had rediscovered historical materialism, or even that he was any sort of materialist at all. As we saw in chapter 2, there is compelling evidence against thinking of Morgan as a materialist and in favor of regarding him as a sort of eclectic with strong idealist leanings. Engels was also incorrect in seeing Morgan as a socialist fellow traveler. While Morgan was indeed critical of the effects of private property on the quality of human life, his statement about the emergence of a new, higher plane of social life was scarcely motivated by the kind of socialist thinking that characterized Marx and Engels. Morgan seemed to have in mind the emergence of the sort of parliamentary democratic mode of government that has actually come to characterize Western societies in the last century. That Morgan's thinking on political questions was fundamentally different from Marx's and Engels's is indisputably shown by his assertion that the United States is a society in which social classes have passed out of existence!

Marx seemed to maintain a somewhat more critical stance toward Morgan. His notes on *Ancient Society* suggest that he did not miss the significance of Morgan's reference to property in terms of an *idea*, and in a letter to Vera Zasulich Marx suggests that Morgan is not a thinker who would be "suspected of revolutionary tendencies" (Shaw, 1984; Krader, 1977). Yet even Marx was on the whole extremely favorable toward Morgan, his view of that thinker not differing appreciably from Engels's. Why were Marx and Engels so laudatory of Morgan? Why did they embrace him as a kindred spirit in the face of what many regard today as such obvious evidence to the contrary? William Shaw has suggested that both Marx and Engels were aware of the contrasts between their own ideas and those of Morgan but chose to minimize them because they saw Morgan's positive contributions as greatly outweighing his deficiencies. As Shaw puts it (1984:225):

No doubt, fully to appreciate *Ancient Society*'s strengths and to perceive its inchoate historical materialism, one should read it, as Marx and Engels obviously did, in contrast with other anthropological studies of the period. And since, more than many books, *Ancient Society* is open to diverse interpretations, Engels (and very likely Marx) were able to read more historical materialism into Morgan than was probably there. It would also seem that Engels pursued the intellectual equivalent of a united front policy with regard to Morgan. On the one hand, Engels's ongoing belief was that the British anthropological establishment had entered a conspiracy of silence against Morgan's subversive ideas. Closing ranks with Morgan was therefore more important than emphasizing differences. On the other and less honorable hand, one might surmise that, by claiming Morgan for their own, Marx and Engels hoped to add to the prestige of their own theory.

It may well have been that Marx and Engels hoped the intellectual appropriation of Morgan would enhance the prestige of their own theory. But certainly the reverse occurrence was not in the cards. Indeed, as Harris has argued, the association of Marx and Engels (and their followers and successors) with Morgan led not only to the decreased prestige of the latter, but to actual efforts to discredit Morgan's theory simply by pointing to its embracement by the Marxists. Thus, "with Morgan's scheme incorporated into Communist doctrine, the struggling science of anthropology crossed the threshold of the twentieth century with a clear mandate for its own survival and well-being: expose Morgan's scheme and destroy the method on which it was based" (Harris, 1968:249).

## THE DARWINIAN CONNECTION

Just as they were strong admirers of Morgan, Marx and Engels were both greatly impressed with the achievements of Darwin's theory of evolution by natural selection. Engels makes a number of glowing references to Darwin in *Anti-Duhring* and, as we have seen, he drew a direct parallel between Darwin and Marx in his eulogy at Marx's funeral. Although many Marxian exegetes have attempted to diminish the significance of Engels's eulogizing remarks, there is no reason not to conclude with Paul Heyer that (1982:11) "we can only assume that if Engels at such a sensitive moment elected to draw the parallel, it must have held meaning for Marx."

Indeed, all the direct evidence given by Marx himself suggests that he would have agreed with this assessment. Earlier we quoted from Marx's letter to Lassalle in which Marx says that "Darwin's book . . . serves me as a basis in natural science for the class struggle in history." Moreover, when Marx first read Darwin's *Origin* he was apparently fascinated by it and talked about its tremendous importance for months thereafter (Heyer, 1982). It is true that Marx did say in a letter to Engels that "it is remarkable how Darwin has discerned anew amongst beasts and plants his English society with its division of labor, competition, elucidation of new markets, 'discoveries' and the Malthusian 'struggle for existence'. . . . In Darwin the animal kingdom figures as bourgeois society" (Marx, 1979[1862]:157). But Marx meant by this statement only that the character of the social and economic order in which Darwin lived had undoubtedly influenced his thinking about nature. Marx did not mean to suggest that Darwin's theory was inadequate or wrong, and there is enormous evidence that he thought no such thing.

Some of the most powerful evidence in support of this last statement concerns the fact that in 1873 Marx inscribed a copy of the second edition of *Capital* and sent it to Darwin, along with a letter that has been lost or destroyed. Darwin wrote back to Marx later that same year thanking him for the book and indicating that he knew little of the subject of political economy and was therefore not quite worthy of receiving such a profound contribution to the subject (Heyer, 1982). If Marx, a man who heaped intellectual contempt on others with apparent ease, actually went so far as to send Darwin one of his works to read (and no doubt to be impressed by), there can be no serious doubt about his opinion of Darwin or his belief in important resemblances between Darwin's work and his own.[4]

To say that there were strong parallels between Darwinism and Marxism, however, is not to say that Marxism ever borrowed any explicit notions from Darwinism. Marx's basic theoretical ideas were already well established by the time Darwin published *Origin*. If there is little basis for the view that the evolutionism of Spencer, Morgan, and Tylor was strongly influenced by Darwinism, there is none at all for the notion, should anyone care to advocate it, that the evolutionism of Marx and Engels fell at any time under such influence. The intellectual traditions that lay behind Marxism were entirely different from those that set the course for Darwinism. Thus Marxism and Darwinism have developed entirely independently of each other, even after their mutual awareness.

CONCLUSIONS

No proper assessment of the contributions made by Marx and Engels to a theory of social evolution can be made until we take a closer look at how contemporary materialist evolutionists have attempted to develop many of their insights. I have already indicated, though, that the evolutionary stages presented by Marx, however we interpret them, are thoroughly inadequate. Apart from the ambiguities and confusions they present, they have a strong Eurocentric bias and thus are highly deficient in providing a worldwide perspective. This Eurocentric bias is strongly evident in Marx's concern with ancient Roman society and with European feudalism, as well as in his view (common in his day among European historians) that Asiatic societies had little transformative potential.

Perhaps the most serious problem with the Marxian stages, though, concerns the criterion on which they are based: the mode of production. Although Marx and Engels made it clear that a mode of production was a sort of concatenation of forces and relations of production, exactly what this means, and how the concept of a mode of production can be operationalized for the purposes of basing an evolutionary scheme on it, remains very unclear. This may have been obvious to Marx himself, for in reality the evolutionary stages he lists are really stages of ownership – of relations of production. The forces of production are there in his stages surely enough, but only in a kind of shadowy and murky way. The problem of just what a mode of production is and how it can be operationalized is even more apparent in Engels's *Origin*. Here we find Engels appropriating Morgan's tripartite scheme of Savagery–Barbarism–Civilization and re-commending its incorporation into the Marxian evolutionary schema. But Morgan's scheme is based mainly on technological criteria and bears little relationship to any of the schemes set forth by Marx. To mix it indiscriminately with Marx's is only to invite further trouble.

None of the difficulties we have been discussing is incapable of resolution, but they were never adequately resolved by Marx and Engels themselves. However, if we turn away from these conceptual and classificatory difficulties, then Marx and Engels can be seen in a more favorable light. In a broad theoretical sense, their work was certainly a vast improvement on the epistemologically confused and causally eclectic formulations of Spencer, Morgan, and Tylor. Not only did Marx and Engels abandon the developmentalism that pervaded the thinking of these others, but they rooted their causal formulations in material forces. Both are major accomplishments. Although Marx's and Engels's materialist formul-ations often leave much to be desired, they certainly constitute a solid base on which to build.

Many modern evolutionists have been highly appreciative of the Marxian tradition. Some have thought of themselves explicitly as Marxists and have tried to develop evolutionary formulations that have hewn very closely to the original Marxian formulations. A greater number though, have borrowed from Marx more generally, more in spirit than in letter, as it were. They have given up the mode of production concept while retaining the notion that understanding technological and economic changes is crucial to a broader understanding of societal evolution. Some of them have considerably broadened the meaning of a material infrastructure well beyond what was intended by Marx and Engels. Such changes have necessitated abandoning the Marxian evolutionary schemes and replacing them with ones that are conceptually sounder and easier to operationalize. The works of these contemporary materialist evolutionists will be systematically explored in a later chapter. It is there that we will genuinely come to appreciate the importance of the foundations that Marx and Engels established.

### NOTES

1 Compare Miller's interpretation in particular with that of S. H. Rigby (1987). Rigby rejects developmentalist interpretations of Marx, but claims Marx was radically inconsistent in his theoretical understanding of history. He allegedly had two contradictory theories of history. One was a "productive force determinism," the other a theory emphasizing the priority of the relations of production over the productive forces. Contrary to Rigby, it is difficult to believe that a thinker of Marx's stature could have been so markedly inconsistent. For this and other reasons detailed in the text, Miller's interpretation is clearly preferable.

2 None of this is to say that Miller is correct, and it must be admitted that there is a certain opaqueness to his presentation of the narrower version of the MPI. Miller's analysis, especially his narrower version of the MPI, is not only carried out at an extremely abstract level of analysis; it is positively confusing on at least one major point. Miller insists that the narrower MPI is consistent with Marx's abstract theoretical pronouncements in that "changes in productive forces initiate social change" (1984:210). One of his principal examples of this notion, as already noted, concerns Marx's discussion of the role of workplace changes in capitalism that give workers opportunities to organize themselves against capitalists. But how is this truly an example of the priority of the productive forces? The question is begged as to why these productive forces themselves changed, and Marx's answer in this instance is that such changes derive from the economic interests of capitalists, and thus from the nature of the relations of production. Miller may well recognize all this, because at another point he does say that the MPI permits a "zigzag dialectic . . . between changes in productive forces and nonderivative social processes [that] is required by all of Marx's concrete discussions of major transformations of the productive forces" (1984:209). Moreover, in the very same paragraph he apparently suggests that the MPI does not give explanatory primacy to the productive forces, even in the broader sense of those forces, and then slightly later he goes on to day that "if the mode of production interpretation is right, structures do select forces quite as much as forces select structures" (1984:212). If Miller is arguing that Marx perceived a complex causal interdependence between the forces and relations of production in explaining major social transformations, then that is a sensible interpretation. But he should say so more explicitly and thus explain more carefully what he means when he repeatedly asserts that the MPI claims that social change is initiated by changes in the

productive forces. (Possibly he means that changes in the productive forces are only proximate causes that are often linked to deeper ultimate causes, but again the whole issue is left in doubt.)

3 The reader has a right to know why I have exempted Engels from the epistemological confusion with which I charged Spencer, Morgan, and Tylor, and especially the second of these. Actually, as already suggested, it is still quite possible that Engels may have been guilty of such confusion. If so, then the difference between him on the one hand and Spencer and Morgan on the other reduces essentially to a matter of emphasis. Spencer's and Morgan's ordinary causal arguments only make sense, I believe, in terms of their developmentalist arguments. But the situation with respect to Engels is different. Even if he were a subscriber to developmentalism, his causal arguments clearly take priority. Again, however, I think it improbable that Engels was a literal developmentalist. As an extremely close friend and associate of Marx's for some forty years, Engels had to be profoundly aware of Marx's hostility toward teleological arguments in regard to nature (and, as I have argued, by extension in regard to society and history). If Engels really had disagreed with Marx on this matter, it would surely have come out during all that time. Engels was fiercely loyal to Marx and would not have set forth a view of his own that he knew to be opposed to Marx's on an item of major concern without calling attention to the fact and excluding Marx from any association with such a view. It is well known that Engels read the manuscript of *Anti−Duhring* to Marx and that Marx raised no particular objection. Marxists antagonistic to Engels have tried to explain this away by saying, for instance, that Marx was too busy with other things really to concern himself with Engels's writings, and that he didn't especially care what went out under Engels's name. This interpretation is extremely improbable. Marx knew that his name and Engels's were strongly associated in the minds of their readers and interpreters, and that what Engels said would reflect upon him. Thus there is every reason to think that Marx did not object to *Anti−Duhring* because, in principle, he found it unobjectionable.

In short, I think we have to proceed as if Marx and Engels were in basic accord with respect to developmentalist and teleological interpretations of history. If we are not going to tar Marx with the brush of developmentalism, then Engels should be excluded as well. The strong personal tie between Marx and Engels provides yet another line of evidence useful in rendering a nonliteral reading of Engels's superficially developmentalist statements. No such countervailing evidence exists in the cases of Spencer and Morgan, and their statements must be taken more literally.

4 For many years it was thought that Marx had written a letter to Darwin asking to dedicate a new edition of *Capital* to him. No such letter has ever been found, but the presumption that one had existed was based on a letter Darwin wrote (with the greeting merely "Dear Sir") on October 13, 1880 indicating that it would be inappropriate for him to give his consent to a matter not requiring it. Recent evidence now suggests that Darwin's letter was written to Edward Aveling, Marx's son-in-law. Aveling had apparently sought Darwin's approval for a book he, Aveling, had written popularizing Darwin's ideas (Heyer, 1982).

# 5

# The Evolutionary Revival

By the middle of the 1930s evolutionism was beginning to show signs of regaining the respectability it had lost for some four decades. The first substantial indications of this renewed respect for evolutionary theorizing could be discerned in the work of Vere Gordon Childe, an Australian-born archaeologist and prehistorian who pursued his academic career in Britain. Childe was shortly followed in his evolutionary endeavors by two American anthropologists, Leslie White and Julian Steward. White produced a version of evolutionary theory in the 1940s and 1950s that was deliberately intended to be a rehabilitation of the evolutionism of the classical evolutionists, especially Morgan. Steward generated a more modest version of evolutionism that was opposed in some important ways to White's version, but that shared much with it nonetheless. These three thinkers may collectively be regarded as staging an "evolutionary revival" in the social sciences, a revival that had become fairly complete by the 1960s. Their influence on later intellectual generations has been very great, and much of what may today be regarded as sound in evolutionary theorizing can be traced to certain of their ideas. This chapter is devoted to explicating and critically assessing their major formulations.

## V. GORDON CHILDE

### Childe's Substantive Contributions

Childe's earliest work of real intellectual substance was anything but an exercise in social evolutionism. In 1925 he published *The Dawn of European Civilization*, a work that subsequently went through six editions and that many prehistorians still regard as his most important. *The Dawn* was an attempt to trace the prehistoric roots of European civilization. It was thus concerned with the unique qualities of one particular civilization, hardly the kind of focus of a thinker preoccupied with evolutionary considerations.

Although Childe never abandoned his concern with European uniqueness, or indeed with the unique features of other civilizations and cultural traditions, in due time he did begin to show a serious interest in the broad similarities in the historical development of societies throughout prehistory. In 1936 he published *Man Makes Himself*, a work intended largely for an audience of intelligent laypersons rather than professional archaeologists and prehistorians, and in 1942 a sequel to *Man Makes Himself* appeared under the title *What Happened in History*. Childe's leading substantive contributions to an evolutionary understanding of prehistory are contained in these two works. That Childe had adopted at least a minimal evolutionary perspective is clearly revealed in the opening paragraph of *What Happened in History*. Here he declares (1954:13):

Written history contains a very patchy and incomplete record of what mankind has accomplished in parts of the world during the last five thousand years. The period surveyed is at best about one hundredth part of the time during which men have been active on our planet. The picture presented is frankly chaotic; it is hard to recognize in it any unifying pattern, any directional trends. Archaeology surveys a period a hundred times as long. In this enlarged field of study it does disclose general trends, cumulative changes proceeding in one main direction and towards recognizable results.

The central contribution of *Man Makes Himself* was Childe's postulation of two great revolutions that had occurred in prehistory in three different regions of the world: Mesopotamia, Egypt, and India. The Neolithic Revolution was a major technological and economic transformation that introduced domesticated plants and animals and gave humankind control for the first time over its food supply. This food-producing revolution had a number of important consequences. For one thing, it provided both an opportunity and a motive for the production and accumulation of an economic surplus, or an amount of goods beyond that necessary for consumption by members of the community. Stored surplus food helps to tide the community over bad seasons, to provide a form of insurance in the event of droughts and crop failures. It can also support a larger population than food-gathering societies could, and thus a second major consequence of the Neolithic Revolution was population increase.

Childe stressed that early Neolithic communities experienced other important technological changes that logically followed the emergence of food production. Because of the beginnings of surplus economic production vessels were needed to store grains and other food products, and thus the manufacture of pottery emerged on a large scale. The earliest Neolithic communities of the Middle East also provide the first indications of textile manufacture. Yet despite the emergence of these new industries, Neolithic societies did not develop any significant form of labor specialization beyond that based on sex. More elaborate forms of occupational specialization were not to appear for some time.

The evolutionary character of Childe's conception of the Neolithic Revolution is clearly revealed by his use of the comparative method and by the high level of abstraction of his description of a Neolithic stage of economic life. In this regard Childe says (1936:94–5):

> The simple food-producing economy just described is an abstraction. Our picture is based on a selection of supposedly distinctive traits from materials afforded by ethnographers' observations of modern "savages" and inferences from particular archaeological sites. The precise stage of economic development here adumbrated may never have been fully realized in precisely this concrete form. Archaeology alone could justify the presentation of a "neolithic" economy as a universal historical stage in the progress towards modern civilization. But all archaeology can do at present is to isolate temporary phases in what was really a continuous process. We have tacitly assumed that similar phases were realized nearly simultaneously in several areas. But in prehistoric times such simultaneity cannot be proved, even in the cases of regions so close together as Tasa in Middle Egypt, the Fayum, and the Delta.

This passage shows that Childe was aware of the limitations of the comparative method and of the need in his day of much more empirical evidence to establish firmly the existence of a Neolithic stage of social evolution. But these difficulties did not stop him from making the kinds of bold inferences and generalizations about historical change that the antievolutionists of the day were so loath to make.

Childe went on to argue that these early Neolithic communities continued to evolve over the millennia along similar lines and eventually underwent a second major technological and economic transformation, one that he dubbed the Urban Revolution. This revolution was made possible by, among other things, the invention of the plow. The plow revolutionized agriculture by dramatically improving soil fertility and by making it possible for a man to cultivate much larger plots of land than was ever possible in Neolithic times. The plow therefore meant larger crops, a greater food supply, and the possibility of producing economic surpluses on a major scale.

As its name suggests, the Urban Revolution inaugurated a transformation in which the city emerged as an especially significant feature of social and economic life. But the city had come into existence, and had become important, only because of other dramatic changes. The production of large economic surpluses made it possible for many individuals to be freed from agricultural work altogether, and thus craft specialization was promoted because craftsmen could live off what others produced. The increasing economic productivity of agriculture also made it possible for large supplies of wealth to be created, and this led to increasing social conflict and the emergence of sharp class divisions. The state emerged as a means of managing this conflict. In short, a much more complex and internally specialized society with deep social, economic, and political cleavages had emerged.

## The Logic of Childe's Evolutionism

Despite the obvious theoretical significance we can glean from them, *Man Makes Himself* and *What Happened in History* were primarily substantive rather than theoretical contributions. They were primarily designed to tell a story about parallel changes in prehistory, not to state abstract theoretical principles. Eventually, though, Childe came to produce an account of evolutionary theory that had more theoretical aims. In 1951 he wrote *Social Evolution*, a short book based on a series of invited lectures. If we combine many of Childe's explicit theoretical statements in this book with the more theoretical parts of his early substantive works, a reasonably clear picture emerges of the logical structure of his evolutionary account of world prehistory.

Let us begin with the question of whether Childe was a unilinearist of any sort. This issue is particularly important in view of Julian Steward's (1955) characterization of Childe's evolutionism as one that concentrated so much on the broad outlines of cultural evolution that it lost almost complete sight of historical divergence and local variation.

In *Social Evolution* Childe attempted to develop a general evolutionary classification system. After deciding that the time-honored archaeological classification of Stone, Bronze, and Iron Ages was not serviceable as a set of evolutionary stages, Childe turned his attention to Morgan's scheme of Savagery-Barbarism-Civilization. He concluded that this scheme was thoroughly inadequate in its details, but that it was nonetheless the best available, and thus he adopted it (minus the substages) as his own. For Childe, Savagery referred to pre-Neolithic food-gathering societies, Barbarism to early food-producers, and Civilization to societies having achieved writing.

This adoption of Morgan's general evolutionary scheme is no doubt one of the things that must have been uppermost in Steward's mind when he characterized Childe's evolutionism in the way that he did. As it turns out, however, there is much more to Childe's evolutionism than this, for he gave the divergent features of historical change just as much attention, if not more attention, than the parallel features. There are numerous statements in *Man Makes Himself* that reveal great concern for the divergent aspects of the Neolithic and Urban Revolutions in the different world regions. In *Social Evolution* evolutionary divergence is given even more emphasis. Commenting on the evolutionary sequences in Temperate Europe, the Mediterranean, the Nile Valley, and Mesopotamia, Childe says that the outcome, civilization, is basically the same but that in each case "the intervening steps in development do not exhibit even abstract parallelism" (1951:161). At slightly later points he says, "So the observed developments in rural economy do not run parallel; they cannot therefore be used to define stages common to all the sequences examined" (1951:162); and, "For within the status of barbarism at least, the observable cultural sequences do not follow parallel lines" (1951:165–6).

These assertions scarely seem like the views of a theorist committed to anything but an especially weak version of unilinearism. When such assertions are placed alongside Childe's lifelong interest in the unique features of European civilization and its prehistory, it becomes almost impossible to understand how Steward could have characterized him in the manner that he did (cf. Harris, 1968; Trigger, 1980). Indeed, it might almost be wondered whether Childe had not virtually abandoned evolutionism altogether in favor of a form of historical particularism. But this conclusion is not warranted either, as we can see when we recognize that Childe's understanding of social evolution was based on a close analogy with organic evolution. As he notes (1951:166):

Organic evolution is never represented pictorially by a bundle of parallel lines, but by a tree with branches all up the trunk and each branch bristling with twigs. In so far as the archaeological picture could be represented by such a figure, it would disclose a process analogous to organic evolution. In fact, differentiation – the splitting of large homogeneous cultures into a multitude of distinct local cultures – is a conspicuous feature in the archaeological record.

Another interesting feature of Childe's evolutionism is the emphasis he gave to diffusion. He not only recognized diffusion as common and important, but actually regarded it as a major mechanism whereby evolution occurred. He often viewed diffusion and independent occurrence as working inextricably together to produce historical outcomes. One of the best instances of such thinking on his part concerns his explanation of the observed similarities among world regions in the transition to urbanism. In a most pertinent passage he says (1936:190):

Some sort of diffusion had evidently been going on. Yet no theory of one-sided dependence is compatible with the contrasts revealed by closer scrutiny. Urban civilization was not simply transplanted from one centre to another, but was an organic growth rooted in the local soil. If we want a modern analogy, the establishment of mechanized industry and factory production by European capitalists in Africa or India will not serve. We must think rather of the rise of that system of production in the countries on both sides of the Atlantic. America, Britain, France, the Low Countries shared a common scientific, cultural, and mercantile tradition long before the Industrial Revolution. Despite wars and custom-barriers, the interchange of goods, ideas, and persons went on continuously. England, indeed, was in the van of the Revolution itself, but the other countries did not merely copy her mechanical inventions or economic organization; they had been experimenting along the same lines, and made independent contributions when the time came. . . .

And so Egypt, Sumer, and India had not been isolated or independent before the revolution. All shared more or less a common cultural tradition to which each had been contributing. And it had been maintained and enriched by a continuous intercourse involving an interchange of goods, ideas, and craftsmen. That is the explanation of the observed parallelism.

Childe's views regarding social progress also need to be considered when analyzing the logic of his evolutionism. Unfortunately, there are certain ambiguities in his thinking (or at least his written statements) that make a definitive interpretation on this score difficult. On the one hand, Childe had an astonishingly simple criterion for assessing the degree to which evolutionary changes represent progress: the sheer size of the population that can be supported by any particular mode of social and economic life. In *Man Makes Himself* Childe argued that the Neolithic Revolution led to human progress because the population increased greatly as a result of it (1936:40): "From the biological standpoint the new economy was a success; it had made possible a multiplication of our species." Likewise, the Urban Revolution represented progress because it resulted in a further multiplication of the human species.

At the same time Childe clearly recognized that such a simple criterion taken alone could not be mechanically applied to assess the existence and extent of progress. He clearly recognized that it was not the quantitative existence of life itself, but also the quality of that life, that had to be considered. Thus we find Childe arguing in various passages that in several respects the Urban Revolution represented a setback for humankind. Most significantly, its generation of deep social and economic cleavages imposed new burdens on the mass of the population. Most people shared little in the new wealth that was produced and were sinking to the level of serfs. Warfare and militarism also increased markedly after the Urban Revolution, a further indication of the arrest of social progress.

For the most part, though, it seems that Childe was an optimistic believer in the ultimate triumph of progress despite the kinds of setbacks that the Urban Revolution produced. This interpretation is clearly suggested by the closing lines of *What Happened in History* (1954:292):

Progress is real if discontinuous. The upward curve resolves itself into a series of troughs and crests. But in those domains that archaeology as well as written history can survey, no trough ever declines to the low level of the preceding one; each crest out-tops its last precursor.

Actually, there is some evidence that Childe had a classically historicist view of progress. Near the end of *Man Makes Himself* there is an especially provocative passage that declares (1936:268):

It is as futile to deplore the superstitions of the past as it is to complain of the unsightly scaffolding essential to the erection of a lovely building. It is childish to ask why man did not progress straight from the squalor of a "pre-class" society to the glories of a classless paradise, nowhere fully realized as yet. Perhaps the conflicts and contradictions, above revealed, themselves constitute the dialectics of progress. In any case, they are facts of history. If we dislike them, that does not mean that progress is a delusion, but merely that we have understood neither the facts nor progress nor man.

Whether Childe actually held firmly and consistently to the kind of historicist view of progress suggested by this passage is difficult to ascertain, since there is little else in his writings so explicit. But be that as it may, a more interesting question is whether or not he was ever committed to a historicist view of *explanation*, that is, one committed to an epistemology of directional or developmental laws.

There is very little evidence to suggest that Childe ever held a developmentalist conception of evolutionary explanation. Not only is there a marked absence of statements in his work to suggest he embraced such an epistemology, but there are numerous passages strongly suggesting precisely the opposite. Consider, for instance, the opening sentence of his summary theoretical work *Social Evolution*. Here Childe denies any credence to conceptions of social evolution that refer to transcendent processes working outside of the basic actions of human beings in particular contexts (1951:1): "In using the phrase 'social evolution,' students of the science of man . . . have mistaken 'evolution' for a sort of generalized magic force that does the work of the concrete individual factors that shape the course of history."

That Childe continually insisted upon paying close attention to the unique features of historical change in different societies and world regions also strongly suggests the absence of a developmentalist epistemology. For Childe, there is no singular "evolutionist process" that is but the unfolding of latent potentialities toward some goal. There is, rather, a whole series of separate histories revealing both important similarities and major differences, the similarities being great enough to allow some important generalizations to be made. There is, of course, no inherent contradiction between an acknowledgement of historical uniqueness and a developmentalist epistemology. As we have seen, the classical evolutionists were perfectly willing to acknowledge uniqueness. Yet Childe stressed it in a way that they never did, and such stress certainly seems incompatible with a belief in a developmentalist process.

Finally, the title of Childe's most famous book – *Man Makes Himself* – is of no small significance. By choosing this title Childe meant to suggest that history is made by men – by the actions of concrete human beings who find themselves in particular circumstances. Human beings are not only made by their societies, but in turn make them as well. This obvious stress upon humans as agents seems thoroughly incompatible with any commitment to a developmentalist belief in transcendent historical laws that push individuals along certain predetermined paths.

If Childe was not a developmentalist, and if he therefore embraced an ordinary causal conception of historical change, what did he propose as the chief causes of evolutionary changes? This is a difficult question to answer with any specificity because Childe devotes the vast amount of his published work to description rather than to explanation. About the best that can be said is that Childe adhered to a very loosely Marxist conception of history, but one that was never carefully spelled out in his writings and thus always remained ambiguous.

Childe apparently always regarded himself as a Marxist, both politically and theoretically. His writings are peppered with references, allusions, and sometimes even forthright discussions of Marx, and he took a particular interest in the rigid unilinear evolutionary scheme of the Soviet prehistorian Nicholai Yakovlevich Marr, eventually denouncing it (Trigger, 1980). He frequently employed the language of dialectics, referring to how certain economic forms of society contained internal contradictions that they had to overcome.

In *Man Makes Himself* Childe aligned himself with Marxism under the label of the "realist" conception of history. His realist view of history, though, seems Marxist only in the simplest and most general sense: as a theory emphasizing economic and technological conditions as the guiding factors in historical change. Childe says that "Marx insisted on the prime importance of economic conditions, of the social forces of production, and of applications of science as factors in historical change" (1936:7). Often Childe's Marxism reduces to little more than a kind of technological determinism. Bruce Trigger (1980) has insisted that Childe was not a technological determinist because he recognized that technology was itself conditioned by social and economic conditions. Trigger is doubtless correct, yet technology is given center stage far more often than not in Childe's theoretical analyses. For instance, he often speaks of the different kinds of social organization that are implied by stone, bronze, and iron tools.

Moreover, his account of the Urban Revolution concentrates upon technological factors as basic to bringing it about. Much emphasis is given to the plow in heralding the agricultural revolution that made urbanism possible, and it is claimed that the Urban Revolution "was possible only because Sumerians, Egyptians, and Indians disposed of a body of accumulated experience and applied science" (1936:202). It is true that Childe does go on to say that "the practical needs of the new economy had, in fact, evoked the innovations" (1936:202), thus seemingly rejecting a technological determinism. Yet most of his discussion of urbanism focuses on technology, and if he wished to make economic factors causally determinant there is no clear indication (other than very general references to "contradictions") as to how broad economic changes themselves occur.

In sum, it can be said that Childe had an ordinary causal rather than a developmentalist conception of social evolution, and that he was consistently a materialist. But beyond this it is difficult to go because of the casual and underdeveloped way in which Childe advanced explanatory arguments. His evolutionism was focused overwhelmingly on descriptions of broad similarities and important differences in sequences of historical change in different societies, and theoretical analyses got very short shrift indeed.

### LESLIE WHITE

No one has done more than Leslie White to revive and rehabilitate the classical evolutionary tradition and to stress the importance of an evolutionary approach to social life. White has insisted upon emphasizing the similarities between his brand of evolutionism and those brands developed by Morgan and Tylor, and for this reason he has rejected the label "neoevolutionist." As we shall see, there are some important affinities between White's evolutionary analyses and those of these classical theorists. On the other hand, there are some major differences that White failed to recognize, a failure that resulted from his incorrect understanding of the causal arguments advanced by Morgan and Tylor. Let us examine White's evolutionism by reversing the procedure we followed for Childe, first looking at White's more abstract theoretical notions, which after all he did publish earlier in his career, and then considering the substantive contributions he made to evolutionism in his book *The Evolution of Culture* (1959).

### *White's Abstract Evolutionary Formulations*

Throughout the 1940s White wrote a series of articles that attacked the antievolutionists for the many misconceptions they perpetuated about the classical evolutionists and that set forth certain basic evolutionary principles.

In these articles White addressed many key questions and concerns regarding evolutionary theory, among them the distinction between evolution and history; the unit or units to which evolutionary accounts apply; the relationship between diffusion and evolution; the problem of evolutionary stages; the scope of evolutionary theories (i.e., unilinearism vs something else); the relationship between evolution and progress; and the causes of evolutionary change.

White's version of evolutionism cannot be understood apart from his more general conception of what culture is and how its existence can be explained. White argued that it is essential to distinguish between Culture and a culture, or between *culture* and *peoples*. Peoples are individual tribes and nations. They are the carriers of the elements of culture – of the technical inventions, rules, forms of consciousness, and social patterns that human beings have created – and the particular cultures of these peoples obviously differ. Culture itself, though, refers to the culture of humankind taken as a whole: the totality of all human inventions and achievements accumulated over the entire history of human experience on earth.

Early in his career White adopted and subsequently never abandoned the uncompromising antireductionism promoted by Durkheim and the Durkheimians: the notion that culture is a reality *sui generis* and can be explained only in terms of culture. Thus White steadfastly opposed any interpretation of cultural forms or traits that attempted to explain them in psychological terms – in terms of the properties of individual persons. In fact, he even went so far as to suggest that culture was such an important reality that the science that studied it should have its own distinct name: culturology.

When White applied these basic ideas to evolutionary theorizing, he began by distinguishing evolution from history, and thus evolutionary accounts from historical ones (White, 1945b). For him, historical accounts were those that attempted to describe and explain unique sequences of events. Evolutionary accounts, though, ignored historical uniqueness and concentrated on *categories* of phenomena. They were concerned with describing and explaining a *temporal sequence of forms*. White went on to argue that anthropologists need not be forced to choose absolutely between these two types of analysis, as both were legitimate. But they were fundamentally different and should never be confused. White, of course, chose to cast his lot with evolutionism, but this did not lead him to argue that an interest in uniqueness was improper and misplaced.

Carrying this argument forward, White claimed that evolutionary accounts dealt only with culture taken as a whole, and never with individual tribes or nations. In fact, he argued that the Boasian belief that evolutionism applied to peoples rather than to culture is what led them into such serious errors, such as the belief that the facts of diffusion make a mockery of evolutionary explanations. As White put it (1945a:343):

The Boas school has confused the *evolution of culture* with the *culture history of peoples*. The [classical] evolutionists worked out formulas which said that a culture trait or complex B has grown out of trait or complex A, and is developing into, or toward, trait or complex C. In other words, they describe a culture process in terms of stages of development. They say nothing about peoples or tribes. . . .

But the Boas school has tried to apply these fomulas that describe a process of cultural development to the culture history of a people. Naturally the attempt failed; the cultural formulas have nothing to do with peoples.

At first glance White's distinction between history and evolution, and between historical and evolutionary accounts, seems entirely reasonable. The distinction between generalizing and particularizing, or nomothetic and idiographic, approaches has long been acknowledged by social scientists. It is easy enough to recognize that phenomena can be approached either in terms of how they are similar to or different from each other. Moreover, White was not claiming exclusive priority for evolutionary accounts, but recognized that evolutionary and historical accounts can be employed complementarily. Unfortunately, though, White was actually claiming something more than this. He was simultaneously making at least two much bolder claims.

First, White was claiming that there actually is a reality that may be called "culture as a whole," to which, and only to which, evolutionary accounts apply. But what is the ontological status of this "culture as a whole?" Is it a "thing" in the Durkheimian sense that White seemed to be suggesting? Carneiro (1973b) has argued that there are two possible meanings that can be ascribed to the phrase "the evolution of culture as a whole." One meaning Carneiro calls the "initial-appearance view." This view holds that, in a situation in which Trait A is said to precede Trait B evolutionarily, then the very first appearance of A occurred earlier than the very first appearance of B. The other possible meaning Carneiro refers to as the "predominance-of-cases view." This view claims that Trait A may be regarded as evolutionarily prior to Trait B if it occurs earlier in a majority of individual societies, regardless of when it first appeared. Which of these two meanings did White give to his conception of the evolution of culture as a whole? It seems that he cannot have meant the second and remained logically consistent, because that involves adding up individual cases, and White explicity rejected the notion that evolution has anything to do with specific societies. It is possible, of course, that he intended the first meaning, but nowhere in his writings is there any explicit statement to this effect. Unfortunately, many of his most significant statements on this matter appear highly equivocal, such as the quote given immediately above. Therefore it is entirely unclear whether White intended one or the other of Carneiro's meanings, whether he might have intended them both, or, indeed, whether he had in mind some third meaning that no one has yet been able to fathom.

But even if this matter could be put to rest, there is another much more formidable one, and that involves White's extraordinary statement that evolutionism has nothing to do with individual tribes or peoples. The unacceptability of this statement, and the confusion it so obviously displays, has been exposed by Marvin Harris, who asks (1968:649):

Does the law of gravitation tell us nothing about particulars? When one predicts a particular eclipse on a particular planet of a particular sun by a particular moon, has this no relation to the general law? White undoubtedly means to say something else, to wit: no general law tells us *everything* about particulars. . . . But if a generalization tells us *nothing* about particulars, it can scarcely enjoy the status of an empirical proposition.

Actually, White's entire analysis in this regard was to some extent much ado about nothing. In the first chapter of *The Evolution of Culture* he declares that "evolutionist interpretations of culture will therefore be both unilinear and multilinear. One type of interpretation is as valid as the other; each implies the other" (1959:31). In making such remarks White seems almost to recognize the inadequacy of his assertion that evolutionist accounts deal only with "culture as a whole." Moreover, the actual substantive analyses in the remainder of this book make continual reference to individual tribes in order to illustrate his general analyses. Indeed, how could he have done otherwise? As Harris has pointed out (1968:643):

White not only attempts to trace the whole course of cultural development . . . but he also reconstructs specific cultural sequences in the light of the general trends manifest in the universal sequence. In Australia, for example, the Arunta system of marriage classes is said to have evolved from the Kariera type of relationship. . . . More commonly, it is White's practice to interpret the significance of various institutions in particular societies on the assumption that the culture has reached a certain level of evolution. Thus, his treatment of social stratification in Polynesia and the Northwest Coast draws heavily on the universalistic generalization . . . that "it is not until kinship has ceased to be the basis of social systems and society has become organized on the basis of property relations and territorial distinctions that true classes of subordination and superordination come into being."

Let us now turn our attention to the question of epistemology and causation in White's evolutionism. Was White a developmentalist? Did he believe in irreducible directional laws of evolutionary change? Mandelbaum (1971) has suggested that directional-law and functional-law modes of explanation seem to have coexisted in White's work. Tim Ingold has taken a stronger position, claiming that "White's conception of the evolutionary process . . . is essentially pre-Darwinian" (1986:82), and holding that his evolutionism was based on the notion of "an 'unfolding of immanences' " (1986:82).

Some reasonable grounds do exist for presuming that White was operating within the framework of developmentalism. For instance, his famous essay "Energy and the evolution of culture" (1943) is, after all, devoted to presenting and elaborating a "law" of evolution. In addition, White has declared that "the temporal–formal [evolutionary] process is deteminative: prediction is possible to a high degree. In the decomposition of a radioactive substance one stage determines the next and the course and rate of change can be predicted. In short, we can predict the course of evolution" (1949b:230). I believe, however, that both Mandelbaum and Ingold have mistaken superficial appearances for the essence of White's explanatory model, which was basically an ordinary causal one.

To develop this argument I must return for a moment to White's conception of culture. Why does culture exist, White asks, and why does it take one form or another? White's answer is that it is *adaptive;* it exists as "a mechanism for serving human needs" (1943:337–8). White divided cultural systems into three basic spheres, each of which serves particular kinds of needs. *Technology* consists of the tools and techniques that people use in obtaining food and shelter and in defending themselves; *social systems* are the organized patterns of social relationships they carry on; and *ideology* consists of the beliefs they hold in common. White was a vigorous materialist and thus regarded the technological component of culture as largely determining the nature of social systems and ideologies.

This materialism was expressed forcefully in White's view that cultures are really thermodynamic systems, or modes of harnessing energy and putting it to use. His basic law of evolution relates the level at which a society has harnessed energy to its overall level of cultural evolution. It states that *culture develops when the amount of energy harnessed by man per capita per year is increased; or as the efficiency of the technological means of putting this energy to work is increased; or, as both factors are simultaneously increased"* (White, 1943:338; emphasis White's). White argued that there had been two great leaps forward in humankind's capacity to harness energy: the Agricultural Revolution, which brought about domestication of plants and the development of animal husbandry; and the Fuel Revolution, which is White's name for the Industrial Revolution of the eighteenth century. Each of these, he argued, was responsible for major transformations in the other components of culture.

Although White's law of evolution, with its clear conception of a directional tendency in cultural evolution, may look very much like an irreducible directional law, there is every reason to suppose that White attempted to account for this directional tendency only in ordinary causal terms. White makes a great many statements throughout his works that I believe easily support this interpretation, but I will be satisfied with the following one because it leaves little doubt. In discussing the consequences of the Agricultural Revolution for cultural evolution, White says (1943:343–4):

The sequence of events was somewhat as follows: agriculture transformed a roaming population into a sedentary one. It greatly increased the food supply, which in turn increased the population. As human labor became more productive in agriculture, an increasing portion of society became divorced from the task of food-getting, and was devoted to other occupations. Thus society becomes organized into occupational groups: masons, metal workers, jade carvers, weavers, scribes, priests. This has the effect of accelerating progress in the arts, crafts, and sciences (astronomy, mathematics, etc.), since they are now in the hands of specialists, rather than jacks-of-all-trades. With an increase in manufacturing, added to division of society into occupational groups, comes production for exchange and sale (instead of primarily for use as in tribal society), mediums of exchange, money, merchants, banks, mortgages, debtors, slaves. An accumulation of wealth and competition for favored regions provoke wars of conquest, and produce professional military and ruling classes, slavery and serfdom. Thus agriculture wrought a profound change in the life-and-culture of man as it had existed in the human-energy state of development.

What else was White stating in this passage but a series of causal relationships between a set of variables? What else was he doing but explaining a directional tendency in cultural evolution in ordinary causal terms? Although White gave great stress to the notion that there is an overall directional trend in the development of culture, it is hard to believe that he thought this trend was explained by some sort of irreducible law of change that was unrelated to specific causal relationships between specific variables at specific times.

Before turning our attention to White's important substantive contributions we need to examine his conception of progress because it is closely related to his energy theory of cultural evolution. White's views here have a strong affinity with Childe's, and they run into the same difficulties. White believed it was perfectly sensible to think of progress as an accompaniment of cultural evolution, and progress in the evaluative sense of "betterment" or "improvement." He proposed that the degree to which cultures had progressed could be assessed objectively, the criterion for such assessment being the degree of survival and security of the members of a society. The best indicator of the level of survival and security was the amount of energy that had been harnessed. Cultures that had harnessed more energy could provide their members longer and healthier lives freer from the insecurities imposed by nature.

Unfortunately, this criterion made it extremely difficult if not impossible for White to assess progress along other than material lines, and in fact its rather mechanical employment led him into very dubious assertions about crucial ethical concerns. For example, in one place he asserts (1947b: 183–4):

The purpose of culture, in its several aspects as well as a whole, is to make life secure, perpetual, and worth-while. We might not be able to say that the ethical code, religion, or form of family of the British who colonized Tasmania was any "better" in and of itself than that of the aborigines they found there. But we can certainly say that the beliefs, ethics, family form, etc., of the invaders were integral parts of a culture that was far superior to that of the poor blacks they exterminated. Cultures – as means of carrying on the struggle for existence – can be compared with each other and evaluated. Their ethical, political, familial, and other aspects, considered apart from cultural wholes, cannot be so treated.

There is actually a great deal of evidence that White did not believe in the kind of relativism being asserted in this passage. At other points he not only made implicit moral judgments about cultures, but actually took a very negative view of several aspects of more energy-intensive cultures, a view that conflicted sharply with his purely thermodynamic criterion of cultural progress. It is principally in *The Evolution of Culture* that we find such an analysis, so let us turn to that work.

### White's Substantive Contributions

*The Evolution of Culture* was originally intended to be only a portion of a much larger work summarizing the main outlines of cultural evolution from Paleolithic times to the present. But the remainder of the work never appeared, and so *The Evolution of Culture* remains White's sole book-length contribution to a substantive analysis of evolutionary changes.[1] The analysis of cultural evolution in it ends, as the subtitle announces, at the time of the fall of the Roman Empire. In this work White took up several prominent themes of major interest to social scientists, anthropologists in particular, but his most significant discussions concerned evolutionary modes of economic life, the cultural effects of the domestication of plants and animals, and the role of the "state-church" in civil society. In these analyses White revealed himself to be strongly under the spell of Morgan and Engels (cf. Harris, 1968).

*The Evolution of Culture* is permeated by Morgan's distinction between *societas* and *civitas*. White argued that there are two, and fundamentally only two, different kinds of economic systems. One of these is found in primitive societies based on kinship, and in it economic relationships are built around social relationships in which human beings are ends in themselves. This kind of economic system does not produce goods for the purpose of maximizing the economic gain of the producers. The well-being of the entire community, rather, is the aim of production. Everyone has equal access to the means of production, and no division of the society into social classes exists. In the other kind of economic system the relationship between goods dominates the relationship between persons. Production takes place in order to maximize the economic gain of the producers.

Private ownership of the means of production exists, and economic life is centered around competition, struggle, and exploitation. This economic system is impersonal and nonhuman – indeed, actually inhuman, immoral, and inhumane.

The transition from the first economic system, which White called primitive society, to the second, which he called civil society, was brought about by the introduction of agriculture, White's Agricultural Revolution. The shift to an agricultural technology led to a whole series of cultural consequences eventually culminating in the economic and political inequalities that White identified as among the most essential features of civil society. An agricultural technology allowed for a substantial increase in food production, and this in turn produced a general increase in population. Increases in population size and density generated an overall structural differentiation and functional specialization of society. Some members of society were released from their roles as food producers and became occupational specialists of various sorts: weavers, metalworkers, potters, carpenters, etc. This growing functional specialization broke down the old economic system based on kinship and mutual aid and led to an economic system built around private ownership and the production of goods for the purpose of economic gain. The struggle for wealth created class divisions of various sorts, the particular type of class structure varying from one society to another.

Because society was now divided into a ruling class and one or more subordinate classes, and because this class polarization intensified with the further intensification of the Agricultural Revolution, a special need arose to manage the tensions such class polarization created. For White, the mechanism that evolved to fulfill this need was the state-church. His essentially Marxist argument is summarized as follows (1959:313–14):

The struggle between dominant and subordinate classes has been chronic and perennial in civil society. The lower classes – the slaves, serfs, industrial proletariat – periodically try to better their lot by revolt and insurrection. If the social system is to be kept intact, if it is not to explode in violence and subside in anarchy, the relationship of subordination and superordination between the classes must be maintained; in other words, the subordinate class must be kept in a condition of subjection and exploitation. It is the business of the state-church to see that this is done.

It is clear that White viewed the transition from primitive to civil society as producing a host of social, economic, and political evils. His judgments of this evolutionary transformation differed little from those of Marx and Engels, with whom he was obviously aligning himself despite his failure to mention them. As I pointed out earlier, this constitutes a very strong implicit qualification of his view that progress can be measured objectively in thermodynamic terms. White's negative evaluation of the cleavages of thermodynamically advanced societies thus signified a serious tension in his work.

Julian Steward's brand of evolutionary theory can be properly understood only in light of his objections to the evolutionary theories of Childe and White. In his most explicit theoretical essay on the subject, Steward distinguished three major types of evolutionism: unilinear, universal, and multilinear evolution. It is unfortunate that Steward persistently used the word "evolution" in this regard, an obvious confusion between theories and the empirical processes they are intended to represent.[2] Nonetheless, to maintain the integrity of Steward's analysis I shall follow his usage.

*Unilinear* evolution for Steward involved the theories of the classical evolutionists, especially Morgan and Tylor. Steward argued that these theories had been shown to contain so many factual inaccuracies that they had not stood the test of time. They therefore had to be abandoned. Some theorists, though, had not given them up, but rather had rehabilitated and reformulated them. Thus the creation by Childe and White of *universal* evolution, of which Steward was even more critical than he was of unilinear evolution. He argued that Childe and White emphasized the extremely broad generalizations of the unilinear evolutionists at the expense of their recognition of divergences and local variations. This meant that the evolutionary sequences postulated by Childe and White were "so general that they are neither very arguable nor very useful" (Steward, 1955:17). Steward went on to complain that the extreme generality of the theories of the proponents of universal evolution gave these theories no applicability to individual cases, that "White's law of energy levels, for example, can tell us nothing about the development of the characteristics of individual cultures" (1955:18). This made universal evolution even less useful than unilinear evolution for, "right or wrong, the nineteenth-century evolutionists did attempt to explain concretely why a matriarchy should precede other social forms, why animism was the precursor of gods and spirits, why a kin-based society evolved into a territorial-based, state-controlled society, and why other specific features of culture appeared" (1955:18).

Steward thus proposed *multilinear* evolution, which he argued would be concerned with the search for laws dealing with significant regularities in cultural change. These laws, though, would hardly have the level of generality of the propositions of Childe and White. They would assume the existence of parallels in cultural development, but parallels of much more limited scope. As Steward put it, multilinear evolution "deals only with those limited parallels of form, function, and sequence which have empirical validity" (1955:19). In essence, the theory of multilinear evolution as Steward proposed it was a kind of nervous compromise between the very general and highly abstract formulations of the classical evolutionists and of Childe and White, and the historical particularism of the Boasians. Steward wanted to be nomothetic, but only so much. He apparently felt that nomothetic statements that took insufficient account of unique historical features of societies were just as bad as highly particularizing arguments that failed to recognize any historical similarities at all.

Before examining how Steward tried to apply his theory of multilinear evolution to cultural changes, two points must be mentioned. First, as both Harris (1968) and Carneiro (1973b) have pointed out, it is extremely unfortunate that Steward referred to multilinear evolution as a "methodology." When this language is combined with Steward's failure to distinguish between evolution as an empirical process and evolutionism as a theory of such a process, then it is obvious that Steward is plagued by some serious misconceptions. Perhaps Steward meant by his attribution of methodological status to multilinear evolution that it is a general intellectual *strategy* designed to ascertain the extent to which significant regularities in cultural change do or do not exist. But it is certainly not a methodology in any conventional sense of that term, that is, a set of methods or techniques for gathering and analyzing empirical data.

Second, there are excellent reasons for questioning Steward's whole concept of universal evolution. As we have already had occasion to note, and as others have pointed out (cf. Harris, 1968), Childe and White scarcely formulated universal propositions or laws that had no application to individual cases or that failed to be sufficiently appreciative of historical variation and divergence. In *Man Makes Himself* and *What Happened in History* Childe made much mention of how historical differences coexist with broad patterns, and in *Social Evolution* the emphasis on historical divergence virtually overrode the stress on similarity of pattern. With respect to White, there was a great deal of explicit recognition of local variation and, his formal statements to the contrary notwithstanding, he extensively applied his general energistic law of evolution to individual cases. In many ways Childe and White were just as "multilinear" as Steward himself.

These difficulties aside, what did Steward's evolutionism look like in practice? Steward's earliest, and still probably most significant, substantive contribution to evolutionary theory was his famous essay "Cultural causality and law: a trial formulation of the development of early civilizations," published in 1949. This article was a landmark in the revival of evolutionism in the social sciences because it actually demonstrated with reliable empirical data the existence of strong parallels in cultural evolution in different parts of the world.

Using archaeological data, Steward claimed that societies in Mesopotamia, Egypt, India, China, Peru, and Mesoamerica had undergone very similar evolutionary sequences in the transition from simple hunter-gatherers to complex agrarian civilizations. Steward delineated five basic stages that each world region had passed through. In addition to a *hunting and gathering* stage, these included a stage of *incipient agriculture*, which began when plant and animal domestication first started to supplement foraging and ended when agriculture became the principal basis for subsistence; a *formative era*, during which cultivation became more intensive and community-wide irrigation projects were constructed; an *era of regional development and florescence*, during which irrigation works were expanded, economic specialization increased, class stratification became fully established, and multicommunity states emerged; and finally an *era of cyclical conquests*, which was marked by the emergence of large-scale militarism, empire building, urbanization, and the elaboration and increasing rigidification of stratification systems.

Typically, Steward was very cautious about the scope of application of the regularities to which he pointed in this essay. He stressed that his evolutionary scheme of stages was rough and tentative. Moreover, it applied only to the arid and semiarid regions where early civilization arose, and thus could not be regarded as a worldwide evolutionary scheme. Steward had not yet adopted the term multilinear, but he apparently felt this work was an exercise in multilinear evolution. Yet as Carneiro has argued, Steward was actually engaged in a kind of analysis much closer to unilinear evolutionism, and his "formulation was of more general application than he was ready to assert" (Carneiro, 1973b:94). Indeed, Carneiro suggests that (1973b:94):

despite Steward's demurral, his sequence of stages seemed to fit the development of civilization in areas where irrigation was not practiced, as well as those in which it was. Steward had never actually said that civilization in humid areas had not gone through the same stages as those he had proposed for arid areas. Now he found that Yucatan, a region of tropical rain forest, "appears to fit the formulation made for the more arid areas to the extent that its sequences were very similar to those of Mesoamerica generally" (1949:17). Already, then, there was an indication that Steward's stages might apply beyond the limits he had originally set for them.

Thus, even though only a few short years later Steward began officially proclaiming the doctrine of multilinear evolution, he actually started his evolutionary career as essentially a practitioner of a weak unilinearism. What happened in between? If Carneiro (1973b) is right, it was the discovery of certain discrepancies between his evolutionary scheme and the empirical evidence. Steward apparently took these discrepancies at face value, which caused him to become very nervous about the boldness of his scheme and to retreat from it. "So it was that without ever realizing he had practiced it, Steward turned his back on unilinear evolution and cast his lot with that mode of evolution he came to call multilinear" (Carneiro, 1973b:96).

The rest of his career Steward basically practiced the kind of limited multilinearism he explicitly advocated. When he returned to comment on the broad parallels in the evolution from foraging to civilization throughout the world, he always stressed the important differences between the evolutionary sequences. Furthermore, his later empirical studies generally had a very limited empirical scope. For example, one of his most famous studies concerned parallel changes he observed in two different tribes, the Algonkians of Canada and the Mundurucu of South America (Murphy and Steward, 1956). In aboriginal times these two tribes were quite different, but they were independently subjected to very similar influences that led to similar evolutionary outcomes. The Algonkians hunted large migratory game and were organized into nomadic bands, whereas the Mundurucu were tropical forest horticulturists residing in semipermanent villages. As a result of their contact by outsiders, both societies came to be integrated into capitalist economic networks, the Algonkians as fur trappers and the Mundurucu as rubber producers. Both groups began to reorganize their economies in order to produce commodities for sale to outside commercial interests. According to Steward, this similar involvement in commerical networks led to essentially the same results. As economic individualism took over, traditional forms of social integration gave way to an emphasis on new kinds of social units. Most importantly, traditional modes of kinship broke down and were replaced by nuclear families as the most important social group.

Let us conclude our discussion of Steward by turning to the kinds of epistemological and causal assumptions he made. With respect to the issue of developmentalism, it is even more obvious than in the cases of Childe and White that Steward was not a developmentalist. We can infer this from the very nature of his explicit theoretical pronouncements, for a nervous-ness about broad generalizations and an emphasis on multilinearity are scarcely the kinds of orientations likely to be held by someone who believes that evolutionary changes are the unfolding of a preordained pattern. But we need not be restricted to indirect inferences, for we find Steward explicitly opposing any such doctrine (Steward, 1977[1956]:59–60):

Few students of evolution today . . . would argue that the universe has any design making progress inevitable, either in the biological or the cultural realm. Certainly there is nothing in the evolutionary process which preordained the particular developments that occurred on our planet. From the principles operating in biological evolution – heredity, mutation, natural selection, and so on – an observer who visited the earth some half a billion years ago, when the algae represented the highest existing form of life, could not possibly have predicted the evolution of fishes, let alone man. Likewise, no known principle of cultural development could even have predicted specific inventions such as the bow, iron smelting, writing, tribal clans, states, or cities.

There can be no serious doubt that Steward had nothing to do with the epistemology of developmentalism and operated instead with a straight-forward ordinary causal epistemology. What kinds of ordinary causes did he propose? Like Childe and White, Steward was consistently a materialist, but a materialist of a rather different sort. For him, *ecological* variables constituted the most important causal forces impelling the evolution of societies. The role of ecology can be seen vividly in his early essay on the development of civilization. Steward adopted Wittfogel's hypothesis that large-scale political controls evolved in arid and semiarid parts of the world in order to manage the irrigation works that were necessary for farming. Demography was also involved in the evolution of the ancient civilizations. Under a particular system of irrigation the limits of agricultural productivity were eventually reached, and the resulting population pressure created intersocietal conflicts of various sorts, including warfare. Warfare led to conquest and larger states, which resulted in the expansion of irrigation works, and this in turn led to a further increase in population. In sum, Steward envisioned the evolution of civilization as resulting from a spiraling process of positive feedback involving several variables but initially set in motion by a particular set of ecological conditions.

Ecological explanations are also highly evident in Steward's other evolutionary works, and so much so that he has come to be acknowledged as the founder of the theoretical approach known as *cultural ecology*. This approach is devoted to exploring the ways in which ecological variables interact with technological and economic ones to produce various cultural outcomes. Steward regarded his emphasis upon ecological causation as yet another basis for holding his version of evolutionary theory to be superior to the versions produced by the other contemporary evolutionists, especially White's. As Steward put it, cultural ecology differs from these other evolutionary "conceptions of culture history in that it introduces the local environment as the extracultural factor in the fruitless assumption that culture comes from culture" (1955:36).

SOME COMPARISONS AND CONCLUSIONS

The three men who were the leading intellectual figures of the evolutionary revival had much in common. Despite a few superficial appearances suggesting otherwise, none of them adhered to a developmentalist or unfolding model of cultural change, and thus all offered explanations of evolutionary transformations that rested on an ordinary causal epistemology. In this particular respect they were similar as well, for all were consistent materialists. They were materialists in different ways, Childe and White emphasizing technology and Steward ecology, but materialists they all were nonetheless. In addition, all explicitly recognized that evolutionary models of change could not be entirely endogenous – that they could not assume that evolutionary changes were purely internal to societies. They were not only well aware of the existence of diffusion and other forms of intersocietal contact, but they gave these factors positive roles in evolutionary change. All three thinkers employed the comparative method in their evolutionary analyses, yet all did so judiciously, and they were well aware of its limitations and pitfalls.

Their chief differences concerned primarily the version of materialist explanation they espoused and, more importantly, the scope of their evolutionary theories. Childe and White were much more willing than Steward to state bold generalizations. Although Steward's first real contribution to evolutionary analysis was a bold exercise in tracing broad evolutionary parallels, he soon backed away from such a sweeping model and embraced a more timid conception of what an evolutionary theory could do. But it is wise not to overemphasize even this difference between the three men. In spite of his bold tracing of parallels, Childe never tired of emphasizing historical divergence between societies, and so much so that one of his major interpreters has been moved to comment that it is "clear that his view of evolution was at least as multilinear as was that of Julian Steward" (Trigger, 1980:174). Moreover, White's protestations that evolutionism had nothing to do with the culture history of individual tribes was inevitably abandoned in practice, and White always noted the existence of many forms of historical uniqueness and the legitimacy of anthropological study of that uniqueness.

In assessing the contributions of these thinkers their obvious deficiencies cannot be overlooked. The most serious defects in Childe's work concern the vagueness of his materialism and the rather grandiose historicist conception of progress that he seemed to hold. There has been much debate among prehistorians and other social scientists about the extent to which Childe actually was a Marxist.[3] Although Childe did think of himself as a Marxist, it is clear that his model of evolutionary change can be called such only in the most general sense of that term. As we noted earlier, his materialist explanations often seemed to reduce to little more than a general sort of technological determinism, and in chapter 4 we dispensed with the notion that Marx was some sort of technological determinist. Moreover, Childe conceptualized technological change itself as virtually equivalent to the "expansion of human knowledge," an unusually narrow formulation for someone alleging to be a Marxist.

We also noted earlier the difficulties with Childe's conception of progress. He believed that history reveals human progress and that it can best be measured in terms of the numbers of people who can be supported by any given mode of economic production. But this crude and simplistic criterion runs headlong into some very uncomfortable facts of which Childe himself was all too aware. The most significant of these is the existence, in those very societies where the largest populations are found, of economic and political divisions that place tremendous burdens on the vast majority of the population. Childe tried to reconcile these apparently contradictory consequences of social evolution by arguing that progress occurred in an overall sense despite stagnations and even retrogressions along the way. But, as many evolutionists of the last twenty years have recognized, this will not do at all, and the whole concept of progress has had to be thoroughly rethought (see chapters 7 and 8).

Similar difficulties are found in White's brand of evolutionary theory. Since White's conception of human progress was basically the same as Childe's in every respect, it is subject to the same criticisms, but with an additional confusion. Near the end of his life White published a short book in which he altered two of his former positions (White, 1975). He began to recognize the difficulties with his earlier concept of progress and thus came to the very pessimistic conclusion that the belief in progress is illusory. The record of cultural evolution, he insisted, has been a record of increasing warfare, slavery, exploitation, and other forms of social conflict. We have made our planet increasingly uninhabitable, and the specter of annihilation now hovers over us.

This change in viewpoint does help to make his general concept of progress a more realistic and consistent one, but unfortunately it led White to draw a totally unwarranted conclusion: that culture must be viewed as unrelated to the satisfaction of human needs. This is obviously a complete reversal of his earlier utilitarian position regarding the function of culture. If culture is not utilitarian, then what is it? White's new answer was that culture has no real function, and therefore all anthropologists can do is describe how cultures are organized and how they operate. As he put it, "cultural systems must be explained in terms of themselves, in terms of their components, their structure. They are explained in terms of the intrinsic properties of their components and the integration of these parts in a unity" (1975:36).

This major retreat into a kind of bland functionalism is doubly unfortunate. In the first place it threatens to make a shambles of White's evolutionism, since the different elements of his overall theory are now badly out of kilter with each other. But even more significantly, White's newfound antiutilitarianism is a complete non sequitur. White concluded that because cultural evolution has been associated with so many social evils it cannot be thought of as adaptive, as being built up in response to human needs. It is entirely correct to say that cultures have not for some time (even several thousand years) been adequately serving many of the needs of the majority of their members (see chapters 7 and 8). But that is a far cry from saying that cultures are not built up in response to the *efforts* of individuals to satisfy their needs. White could have concluded that, because of various forms of scarcity and the existence of many different kinds of needs, after a certain point in cultural evolution it was no longer likely that cultures would reflect the needs of everyone equally. He could also have concluded that many cultural systems were built up closely in accordance with the particular needs of elite groups that had emerged. These conclusions would have been perfectly consistent with the notion of culture as utilitarian (although certainly a modified and broadened utilitarianism), but at the same time they would have made it possible to deny that cultural evolution produced some sort of progress in the sense of greater "adaptedness." They would have allowed White to avoid sliding into a sterile functionalism that is completely unequipped to explain the causes of cultural phenomena, including broad trajectories of cultural evolution. In short, they would have permitted him to escape the kind of intellectual castration to which he submitted.[4]

White's materialism also leaves much to be desired. Because White openly adopted a technologically determinist model of cultural evolution, he cannot be charged with the vagueness that I attributed to Childe's model.[5] But this explicit technological determinism is itself open to severe criticism. As chapter 7 will attempt to show, although technological change is highly correlated with many other important evolutionary changes its role as a causal agent has been greatly overrated. Much evidence now suggests that changes in technology are as often, if not actually more often, dependent upon other cultural changes as causative of them. The very close correlation between technological change and other social transformations misled White and many of his followers into making it causal. We have only just recently begun to extricate ourselves from this misconception.[6]

Another problem with White's evolutionism is the crudeness of many of his formulations. The simplicity of his technological model of evolutionary change is one major kind of crudeness in his work. This is a problem related to, but yet significantly apart from, the explanatory inadequacy of the technological determinism to which I just pointed. It concerns his implicit (and often explicit) assumption that cultures are conceptualizable largely as thermodynamic systems. Consider, for example, the following statement (1943:344): "So far as general type of culture is concerned, there is no fundamental difference between the culture of Greece during the time of

Archimedes and that of Western Europe at the beginning of the eighteenth century." What White meant by this astonishing statement is that the same overall level of technology was possessed by the early Greeks and the Western Europeans just before the Industrial Revolution. It is very doubtful whether even that notion could be adequately defended, but the more serious problem is that White could make such an assertion only by completely ignoring the many important nontechnological differences between ancient Greece and early modern Europe. Such a procedure cannot be recommended as one likely to produce a very sophisticated and meaningful view of cultural evolution.

White's crudeness extended also to the extreme generality of his conceptualization of evolutionary "stages." Much of his discussion in *The Evolution of Culture* was built around Morgan's distinction between *societas* and *civitas*. This is by no means an altogether useless formulation, but it is hardly precise enough to capture the essence of the evolutionary changes from simple hunting and gathering bands to complex agrarian civilizations. The same kind of problem crops up in White's treatment of what he calls the Agricultural Revolution. Here he compressed thousands of years of change under a single heading and ignored many very important differences between societies depending in one way or another on agriculture for subsistence. He made it appear as if there were a sudden transformation from egalitarian bands to highly complex societies characterized by intensive social stratification and an oppressive state, quite a serious distortion of the character of the evolutionary changes that did take place.

Finally, we cannot overlook the egregious error White made in asserting that general laws do not apply to particulars, and thus that evolutionary analyses cannot be applied to the history of individual tribes and nations. It is fortunate that White largely disregarded this misguided notion in his own substantive work, for it is difficult to imagine the effect had he not. But White cannot be completely exonerated, because his proclamations badly misled others and have created a serious and unnecessary impediment to a proper evaluation of his work.

Criticism of Steward can be much briefer and more straightforward. He largely avoided the trap regarding the problem of progress into which Childe and White fell. Indeed, he pointed out that (1955:13–14), "The concept of progress is largely separable from evolution." Steward's materialism also seems on much firmer ground, both because of the clarity and consistency with which he applied it, and because of its empirical suitability. Steward carried out many impressive studies designed to show the effects of ecological conditions – or, more specifically, the effects of the interaction of those conditions with technological and economic ones – on a host of social and cultural phenomena. These studies have been carried out with sophistication and a powerful appreciation of subtleties, and they strongly suggest an important evolutionary role for ecology.

The main problem with Steward's work is simply the timidity of his generalizations, his unwillingness to develop the kinds of general evolutionary models that really excite the blood. As we have already noted, Steward let empirical evidence dominate theory far too much, retreating rapidly from bold theoretical generalizations when they ran into even moderate empirical anomalies. He thus produced a form of evolutionary theory notable for its limited and narrow scope. I believe that a clear reading of the evidence that has now accumulated will show that Steward was unnecessarily cautious.

Yet despite all these criticisms, the contributions of Childe, White, and Steward have been far more positive than negative. All three thinkers departed to one extent or another from the particularist tradition that was intellectually hegemonic in their time, and they made use of the best available archaeological and ethnographic evidence to show how realistic evolutionary generalizations could be formulated and defended. They did this, moreover, by adopting an ordinary causal epistemology of explaining historical change, and thus without lapsing into the mystical developmentalism to which the classical evolutionists were highly prone. In addition, they collectively contributed to the revitalization of the materialist tradition most closely associated with Marx and Engels, but that had fallen into terrible disrepute in the early decades of the twentieth century. Their materialism, though, was pursued outside of or on the fringes of Marxism,[7] and in a much more satisfactory empirical manner. In essence, they established a new version of materialist evolutionary analysis that, while unacceptable in many ways, was moving in the right direction. They set social scientists along a path that allowed many of their own errors to be corrected and many new theoretical leads to emerge. Through their influence, it has been possible for social scientists to produce a materialist evolutionary model that is more empirically defensible and less conceptually vulnerable to the criticisms of today's antievolutionists. In chapter 7 we shall have occasion to examine the major works of the most important contributors to this model.

NOTES

1 Robert Carneiro and the late Beth Dillingham, White's literary executors, have helped me learn the details of what happened. The manuscript for *The Evolution of Culture* that White originally submitted to McGraw–Hill was longer than the publisher would agree to publish. This manuscript contained a long treatment of the "fuel revolution," White's name for the Industrial Revolution. This section of the original manuscript now exists as a separate manuscript of 428 pages entitled *The Fuel Revolution,* and is in the possession of Carneiro at the American Museum of

Natural History. White also wrote much of yet another manuscript, *Modern Capitalist Culture*, to which he continued to add throughout the 1960s and into the early 1970s. This manuscript, a much longer manuscript of approximately 1,300 pages, is also in Carneiro's possession.

White approached different publishers about *The Fuel Revolution*, but no contract to publish the work was ever signed. There is no evidence that he ever approached a publisher about *Modern Capitalist Culture*. Through Carneiro's kindness, I have been able to read both of these manuscripts. *The Fuel Revolution* is a highly detailed examination of the Industrial Revolution in England, and then its "spread" to France, Germany, Russia, Japan, and the United States. There are also chapters on industrialization in China, India, Latin America, and Africa. *Modern Capitalist Culture* is a much less polished manuscript that contains discussions of, *inter alia*, the historical development of European capitalism, the general character of "capitalist–democratic" culture, the development of capitalism in the United States, the state–church in capitalist-democratic society, "jungle capitalism," class relations, and the development of welfare systems.

Carneiro is still hopeful that *The Fuel Revolution* will eventually be published, but it is unlikely that *Modern Capitalist Culture* will ever see the light of day.

2 This same terminological confusion is also found in White's works. White frequently spoke of the existence of an "evolutionist process."

3 For various interpretations of the role of Marxism in Childe's works see Clark (1976), Thomas (1982), Gathercole (1971), McNairn (1980), Peace (1988), and Trigger (1980). The last of these provides several additional references.

4 The problem being discussed is obviously the crucial one of the meaning of the concept of "adaptation" and its applicability to evolutionary analyses. This problem gets the much fuller airing it deserves in chapter 8. It is also touched on in chapters 6 and 7 with respect to the evolutionary theories of Talcott Parsons, Marvin Harris, and others.

Actually, White did show some indication of being able to salvage something from the ruins he left behind. Later in the same book he begins to suggest that cultural evolution is much determined by how different individuals and groups pursue their *interests* and how the opposition of interests is resolved. This conflict model was of course very much present in White's earlier work, although it coexisted uncomfortably with his thermodynamic conception of progress and seemed to be subordinated to it. But in the later work it has come to the forefront.

It is unfortunate that White refers to this "new" approach by the pretentious name "method of vector analysis" (vectors, it appears, are simply interests). It is also a pity that he never recognizes that there is no contradiction between talking about interests and their role in cultural evolution and talking about culture as serving human needs. When people pursue their interests, and when some of them end up dominating others and structuring society according to those interests, what are they doing except striving to satisfy certain of their needs? We may not like the way they do it and the end results it produces, but they are doing it nonetheless.

5 White was very clear about his technological determinism, but he did not always apply it consistently. In *The Evolution of Culture* he actually embraced an ecological argument to explain the origin of agriculture, suggesting that hunter-gatherers had the essentials of agricultural knowledge many thousands of years before they

practiced it and thus that they had to be pushed over the threshold into agricultural practice by some sort of environmental disequilibrium. In developing this argument White not only abandoned technological determinism but even went so far as to violate his Durkheimian dictum that "culture can only be explained in terms of culture." White should be commended for showing such flexibility, though, because his explanation would today be regarded as far superior to theories of agricultural origins that make technological change (in the form of "increased knowledge") fundamental.

6  The severe limitations of White's technological determinism are also highly apparent in his unpublished volumes. *The Fuel Revolution* is a tedious and repetitive discussion of industrialization in one country after another. White apparently understood this form of technological change as virtually its own cause, as there is little explicit discussion of the social, economic, and political context in which certain levels of industrialization do or do not occur. *Modern Capitalist Culture* in many ways compounds these difficulties. The fuel revolution is discussed once again, but the causal relationship between industrialization and the expansion of capitalism is never really grappled with. Presumably we still have a simplistic technological determinism, as would be suggested by White's startling statement that "the steam engine was . . . the prime mover of modern imperialism."

7  In spite of Childe's Marxist self-identification, I would regard him, as perhaps clear already, as actually only on Marxism's fringes. I would also place White on Marxism's fringes rather than outside the tradition entirely. He did have a strong admiration for Engels and some of his analyses in *The Evolution of Culture* sound loosely Marxist, and so it is clear that he was influenced by Marxism. Steward, of course, was outside the Marxist tradition altogether.

# 6

# Sociological Neoevolutionism

The evolutionary revival discussed in the last chapter was a distinctly anthropological phenomenon, which is simply to say that it was brought about by scholars who identified themselves professionally with that field of study. As it happens, though, sociology was to experience some two decades later an evolutionary revival of its own, but one that produced a brand of evolutionary theory that was markedly different from the materialist evolutionism of Childe, White, and Steward. The evolutionary revival in sociology took place largely under the influence of Talcott Parsons, at that time sociology's theoretician *par excellence.* I should like to call the brand of evolutionary theory produced under Parsons's influence *sociological neoevolutionism,* a usage suggested by Anthony Smith (1973) in his major critical discussion of this approach. It is perhaps also conveniently identified as *functionalist evolutionism* for, as we shall see, it is a version of evolutionary theory that is built directly on functionalist theoretical premises.

It seems that when sociologists think of "evolutionary theory" it is sociological neoevolutionism that they primarily (or even exclusively) have in mind. Or, if they are thinking more broadly, they readily assimilate other contemporary versions of evolutionary theory to sociological neoevolutionism (cf. Nisbet, 1969; A. D. Smith, 1973). The result is a massive theoretical distortion. Sociological neoevolutionism is unique among all contemporary brands of evolutionism. Naturally it shares some elements in common with these other evolutionisms, but its differences from them are of greater consequence. Its deficiencies and inadequacies – and it will be argued that these are glaring in the extreme – are rather distinctively its own, and these intellectual flaws cannot automatically be assumed to be typical of other versions of evolutionism, or of some sort of "evolutionism in general." And so to celebrate the demise of sociological neoevolutionism does not require abandonment of an evolutionary perspective.

PARSONS'S EARLY CONCEPTIONS OF SOCIAL CHANGE

It is well known that the bulk of Parsons's social theory is little concerned with social change. As of the early 1950s he had no developed theory of change at all, his ideas on the subject being highly sketchy and merely suggestive. However, at this stage he did develop a theoretical formulation that was to become a significant part of his theory of social evolution: his famous pattern variables. The pattern variables, of course, were initially conceived as having nothing to do with social change, and were only static categories deemed useful for the identification and classification of modes of social action. To recapitulate them briefly, they are:

1  affectivity vs affective neutrality, in which cultural definitions of role relationships prescribe either the appropriateness of the emotional involvement of the parties or the appropriateness of a more emotionally detached relationship;
2  self-orientation vs collectivity-orientation, in which cultural definitions of roles permit the pursuit of individual interests or proscribe such pursuit in favor of having a regard for the good of the group as a whole;
3  universalism vs particularism, in which actors are judged either by abstract, impersonal criteria or by their relationship to concrete persons and their imbeddedness in particular social groups;
4  achievement vs ascription, in which emphasis is placed on permitting and encouraging individual social strivings as a criterion for role performance or on the social locations of individuals at birth as a basis for such performance;
5  specificity vs diffuseness, in which a social role absorbs only a part of an individual's identity or all (or much) of that individual's identity.

At a slightly later point, and especially in his *Economy and Society* (Parsons and Smelser, 1956), Parsons developed the theoretical formulation that is probably most often associated with his work: the famous AGIL paradigm of the functional imperatives of social systems. The AGIL system as a theoretical device referred to the *functional differentiation* of social systems, but in *Economy and Society* Parsons and Smelser also developed a conception of the *structural* differentiation of social systems, that is, a conception holding that in many societies there are specialized social structures designed to perform specific functions. For example, the economy is devoted to the adaptation function in all societies, but in modern societies the economy is structurally distinct from other social structures. Parsons and Smelser did not let the concept of structural differentiation remain a purely static one, for they used it to develop a theoretical model designed to apply to changes in modern economic life, such as the separation of ownership from control in the American corporation. They even suggested that the model may be extended more generally to understand a longer process of historical change leading to modern society. Moreover, there are some suggested linkages between the structural differentiation model and the earlier pattern variables, and thus an indication that the pattern variables could be used as more than just classificatory devices.

It is clear that as regards a theory of change this work marks a considerable advance over the largely static and classificatory efforts of Parsons's earlier works. It was not to be long before Parsons was to offer the first installment of his general theory of social evolution, which as we will see is about as elaborately developed a theory of change as there is in the social sciences. But before examining Parsons's evolutionary theory, let us first consider a major work that preceded that theory but that was based directly on Parsons's developing change formulations.[1]

## SMELSER'S *Social Change in the Industrial Revolution*

Neil Smelser's *Social Change in the Industrial Revolution* (1959) is based directly on the theoretical model he and Parsons developed in *Economy and Society*. It attempts to apply this model to understand various social changes associated with the Industrial Revolution in England. Smelser assumes that the most important changes in social and economic life during the Industrial Revolution involved processes of structural differentiation – processes whereby certain social units split apart into two or more distinct units having specialized functions. The process of structural differentiation is said to follow a definite developmental sequence, which can be represented approximately as follows. First, there is some sort of dissatisfaction with the goal-attainment capacities of a social system or subsystem. This dissatisfaction is expressed in various symptoms of disturbance, these being largely negative emotional reactions to prevailing social conditions. These emotional reactions lead people to mobilize resources and develop new ideas directed toward overcoming the dissatisfactions. Serious efforts will be made to implement some of the new ideas, and to the degree that these efforts are successful there will eventually occur an institutionalization of new social patterns. This brings the differentiation sequence to a completion, and the more differentiated social system that has resulted is alleged to function more effectively than the older, less differentiated one.

Most of *Social Change in the Industrial Revolution* involves the exhaustive application of this theoretical model to the evolution of spinning and weaving in the cotton industry and changes in family patterns during the industrialization process. Smelser's analysis of changes in the family is especially revealing of the theoretical logic that permeates his book. Perhaps the most interesting part of Smelser's discussion is his treatment of how agitation among factory workers for a shorter working day and better conditions led to the differentiation of family roles. One law that was passed as the result of the agitation of factory workers was the Factory Act of 1833. This Act prohibited the employment of children under nine in factories and limited the working day of children under 13 to eight hours. It also specified that children employed in the factories had to spend a minimum of two hours each day in formal schooling. What is the significance of this Act, and how is its passage to be explained? Smelser's answer is that (1959:294–5):

it resulted in a greater *structural differentiation* in the family economy. This differentiation moved along two distinct lines: (1) Whereas technological innovations had been weakening the economic link between parent and child for some years, the Act of 1833 broke this link definitively by removing the possibility that the child could remain at his father's side during the entire work-day. Thus it encouraged further segregation of the economic roles of adult and child. Further, it differentiated other characteristics of the parent-child relationship – socialization, moral training, etc. – from the economic roles of family members. . . . (2) The Act pushed the differentiation of formal education from the family economy to a new level. . . . To require a manufacturer to guarantee that his child employees receive a minimum of formal education – either in a manufactory or some other school – marked an increase of educational specialization.

For Smelser, then, the significance of the Factory Act of 1833 is that it produced a more differentiated family economy in the context of an increasingly differentiated social system, and this differentiation improved the functioning of the systems in question. Presumably, this improved functioning serves as the basis for actually explaining the events in question.

It is clear that Smelser regards the process of structural differentiation as the master process of social change, for he tells us near the end of the book that he has been relating the social phenomena under consideration to *"one* major explanatory principle, namely . . . a process of structural differenti-ation"* (1959:384). The key question now becomes: what kind of explanatory principle is this differentiation principle? It is hard to resist the conclusion that it is a principle that rests upon a developmentalist explanatory logic. In reviewing many of the causes of industrialization and economic growth in England proposed by historians, Smelser admits that most or perhaps even all of these proposed factors have been important, and so he acknowledges the significance of ordinary causal explanations. However, he goes on to say that one cannot produce a sensible explanation by simply adding up these causes, for that would distort their meaning. The proposed causes make sense only when viewed as part of some larger developmental process (1959:62):

the notion of simple cause or determination may be misleading because it implies a "before–after" relationship. In fact industrial development involves an interplay of qualitatively different factors which "add their value" to growth at different stages and in different weights. It is hoped that the model of structural differentiation, *which characterizes industrial change as an unfolding sequence,* . . . will provide a framework in which the value-system, technology, natural resources, capital, and so on, may be relegated to their appropriate contributory roles.

This especially pregnant passage may be taken to suggest that Smelser's approach to evolutionary change is strikingly similar to that of the classical evolutionists, that is, it is a peculiar mixture of ordinary causal and developmentalist explanatory logics. Moreover, like the theories of the classical evolutionists, Smelser's is one in which the developmentalist logic dominates. Christopher Lloyd also senses the developmentalist emphasis to Smelser's theory. As he comments (1986:213):

it is not really a causal theory. . . . Nowhere was there a discussion by him of the structural causes of the process. . . . The theory is simply one of stages in a process with a beginning and an end. Differentiation is both the process and (apparently) its own cause.

These serious problems aside, a further question can be raised about the usefulness of describing many of the social changes accompanying industrialization in terms of the concept of differentiation. Think again of Smelser's analysis of the meaning of the Factory Act of 1833. This Act is to be understood as important because it led to a greater structural diffentiation. But is that a sensible way of even *describing* what occurred, let alone explaining it? Would it not be just as plausible, or even more plausible, to say that new *kinds* of social patterns emerged in response to various social struggles, conflicts, and dissatisfactions? Even if it could be shown that these new patterns were in fact more differentiated than previous ones, what is to be gained by saying so? What is there about the fact of differentiation that somehow gives it more importance than other characteristics of the new patterns?

These are difficult questions, and it is by no means clear what the answers are. But let me not pursue my criticism of Smelser any further, for these same concerns will appear again even more dramatically in my analysis of Parsons. As we will see, Parsons not only makes structural differentiation his master principle of social evolution, but he does so in a much more all-embracing and developmentalist manner than Smelser.

PARSONS'S THEORY OF SOCIAL EVOLUTION

By the mid-1960s Parsons had come to produce not only a general theory of change, but a large-scale and complex theory of long-term social evolution, one designed to explain the transformation of human societies from the earliest bands and tribes to the most recent industrial states. As already indicated, the master principle of Parsons's evolutionary theory is that of structural differentiation. But Parsons adds to this notion another critical one: the concept of *adaptive capacity*. Societies are goal-oriented systems that seek ways of adapting themselves to their environments. The key to adaptation is differentiation, and there is a tendency in social systems for them to become more differentiated. By differentiating, social systems increase their adaptive capacity, or undergo what Parsons calls *adaptive upgrading*. They improve the overall level of their functioning. For Parsons, the evolution of human social life is basically a long story about the increasing differentiation and adaptiveness of goal-seeking social systems.

Despite these new wrinkles, an older Parsonian concern has not gotten lost in the shuffle. The famous pattern variables are still to be found alive and well and have ended up being synthesized into the differentiation-increasing adaptation model. As it has turned out, for Parsons increasing differentiation also happens to be a process that closely parallels the transition from one of the pattern variables to its opposite.

*Evolutionary Universals*

Parsons's first systematic development of an evolutionary theory of change occurred in his article "Evolutionary universals in society" (1964). This article developed the concept of an *evolutionary universal*, which is "a complex of structures and associated processes the development of which so increases the long-run adaptive capacity of living systems in a given class that only systems that develop the complex can attain certain higher levels of general adaptive capacity" (1964:340–41). In other words, it is a structural innovation that improves the level of functioning of a system and serves also as a prerequisite for further evolutionary advances. Parsons makes an explicit analogy with what he takes to be evolutionary universals in the biological world. Vision is held to be one of these, and in the case of human biological evolution the hands and the brain are regarded as important evolutionary universals.

Parsons proposes that six evolutionary universals have been especially significant in the historical development of human societies. The first of these is *social stratification*. Its significance lies in its capacity to overcome the evolutionary limitations of ascription. A second evolutionary universal is a system of *cultural legitimation*. Most broadly, this involves a set of ideals whereby a society defines its own identity and distinguishes itself from other societies. It also concerns those ideals whereby particular groups within a society can justify their social position and advantages vis-a-vis other groups.

A second pair of evolutionary universals that becomes important at a later stage of social evolution is *administrative bureaucracy* and *money and markets*. The key characteristic of bureaucracy is its institutionalization of authority in offices. The evolutionary significance of bureaucracy for Parsons is rooted in Weber's conception of bureaucracy as "the most effective large-scale administrative organization that man has invented" (1964:349). Money and markets are also a major evolutionary accomplishment. Markets allow for the much more efficient acquisition and deployment of resources; money is a great mediator of the use of goods and services. Markets and money allow resources to be freed from ascriptive bonds.

There is yet a third pair of evolutionary universals that comes into play at the most advanced stage of social evolution. *Generalized universalistic norms* are abstract legal rules that apply to an entire society rather than to one or more specific groups within it. Rome was the first premodern society to develop a universalistic legal system, but this system has become crystallized and fully systematized only in modern times. In particular, it is the English common law that represents the most developed version of a universalistic legal order. Parsons believes that this system has been "decisive for the modern world" and that it is "the most important single hallmark of modern society" (1964:353). The *democratic association* is the other of this modern pair of evolutionary universals. It involves elective office, the franchise, and collective decision-making. The use of power now rests on a broad social consensus, and thus is a generalized medium for the attainment of societal goals.

### Primitive, Intermediate, and Modern Societies

The full development of Parsons's theory of social evolution is contained in a pair of books, *Societies: Evolutionary and Comparative Perspectives* (1966) and *The System of Modern Societies* (1971). These books identify and describe in detail three major stages of social evolution.

*Primitive* societies are most significantly characterized by their undifferentiated structure. Social life is strongly rooted in kinship and other social institutions are not differentiated from it. In the truly most primitive societies, the members of the society have no well-developed conception of themselves as a distinctive entity – no clear cultural boundedness. They are also characterized by the general status equivalence of different kinship groups. The transition to a more advanced type of primitive society is marked by the emergence of a hierarchical ordering of these groups. Accompanying the rise of this early form of stratification is the emergence of a clear cultural boundedness of the whole society, usually in the form of religious legitimation.

The transition from primitive to *intermediate* societies is marked by the development of written language. Intermediate societies contain two subtypes, *archaic* and *advanced intermediate* societies (the latter are also known as *historic empires*). Archaic societies are characterized by a higher level of cultural legitimation than found in advanced primitive societies. This cultural legitimation is still religious, but it now involves a literate priesthood. The emergence of a priesthood, of course, represents a differentiation of a select group of religious specialists from the remainder of society. Archaic societies are also characterized by the development of an administrative apparatus of a sort well beyond the type possessed by even the most advanced primitive societies. Moreover, there is a substantial differentiation of political and religious leadership roles. Parsons considers ancient Egypt and Mesopotamia to be the leading examples of archaic societies.

The historic empires are distinguished from archaic societies by their innovations in the realm of culture – by their *philosophic breakthroughs.* Parsons regards four civilizations – China, India, the Islamic empires, and Rome – as the great historic empires. China developed an innovation that was entirely new in social evolution. This involved the creation of a governing class – the mandarins – whose status was defined in cultural terms. China, though, had definite evolutionary limitations. One of these involved its degree of rationalization of law, which was little developed beyond that of Mesopotamia and was still characterized by a strong particularism. In addition, its economy was weakly differentiated because it had failed to develop a monetary system sufficient to support an elaborate market system.

India went much further than China in producing a rationally consistent religio-philosophical system, but in fact it went too far in this direction. This "drained away cultural impetus for social development, leaving the society at the mercy of relatively archaic social configurations" (1966:80). As a result, India was unable to develop any highly stable, long-term political structure. The Islamic empires were also characterized by important religio-philosophical innovations. These centered about the *Umma,* or the solidary community of the faithful. The evolutionary failure of the Islamic empires, though, lay in their failure to "undergo the crucial processes of differentiation, inclusion, and upgrading that could have transformed the *Umma* into a total society permeated by universalistic norms" (1966:86).

Where all these historic empires failed, Rome succeeded. Its greatest achievement, for Parsons, was its highly universalistic legal system, a system that he claims was the most evolved system of law until modern times. The universalism of its legal system was closely associated with a concept of citizenship and with a general democratization of the society. In addition to these political achievements, Rome also made major strides in the economic sphere, for it had an elaborate system of money, credit, and markets.

The evolutionary transition to *modern societies* was only made possible, according to Parsons, by the existence of two earlier "seed-bed" societies, Israel and Greece. These societies made major cultural innovations that contributed crucially to the evolution of modernism. Israel's contribution lay in the religion of Judaism and its conception of a single universal God whose normative order was applicable to all mankind. Moreover, Judaism planted the seeds of religious individualism that would be carried over into Christianity. One similarity between ancient Greece and Israel involved the Greek conception of a pan-Hellenic culture that was broader than any single sociopolitical community. This highly universalistic conception of normative order was strongly promoted by its leading intellectuals, such as Plato and Socrates.

Thus Parsons believes that Israel and Greece contributed much to modern society even though they were not aligned on the direct evolutionary path to it. Rome, however, was on this direct path, and its most significant evolutionary contribution was, as we have seen, its elaborate universalistic legal system. In addition, Christianity was an outgrowth of the Roman empire and of Judaism within it. Christianity also provided crucial foundations for future evolutionary developments because it continued and significantly elaborated the religious individualism begun by Judaism.

Modernism first began to crystallize in the northwest corner of Europe, particularly in England, France, and Holland, and thus these three nations were the "spearheads" of early modernity. Parsons attributes greatest evolutionary significance to England, for it "had become by the end of the seventeenth century the most highly differentiated society in the European system" (1971:67). The highly differentiated character of English society is viewed by Parsons as having emerged on a number of fronts. One was economic. Commercial farming arose, and thus landowners began to employ tenant farmers. This "differentiated [the owners'] own functions as social and political leaders in the local community from those of economic production in which their land was a factor of production" (1971:66). An important set of economic changes was also occurring in the towns. These changes especially involved the disintegration of the particularistic system of medieval guilds. Other aspects of differentiation in English society involved religion, government, and law. Protestantism began to break down the traditional fusion of religion and government, and government began to separate itself from the societal community. There thus emerged "a government in which highly influential elements of the societal community were constituents of representative bodies rather than members of government" (1971:67). Connected with this trend toward parliamentary government were legal changes that began to emphasize the rights of individual members of the societal community.

The key developments in the transition to modernity were the industrial and democratic revolutions. The Industrial Revolution produced a massive differentiation in the economic structure of society and greatly extended the market system. Labor became freed from the diffuse and particularistic context in which it had been imbedded in medieval society, and the occupational role began to emerge as the primary basis for the organization of a labor force.

The massive differentiation of the economy produced by the Industrial Revolution created the functional imperative for new integrative mechanisms, and the democratic revolution occurred largely in response to this new societal need. The democratic revolution ushered in a value system emphasizing equality of opportunity, and "to the extent that this emerging value pattern was institutionalized, achievement and achievement capacity became the primary criteria of eligibility for differentially valued statuses" (1971:81).

The modernity of the twentieth century is most clearly exemplified by the United States. It is, in Parsons words, the "new lead society" of contemporary modernity. The United States has gone further than any other society in terms of its level of differentiation and its replacement of ascription by achievement and particularism by universalism. Ethnicity and social class have been increasingly abolished as criteria for social roles, and the greater inclusiveness of the American societal community is well represented by its great elaboration of the concept of citizenship. The United States has also experienced major educational and economic transformations. It has undergone an educational revolution that has contributed greatly to the occupational upgrading of the society, especially in terms of the emergence of the professions. The professions have assumed a critical role in the occupational structure. In terms of economic changes, one of the most important has been the separation of the ownership of corporations from their control.

THE LOGICAL STRUCTURE OF PARSONIAN EVOLUTIONISM

## *The Explanatory Logic of Parsons's Theory*

Let us now turn to a consideration of the logical structure of Parsons's theory of social evolution, beginning with the kind of explanatory logic on which it depends. There is every reason to think that this explanatory logic shares much in common with the classical evolutionists. Parsonian evolutionism is, in other words, a mixture of developmentalist and ordinary causal explanation.

I want to start with the ordinary causal arguments in Parsons, because these are highly characteristic throughout his evolutionary works. In regard to both his general social theory and his theory of evolution, Parsons has been referred to again and again as a cultural idealist. However, this is not how he sees himself, for near the end of *Societies* he identifies himself as a causal pluralist (1966:113):

*no* claim that social change is "determined" by economic interests, ideas, personalities of particular individuals, geographical conditions, and so on, is acceptable. *All* such single-factor theories belong to the kindergarten stage of social science's development. *Any* factor is always interdependent with several others.

Parsons does go on to say, however, that to favor a causal pluralism does not prevent one from establishing a hierarchical ordering of the relative importance of various causal factors. All are important, but some may be more important than others. And what kind of rank ordering does Parsons create? In fact he produces one that elevates human ideals and values and their associated moral rules to supreme importance. As he puts it, "I am a cultural determinist, rather than a social determinist. Similarly, I believe that, within the social system, the normative elements are more important for social change than the 'material interests' of constitutive units" (1966:113).

It would definitely appear, however, that Parsons gives considerably more weight to ideational factors than he would have us believe. They are much more than simply at the top of a causal hierarchy. Indeed, the simple fact of the matter is that Parsons's preferred explanations in his pair of books on social evolution almost always give pride of place to symbolic codes, legal norms, religious or philosophical systems, or some other phenomenon that is primarily mental or ideational. For example, a crucial prerequisite for the transition from primitive to advanced primitive societies is a system of cultural legitimation that gives the societal community a sufficient degree of boundedness. Likewise, the emergence of stratification requires that socially dominant groups formulate a system of ideals for legitimizing their superior position.

When we turn to Parsons's discussion of archaic societies and historic empires, a similar idealist emphasis is found. One of the most important evolutionary features of archaic societies is their elaborate cosmologies, cosmologies that require a much more extensive form of cultural legitimation than necessary at an earlier evolutionary stage. The great evolutionary significance of the historic empires involves their philosophical breakthroughs. In two cases (India and Islam) these breakthroughs center on religio-philosophical systems, whereas in another (Rome) the great breakthrough is said to involve a system of legal norms.

The story is the same with respect to the so-called seed-bed societies. Israel's greatest evolutionary contribution is its universalistic religion, while Greece's involves a more secularized philosophical system of justice. Moreover, Judaism led into Christianity, which is of enormous evolutionary significance for Parsons because of its universalizing and individualizing qualities. In fact, it is Christianity that prevented medieval society from regressing even further than it did.

When we get to modernity, we find that the influence of Protestantism is very great, as is especially the democratic revolution. And what is the substance of the democratic revolution? Parsons tells us that it is essentially an upheaval in values, one that led to greater emphasis on equality of opportunity. The move toward citizenship is part of this democratic revolution as well, and what is citizenship for Parsons but basically a set of philosophical concepts embodied in a constitution.

Thus it is not difficult to make a case for Parsons's ordinary causal explanations being primarily idealist ones. It is clear that Parsons regards the most important achievements in long-term sociocultural evolution as being in the area of symbolic codes, values, and norms, and that these achievements, once they arise, contribute crucially to yet further achievements. Yet it is also clear that Parsons offers little or nothing in the way of explaining many of these evolutionary outcomes. That is, even though Judaism, for example, is said to be an important evolutionary phenomenon influencing the development of Christianity, how do we account for Judaism's origination of what Parsons claims is its most important doctrine, viz., its universalism? Or, to take another example, Roman universalistic law is said to contribute much to the universalism of modern times, but then how are we to understand the origin of Roman legal norms in the first place? Parsons is remarkably silent on these obviously crucial questions and others like them.

Sometimes Parsons answers questions like these in classically functionalist terms, as when he "explains" the democratic revolution in terms of the new functional need for integration brought about by massive economic differentiation. But more often he is simply silent. How do we explain this theoretical absence? Is it that Parsons does not recognize that he has failed to account for something so important? Or could it be that Parsons simply regards many cultural outcomes as essentially arbitrary occurrences that happen to have fortuitous results, as some idealists are prone to argue (cf. Sahlins, 1976)? I think that the first possibility is highly implausible for a thinker of Parsons's stature. As for the second possibility, I think this would be ruled out of court immediately by Parsons's insistence on the *non-random* and *directional* character of social evolution.

There is a third possibility, though, and that is that Parsons sees no need to offer ordinary causal explanations for many evolutionary occurrences because he believes he has already implicitly "explained" them as part of a grand developmental scheme, one that harkens back to the developmentalism of the classical evolutionists and even beyond them to the German idealist philosopher Hegel. Was Parsons a developmentalist whose ordinary causal arguments made sense only when placed in the context of a more all-embracing explanatory principle? There can be little doubt that he was certainly a *historicist*, for historicist reasoning is basic to his whole concept of an evolutionary universal, a notion that is at the very heart of his theoretical system. His six evolutionary universals seem to make sense only in terms of their role in a larger historical whole – in terms of their contribution to later developments. Moreover, throughout his pair of books on evolutionary theory we find the same kind of historicist reasoning employed repeatedly. Rome's contribution to modernity is its universalistic legal system, which was an essential prerequisite for modern legal systems. Likewise, Greece's historical role was its development of a secular system of justice. And so on and so forth.

But does this rather obvious historicism translate into a full-blown developmentalism? I think that it does, and that it is the essential ingredient that ties together the various aspects of his theoretical system.[2] And I believe it is the closing paragraph of *The System of Modern Societies* that provides the most explicit indication of this developmentalism. In this paragraph Parsons says (1971:143; emphasis added):

We should expect that anything like a "culminating" phase of modern development is a good way off – very like a century or more. Talk of "postmodern" society is thus decidedly premature. Taking into account the undeniable possibility of overwhelming destruction, our expectation is nevertheless that *the main trend of the next century or more will be toward completion of the type of society that we have called "modern."*

Although I have italicized much of the last sentence of this quotation, it is obvious that the key word here is "completion." Completion?! Does Parsons mean it? Does he expect to be taken literally? I think that the whole tone of his evolutionary analyses suggests that he does, and that can only mean that he sees human history as evolving toward some ultimate goal. We are not there yet, he says, but it is obvious that he thinks we have gotten very close, and the most important consideration is that he thinks there is a "there" to get to.

To take this argument just one step further, let us note that the imbeddedness of idealist arguments in a developmentalist explanatory logic is hardly a new phenomenon in social theory. For, after all, that is just what we saw in the case of Morgan, and it was even more pronounced in the case of Hegel before him. For Parsons, then, like Morgan and Hegel earlier, the evolution of human society is fundamentally the evolution of the powers of the human mind in accordance with a rational plan.[3]

## Advancement and Progress

The implications of the preceding arguments for the question of whether or not Parsons equated evolution with progress should be more than obvious. Since the master principle of evolutionary transformation is social differentiation, and since more differentiated social systems have greater adaptive capacity, it is clear that Parsons believes that evolution is inextricably associated with advancement and progress. Indeed, this identification of social evolution with social advancement is a keystone of his theory, and it would appear that Parsons is really making the teleological argument that evolution occurs *in order to bring about advancement.* Thus Parsons does not in the least shy away from making explicit value judgments about different social and cultural systems. As he tells us (1966:109–10):

To be an evolutionist, one must define a general trend in evolution – one cannot be a radical cultural relativist who regards the Arunta of Australia and such modern societies as the Soviet Union as equally authentic "cultures," to be judged as equals in *all basic* respects. Our perspective clearly involves evolutionary judgments – for example, that intermediate societies are more advanced than primitive societies, and modern societies . . . are more advanced than intermediate societies. I have tried to make my basic criterion congruent with that used in biological theory, calling more "advanced" the systems that display greater generalized adaptive capacity.

A more contentious question concerns whether or not Parsons's conception of evolutionary advancement is also highly ethnocentric. After all, it is one thing to place social systems in an evaluative hierarchy, but quite another to do so in a way that springs from one's own cultural biases. Parsons himself has vigorously denied an ethnocentric bias to his formulations, and he offers three arguments in his defense. First, he says that the adaptive capacity of a society, though of crucial importance to him, may not be so in the judgment of many other people. Others may focus on other dimensions of social life as a basis for evaluating societies. Second, he says that modern societies may well not be the be-all and end-all of social evolution, for they may give way to a "postmodern" phase of evolution. Finally, modern societies themselves are said to contain many elements that were originally obtained from non-Western sources.

None of these arguments is especially convincing. The first is evasive in the extreme, for does Parsons actually expect us to accept that he himself really believes that his concept of adaptive capacity can be employed in such a highly relativistic way? The second and third, even if highly accurate characterizations, do not really address the problem of ethnocentrism in a straightforward way. Thus, in spite of these disclaimers, it is still very difficult to escape the conclusion that Parsons's judgments about evolution-ary advancement are deeply permeated by his biases in favor of his own particular society (and his own social position in it). What societal characteristics receive most favorable endorsement in Parsons's theory? The answer is, precisely those that Parsons believes to be most heavily concentrated in the contemporary United States, the society that he refers to as the "lead society" of contemporary modernity. And where did this "lead society's" principal societal characteristics originate historically? The answer is, in England and, more distantly, in ancient Rome. Is this not an American-centered or, more broadly, a Eurocentric perspective?

When we look more closely at some of Parsons's pronouncements about the details of modern societies themselves, we find still further evidence of ethnocentrism, and this time of a sort that is closely associated with Parsons's own social position. Take, for example, Parsons's discussion of the modern professions. Parsons gives enormous approval to the develop-ment of these versions of the modern occupational role. He believes that they contribute greatly to the adaptiveness of modern societies because they are built around achievement rather than ascription, and because they are oriented to serving the social collectivity rather than the self. And what is the profession *par excellence*? It turns out to be the academic profession, the very one to which Parsons himself belongs. Can such a judgment made by an American professor teaching at Harvard University conceivably be thought of as free from cultural biases?

### The Problem of Unilinearism

Given the importance that Parsons gives to advancement and progress in social evolution, it might naturally be assumed that his version of evolutionism is a unilinear version. Yet he denies this too, and insists upon separating his evolutionary theory from the theories of the classical evolutionists, especially Spencer's. His, he says, is much more sophisticated and avoids the unilinear trap of the classical theorists (1966:110):

The present analysis differs significantly from most older evolutionary theories in that the developmental dimension I have used is fully compatible with the idea that there is considerable variability and branching among lines of evolution. The evidence we have reviewed indicates that, in the earlier stages of evolution, there have been *multiple* and *variable* origins of the *basic* societal types. Thus, we need not postulate one primitive origin of all intermediate societies. . . . At all stages, the importance of such variability can be adequately treated, we argue, only by an analytic theory of variable factors and components. The impressive development of such theory since Spencer's time enables us to construct a much more sophisticated evolutionary scheme than his.

Once again, however, Parsons seems to overstate his case considerably. Although he has not produced a strong version of unilinear evolutionism, there is no doubt that his evolutionary theory is unilinear in the weak sense. Despite the disclaimers about variability and multiple origins, the fact remains that virtually the entirety of Parsons's evolutionary analysis is preoccupied with the main trunk of evolutionary development – the continuous differentiation and adaptive upgrading leading up to modern times. The only concern at all that Parsons has with divergent developments is directed toward the way in which these developments feed back into the main evolutionary trunk. This is precisely the significance of his analysis of ancient Israel and Greece. They are not analyzed for their own sake, but only in terms of their ultimate contribution to modernity.

It is thus extremely difficult to agree with Parsons's own assessment that his evolutionism represents a significant improvement over that of the classical evolutionists with respect to the problem of unilinearism. In fact, in many ways his theory is even more unilinear than theirs, for they not only frequently discussed divergent developments, but often did so for their own sake instead of simply for their contribution to the main line of evolutionary development.

### PARSONS'S THEORY OF SOCIAL EVOLUTION: A CRITIQUE

I have already implied many criticisms of Parsons' evolutionary theory: its developmentalist and teleological structure, its idealist bias, its ethnocentric emphasis on advancement and progress, and its unilinearism. But I now want to subject Parsons's theory to a much more systematic critical scrutiny, beginning, as seems logical, with his master evolutionary principle.

## The Concept of Differentiation in Parsons's Theory

As we have seen, the critical concept for Parsons's theory of social evolution is that of differentiation, a concept that he inherited from the functionalist evolutionary tradition of Spencer and Durkheim. The concept plays a double role in his theory; it is, as Anthony Smith (1973) has noted, both the process and the causal motor of evolutionary change. Because the concept does double duty in this fashion, to assess its adequacy we must ask two basic questions about it: is increasing differentiation an important characteristic of evolutionary change? and, if so, is the tendency toward increasing differentiation capable of explaining anything about social evolution?

In regard to the first question, Charles Tilly (1984) suggests that, although increasing differentiation can be shown to be a significant aspect of much social change, it is nonetheless not nearly as significant as Parsons conceives it to be. Furthermore, *de*differentiation is also a prominent feature of numerous important social changes. As Tilly notes (1984:48):

many social processes . . . involve dedifferentiation: linguistic standardization, the development of mass consumption, and the agglomeration of petty sovereignties into national states provide clear examples. Furthermore, differentiation matters little to other important social processes such as capital concentration and the diffusion of world religions. Indeed, we have no warrant for thinking of differentiation in itself as a coherent, general, lawlike social process.

Anthony Smith takes a similar view, noting that increasing societal specialization is a substantial trend in the history of human societies, but also cautioning that "we should be careful not to elevate this trend into a sort of master-principle of historical development" (1973:136). But of course this is exactly what Parsons has done, and with a vengeance. In fact, Parsons wants to find differentiation everywhere, even when the changes in question need not (or perhaps even *cannot*) be meaningfully described in such terms. Take for example, his description of the democratic revolution as a major example of differentiation, one that allegedly differentiated the polity from the societal community. It is perhaps not inaccurate to make such a description, but does describing the process that way convey what is most significant about it? That seems unlikely. Or take the shift toward the modern occupational role, which Parsons interprets as a differentiation within the economic sphere. Is it the differentiated character of this process that is most important? Serious doubts would seem to be in order. Could this process be accurately characterized without even using the concept of differentiation? More than likely it could.

But regardless of the extent to which differentiation is an important feature of historical social change, there remains the more crucial question of the explanatory usefulness of the differentiation concept. In this regard I am in complete sympathy with Anthony Smith's judgment that it is extremely difficult "to make a case for the explanatory potential of the concept" and that "the idea that we should view differentiation as . . . *the* motor of change . . . must be entirely discounted" (1973:145). The reason for such a negative judgment can be stated quite straightforwardly. Parsons's argument for the explanatory significance of differentiation is an entirely teleological one, and thus completely unacceptable. Differentiation occurs because it leads to adaptive upgrading, an increasing adaptive capacity of the social system. But not only is this assertion unacceptable because of its teleological character, it employs an extremely vague and troublesome concept of adaptation. And since the concept of differentiation is meaningless in Parsons's evolutionary theory without being attached to his concept of adaptive capacity, this latter concept must also be carefully scrutinized. If it is found wanting, as I shall argue, then this is all the more reason to reject the theoretical utility of the differentiation concept.[4]

## Parsons and Adaptive Capacity

Parsons's use of the concepts of adaptation and adaptive capacity seems so severely flawed as to constitute a fatal weakness in his theory. In the first instance, the Parsonian concept of adaptive capacity rests on a highly reified notion of societies. For Parsons, what adapts is a social system, or at the very least one of its principal subsystems. It is never individual human beings who are the referents for Parsons's concept of adaptive capacity, but always abstract "systems." This classically functionalist notion has been shown time and again to be thoroughly inadequate, and the reason is that it presumes the existence of something that cannot logically have an existence. It presumes the actual existence of a social system as a thing apart with "needs" and "imperatives" of its own. But social systems do not exist as things apart, and they do not have needs or imperatives. Only individual human beings do, and thus it is only to them that the concept of adaptation can apply if it is to be applied at all.

But beyond this overwhelming difficulty, there is another fatal weakness in the Parsonian concept of adaptive capacity: its paralyzing vagueness. This vagueness has been remarked upon by numerous scholars (cf. Giddens, 1984; Zeitlin, 1973). Parsons tells us that adaptive capacity has to do with the ability of a social system to function effectively with respect to its environment, and that this involves active mastery of the environment rather than simply passive adjustment to it. It is not at all clear what this is to be taken to mean. The term "environment," for example, is altogether ambiguous. We are left in the dark as to whether this means the physical environment or the social environment, and as to what the nature and dimensions of this environment are. Consider also the problems with the concept of "mastery." What does it really mean to suggest that social systems evolve toward increasing mastery? Anthropological studies of the simplest human societies, band-organized hunter-gatherers, show conclusively that the members of such groups have detailed knowledge of their natural environments and that they have been able to work out very delicate mechanisms for remaining in close harmony with them. Yet in contemporary industrial societies the amount of destruction done to the environment has been so severe that it is thought by many that environmental and social disaster await. It would thus appear that in one very real sense evolutionarily earlier societies show a much greater environmental "mastery" than evolutionarily later ones. Irving Zeitlin has implied a similar point in asking, "How can one speak of greater adaptive capacity in the present period of history, when all men live in the shadow of a possible nuclear holocaust" (1973:56)?

Given these conceptual and empirical difficulties, what then could Parsons have had in mind in declaring evolutionarily more recent societies to have greater adaptive capacity? I think there is only one realistic answer to that question, and that is that these societies more closely approximate Parsons's preconceived notions as to what a properly structured society ought to look like. This returns us to the problem of Parsons's ethnocentrism, for I think this is precisely what is guiding his judgments about adaptive capacity. If I am correct, this means that Parsons's concept of adaptive capacity is a purely value-laden one that thoroughly distorts our understanding of the nature and causes of trajectories of social evolution.[5]

## The Idealizations in Parsons's Evolutionary Theory

The problem of value-ladenness also seems to be central to Parsons's characterization of social evolution as marking a gradual shift from one kind of action-orientation to another – from one pattern variable to its opposite. In order to criticize Parsons's evolutionary use of the pattern variables, let me select just two of them, ascription vs achievement and self-orientation vs collectivity-orientation.

Parsons claims that the general course of social evolution is marked by a gradual movement away from ascriptive social bonds toward achievement. I think a good case can be made that things have happened quite differently. Parsons believes that the simplest societies are strongly rooted in ascriptive ties because of the importance these societies give to kinship. Kinship ties are, of course, ascriptive, and Parsons is quite right to note that they are of crucial importance in these kinds of societies. However, he has overlooked other dimensions of such societies in which achievement rather than ascription prevails. A notorious feature of societies that anthropologists generally call band and village societies is their egalitarian and unstratified character. There are no class divisions – no groups with unequal access to the means of production. This does not mean that such societies do not have important positions of leadership. They do, but the crucial thing about such leadership positions is the extent to which they are openly contested by members of the society. Band and village societies generally lack hereditary restrictions on the capacity to exercise leadership, and so it is achievement rather than ascription that determines who the leaders are.

An excellent example of what I am talking about is provided by Marshall Sahlins's (1963) analysis of patterns of leadership in two kinds of societies found in the southern Pacific that may be said to differ in evolutionary terms. In Melanesia, there tended to be societies in which there were no developed stratification patterns in the sense of the existence of discretely identifiable social classes. These societies had leaders known as "big men," who were men of considerable social rank who exercised important economic and political functions. To attain the status of big man, a man had to compete with other aspirants, since there were no hereditary mechanisms for the transmission of leadership roles. To get to be a big man a man had to demonstrate his abilities to the entire village, and big men could easily lose their leadership roles if their abilities or motivation for leadership declined. It is clear that this kind of leadership pattern was based on achievement rather than ascription.

In Polynesia, on the other hand, there tended to be found societies that Sahlins regarded as farther along on an evolutionary scale. These societies were stratified into hereditary social classes, and the top leadership roles were those of chiefs rather than big men. Chiefs were leaders who were capable of exercising considerably more power than that available to big men. No open competition for the role of chief existed, and a man could attain the position of paramount chief (or village subchief) only by inheriting it in a family line. The Polynesian pattern of chiefly leadership was obviously based on ascription rather than achievement.

Sahlins believes that the hereditary chiefly pattern typical of aboriginal Polynesia actually evolved from a pattern much like the big-man system found throughout Melanesia in recent times. If so, then what we are witnessing is the actual evolution from achievement to ascription, the very opposite of the proposed Parsonian pattern. But the illustration Sahlins provides is only one among many that can be drawn from the works of anthropologists. It is well known among anthropologists that many important social roles in the simplest societies are openly contested, and that in more evolved societies the hereditary placement of individuals into social roles is commonplace.

Much the same sort of argument can be made with respect to the self-orientation/collectivity-orientation pattern variable. Parsons has insisted that social evolution has traveled a path of increasing concern for the collectivity over the self. Yet, despite the fact that Parsonian evolutionary theory draws on Durkheimian notions, Durkheim himself stressed that small-scale societies are grounded in mechanical solidarity, a social pattern in which the individual self is rather completely assimilated into the collectivity. In fact, compelling evidence suggests that all preindustrial societies emphasize a collectivity-orientation over a self-orientation, and that the real predominance of the self-orientation did not begin to emerge until the transition to modernity a few hundred years ago. One of the most important features of modern societies stressed by many sociologists is their "individualism."

Parsonian defenders might object to this line of reasoning by claiming that the self-orientation/collectivity-orientation distinction has more to do with the use of power than with the psychological relationship between self and society. Perhaps so, but serious problems with the Parsonian evolutionary analysis remain nonetheless. In societies of the big-man type, for instance, political leadership exercised by big men must serve the larger interests of the collectivity, otherwise big men cease to be big men. Big men are regarded as public servants, and one of their primary responsibilities is the redistribution of economic products to the entire community. Self-oriented big men last only a short while in their roles. Contrast this situation with the use of political power by Polynesian chiefs, which is indeed strikingly more self-oriented. In the great agrarian civilizations, the self-interested use of political power is carried to an even greater extreme. Parsons would have us believe, of course, that in the transition to modernity all this changed, and that power became a "generalized societal medium" to be used in behalf of the entire society. But such a notion would be extremely difficult to defend and is really little more than an extraordinary idealization of modern society.

Such a tendency toward idealization should no longer surprise us, though, and in fact is fully consistent with the marked ethnocentrism that pervades Parsonian evolutionism. It is this aspect of Parsons's theory of evolution that catches the eye of Irving Zeitlin, who connects it with Parsons's functionalism and idealism. Suggesting that Parsons's evolutionary theory is actually very much a hidden polemic against Marxism, Zeitlin claims that the most serious absences in the theory are those concerning the social role of conflict, domination, and material self-interest (1973:54):

There is no discussion whatsoever of the connection between economic surplus and classes. No attention is given to the proposition, now generally accepted among social scientists, that with the emergence of a significant surplus over and above subsistence requirements of the producers themselves, a group other than the producers manages in various ways to gain control of the surplus as well as the productive resources; and that a system of domination thus emerges that ensures the maintenance of the producers' subsistence at a minimum level and continued economic and other advantages for the rulers. This economic basis of stratification, the resulting conflicts of material interests, the struggles over access and control of the surpluses and key resources, the use of force and the threat of force to gain or retain control of resources, war within and among societies, the institutionalization of political power to maintain the privileges of the dominant class – all this receives no treatment in Parsons' conception of social change and "evolution."

And so we see yet another serious distortion produced by Parsons in his effort to understand the broad evolutionary trajectory of human societies.

### Talcott Parsons: The American Hegel

Earlier we noted that Parsonian neoevolutionism is rooted to a considerable extent in the evolutionary tradition of Spencer and Durkheim. It should be more than obvious that Parsons is working within a theoretical tradition in which Spencer's conception of increasing social differentiation and Durkheim's (1933[1893]) view of the shift from mechanical to organic solidarity are classical exemplars of how best to understand evolutionary change.[6] But Parsons himself actually stresses his links to a different tradition of classical social theory. At the beginning of *The System of Modern Societies* he suggests that his evolutionary theory owes most to "German idealism, as it passed from Hegel through Marx to Weber. Although it is fashionable today to ridicule Hegel's glorification of the Prussian state, he did develop a sophisticated theory of general societal evolution and its culmination in the modern West" (1971:1).

Parsons goes on to emphasize the indebtedness of his theory to Weber, particularly in terms of Weber's conception of the increasing rationalization of the West, and Hegel is not mentioned again. This seems sensible enough, for certainly there are unmistakable earmarks of Weber's direct influence on Parsons (at least with respect to Parsons's interpretation of Weber). On the other hand, there is a sense in which the influence of Hegel on Parsons was actually greater. After all, Weber was not at all sympathetic to evolutionary interpretations of history, especially those of such enormous sweep as Parsons's. Moreover, it is well known that Weber's view of the present and future state of the West was a melancholy and pessimistic one, and the contrast between this view and Parsons's cheery optimism is stark.

Yet on both these counts the views of Parsons and Hegel are strikingly similar.

Consider the comparisons that can be made between Parsons and Hegel. Most obviously, both had strongly historicist and developmentalist modes of explaining historical changes. Hegel thought that history unfolded as part of a rational developmental process that had an ultimate endpoint (see Hegel, 1953[1837], 1956[1899]). History was governed by reason (for Hegel, Reason) and would culminate in freedom (Freedom), which consisted of mankind's complete knowledge of itself. Parsons thinks much the same thing. History (social evolution) has an endpoint, which is the modern (actually, "postmodern") society. This society is more rationally organized than any previous one, and it too holds out much greater freedom (especially in the form of universalism and an emphasis on achievement).

Similarily, both Hegel and Parsons held the view that at every major stage of historical development there is a single society that is ahead of all the others – that has progressed further toward the fully rational society. Hegel thought that in ancient times it was Rome that held this position, while in modern times it was Germany (Prussia). Likewise, Parsons gives Rome pride of place among the historic empires, and the United States is identified as the "lead society" of contemporary modernity.

Hegel and Parsons are also linked by their theoretical idealism, a point specifically mentioned by Parsons. For Hegel historical development is the unfolding of the Absolute Idea, and societies and civilizations are to be identified principally by their achievements in the realms of art, religion, and philosophy. Parsons certainly holds no metaphysical notion of an Absolute Idea, but he does, despite his disclaimers, offer a strongly idealist interpretation of the nature of human societies. For Parsons, the great achievements in social evolution belong mostly to the realm of ideas, and these achievements are said to be essential for further developments. But let it not be forgotten that the idealisms of both Hegel and Parsons make sense only within a larger conception of the causes of historical change, a conception that emphasizes history as the logical unfolding of inherent potentialities toward some ultimate goal.

Another similarity between Hegel and Parsons concerns the role they ascribed to individuals in historical change. For both, individuals are not agents who create historical events, but mainly tools who are "used by" larger forces to achieve grander goals than anything imagined by individuals. Hegel's concept of the "cunning of reason" is the main expression of his view of the relationship of individuals to the historical process. Parsons has nothing quite so grand, but his concept of structural differentiation shows clearly how much emphasis is given to abstract social structures over human individuals.

Finally, it can be said that both thinkers had views of history that were similarily "unilinear." For both there is a main thrust to history that must be distinguished from numerous "historical sideshows." Neither is interested in these sideshows, but really only in the historical events that contribute to the onward-and-upward directional movement of history. Indeed, given the strong developmentalism of both thinkers, how could it be otherwise?

Of course, there are also major differences between the two thinkers that should not be ignored. Hegel's philosophy of history was really devoted to a theodicy – a justification of the role of God in history – and it would be difficult to argue for anything like this underlying Parsons's evolutionary theory (Parsons has, however, been called a deeply religious thinker). Hegel also gave a historical role to what he called "world-historical individuals." These were men – such as Alexander, Caesar, or Napoleon – who had a glimpse of the contribution they and their society could make to history, and who were prepared to act on this understanding. There is really no parallel to this in Parsons's evolutionary theory. In addition, Parsons's theory is offered as a scientific and explicitly evolutionary theory, and close links are suggested between the processes of biological and social evolution. Nothing like this, obviously, is to be found in Hegel. Finally, we should not overlook the explicitly *dialectical* foundations of Hegel's philosophy of history. This image of history moving forward as the result of a continuous series of negations and syntheses is something completely lacking in Parsons.[7]

Nevertheless, the similarities between Parsons's theory of social evolution and Hegel's philosophy of history are striking, and these similarities should give us pause. Although Parsons's evolutionary theory avoids some of the more horrendous metaphysical dimensions of Hegelianism, it is still rooted in many of the same philosophical and theoretical assumptions, assumptions that scarcely bode well for acquiring an adequate understanding of the character of social evolution. It has often been suggested by critics of Parsons that his evolutionary theory is scarcely an advance beyond the theories produced by Spencer and the other classical evolutionists.[8] Indeed, more might be said, and that is that in several crucial respects Parsonian evolutionism is not even much of an intellectual advance beyond the thinking of a German philosopher whose ideas about the broad course of historical change were themselves inferior to those of the classical evolutionists.

THE CURRENT STATUS OF SOCIOLOGICAL NEOEVOLUTIONISM

The sociological version of evolutionary theory that is best represented in the work of Talcott Parsons has suffered from enormous criticism and began a sharp intellectual decline sometime during the early 1970s. The regeneration of Marxism, and the emergence from more traditional Marxism of dependency and world-system theories of economic development and underdevelopment, have pushed sociological neoevolutionism far into the background. Yet this perspective has by no means died out entirely. Parsons and other sociological neoevolutionists have always had numerous defenders and elaborators, and in the past decade there has even begun a sort of "Parsons revival." This revival is most closely associated with the work of Jeffrey Alexander (1983) in the United States and of several German sociologists. The thinker who is most concerned with building upon Parsons's evolutionary theory is the German theorist Niklas Luhmann, himself a former student of Parsons. In his *The Differentiation of Society* (1982), Luhmann sketches out some of his most basic notions concerning a theory of social evolution. Most of these notions seem to have been borrowed directly from Parsons. There are strong emphases, for instance, on the adaptive significance of universalistic symbolic codes, on the evolutionary importance of stratification, and on the emergence in modern times of increasingly "open" stratification systems. Most importantly, and as the title of Luhmann's book indicates, it is social differentiation that is held up as the key to evolutionary changes.

To be fair to Luhmann, it must be stressed that his evolutionary views are not simply uncritical imitations of those of Parsons, and he does distance himself from Parsons at certain points. This is perhaps most evident in Luhmann's explicit recognition of the difference between classifying societies according to modes of differentiation and building a genuine theory of evolutionary transformations. Yet despite such an important awareness, it is clear that the main thrust of Luhmann's ideas regarding a theory of evolution are strikingly similar to the functionalist assertions of Parsons. In Luhmann's differentiation theory, then, sociological neoevolutionism is still alive and well.

Parsonian neoevolutionary ideas have also been preserved in the more recent works of Jürgen Habermas, except that Habermas has attempted to develop other aspects of Parsonian evolutionism. Habermas's major contribution to a theory of social evolution is his *Communication and the Evolution of Society* (1979; some of these ideas are developed more fully in his more recent *The Theory of Communicative Action* [1984]). He intends his evolutionary theory to be a "reconstruction" of historical materialism, thus regarding himself as still working within the Marxian tradition. But this is extremely difficult to accept, for there is very little traditional Marxism (by whatever interpretation) remaining in Habemas's mature thought. On the contrary, we find him recommending the cognitive–developmental psychologies of Piaget and Kohlberg and the idealist assumptions of Parsons as proper foundations for a theory of evolution. Just as Piaget and Kohlberg claim that individual cognitive and moral development progress through an invariant sequence of stages, so Habermas claims that societies progress through an invariant stage sequence in which they achieve more adequate modes of "communicative action." This is given an interesting Parsonian twist so that modes of communicative action are seen to be closely intertwined with normative structures and modes of social integration. Societies, in short, go through an "evolutionary learning process" in which they respond to "evolutionary challenges" and enhance their overall adaptive capacity by producing more adequate cognitive and moral structures, which for Habermas are basically world views.

Habermas marks off four major evolutionary stages. *Neolithic societies* are dominated by mythological world views and by the legal regulation of social conflict in terms of a preconventional morality. *Early civilizations* also have mythological world views, but these now play important legitimizing roles for positions of authority. Conflict is regulated by a conventional system of morality in which rulers represent and administer justice. *Developed civilizations* have broken with mythological thought and have begun to develop rationalized world views. Conflict is regulated by a conventional morality, but this is embodied in systematized law rather than attached to the person of the ruler. Finally, *modern societies* are grounded in postconventional political and legal principles and a universalistic doctrine of social legitimation.

The similarities between this scheme and Parsons's idealist evolutionary scheme are striking, and there is no doubt that Habermas has borrowed extensively from Parsons in this regard (despite blending in strong cognitive–developmental underpinnings). And like Parsons (and Piaget and Kohlberg as well), there is no doubt that Habermas's theory rests on a developmentalist explanatory framework. Habermas tells us again and again that there is a developmental logic to the cognitive and moral structures that individuals learn and that are transferred to societies in the form of world views. Each successive societal world view is not only a more adequate structure for integrating society and solving its adaptive problems, but indeed for Habermas seems to arise precisely *because* it enhances the adaptive capacity of society.

As in the case of Luhmann, Habermas maintains a certain distance from Parsonian evolutionary ideas. Contrary to Luhmann, he rejects the concept of differentiation as an evolutionarily meaningful one (although he does sometimes smuggle it back in in markedly Parsonian ways). In addition, his theory is not associated with as uncritical a view of evolutionary progress as Parsons's. As a representative of the Frankfurt School, Habermas is obviously much more aware of the disagreeable features of modern capitalism. In the main, however, the Parsonian heritage in Habermas's evolutionism is unmistakable. What an extraordinary outcome for a thinker who started his career as a Marxist![9]

NOTES

1 Other major works that preceded Parsons's full-blown evolutionary theory, but that drew on his early ideas on social change, include Bert Hoselitz's *Sociological Aspects of Economic Growth* (1960) and S. N. Eisenstadt's *Modernization: Protest and Change* (1966; cf. Eisenstadt, 1968, 1973). These well-known contributions to so-called moderniz-ation theory elaborate a distinction between "traditional" and "modern" societies in order to explain variations in levels of economic development among contemporary nations (Hoselitz frames the distinction between "traditional" and "modern" by drawing explicitly on Parsons's pattern variables). What is perhaps Eisenstadt's single most important work, *The Political Systems of Empires* (1963), is grounded in neoevolutionary theoretical assumptions but is not a work focusing on modernization per se. Eisenstadt's essay "Social change, differentiation, and evolution" (1964) is an important general theoretical contribution.

   Mention should also be made of Robert Bellah's "Religious evolution" (1964). This famous essay on the evolution of religion makes use of Parsons's concept of differentiation.

2 Much the same argument is developed by Anthony Smith in his well-known critique of sociological neoevolutionism, *The Concept of Social Change* (1973). Smith is extremely critical of Parsons for largely avoiding any discussion of actual causal mechanisms of evolutionary transformation. He also asserts that sociological neoevolutionism in general rests firmly on the notion that "to change is to unfold the potentialities of [a] structure" (1973:50).

   For a contrasting interpretation of the explanatory structure of Parsonian evolution-ism, see Haines (1987).

3 Near the end of this chapter I will offer a systematic and explicit comparison of Parsons and Hegel.

4 In one sense, though, the concept of differentiation cannot be so summarily dismissed. If we accept that the evolution of human societies is broadly characterized by increasing differentiation, then we are still left with the problem of accounting for the existence of such a pattern. This is all the more important when we recognize that biological evolution is also characterized by increasing complexity. There are two quite different ways we might approach this problem. We could assert that differentiation is a fairly uninteresting by-product of social (and biological) evolution that has garnered far more attention than it deserves. Or we could suggest that differentiation is an evolutionary phenomenon of considerable importance, but one whose significance has been improperly understood by Parsons and the sociological neoevolutionists in general. In chapter 8 I shall attempt a resolution of the dilemma I have posed in the context of a consideration of the significance given to differentiation by biological evolutionists.

5 These overwhelming difficulties with Parsons's employment of the concept of adaptation do not require, as a number of social scientists seem to think, abandonment of the concept itself. As I will attempt to show in chapter 8, the concept is a perfectly good one that is both useful and essential for social–scientific analyses, including evolutionary ones. But it is fraught with dangers and thus should be used only with the greatest care.

6 Parsons says little about the relationship of his evolutionary ideas to those of Spencer and Durkheim, but Smelser (1968) points to an explicit connection between sociological neoevolutionism and the earlier works of Spencer and Durkheim (see in particular p. 137 and pp. 197–8).

7 On the other hand, Hegel did suggest that dialectical change led to increasing diversity and the unification of diversity, and that such a process was fundamental to the unfolding of Reason in history. Is not Parsons saying something strikingly similar?

8 Indeed, in some crucial respects Spencer would hold the upper hand. Spencer's most important insights, such as those regarding the role of population pressure and warfare in social evolution, are superior to anything produced by Parsons.

9 Something much like sociological neoevolutionism is also basic to the so-called theory of postindustrial society. The best-known version of this theory, Daniel Bell's *The Coming of Post-Industrial Society* (1973), is still a very influential view in the social sciences despite the widespread criticism it has received. The connection should not be overdrawn, for certainly the more blatant teleological and developmentalist biases of Parsons are missing (or at least highly tempered) in Bell's work, and Bell has insisted that "there are no unilineal sequences of societal change, no 'laws of social development'" (1973:xii). Yet the similarities between Bell and Parsons are too important to overlook. Like Parsons, Bell claims that he is a causal pluralist but then ends up stressing the significance of developments that are largely within the realm of ideas. The transition to the postindustrial society is, for instance, the transition from an "economizing mode" to a "sociologizing" one. These "modes" are broad mental conceptions that Bell thinks underlie the structure of society. Bell's conception of the increasing openness of the class structure of the postindustrial society, and of the great importance of a "knowledge class," is also strikingly like Parsons's conception of modernity, where achievement, educational expansion, and the social role of academicians are prominent social virtues.

# 7

# Anthropological Evolutionism Since 1960

If evolutionary theorizing in sociology in the past three decades has been dominated by Parsonian functionalism and idealism, the situation has been quite different in anthropology. For here it has been the materialist evolutionary tradition of Childe, White, and Steward that has been most influential. Indeed, the anthropological evolutionism during this time may be characterized as a kind of "second generation" of the evolutionary revival, for the theorists in question have all been students or close followers of either White or Steward or both. The most important of these theorists are Marshall Sahlins, Elman Service, Robert Carneiro, Gerhard Lenski, and Marvin Harris. It has been they, Lenski and Harris in particular, who have made the most notable recent contributions to broad theoretical questions. There are considerable differences among these thinkers, and they have been faithful to the materialist evolutionary tradition in different ways and to different degrees. Nonetheless, it is that tradition in which they are rooted and that accounts for the direction in which their ideas have developed. And the very best of these ideas, I will argue, are to be greatly preferred to the developmentalism, functionalism, and idealism of the Parsonians.

Discussion of the evolutionary contributions of Marshall Sahlins is somewhat hampered by the fact that it is a position with which he is no longer associated. In the late 1960s Sahlins began to shift his theoretical sympathies to a kind of structuralism and to severely criticize many of the assumptions of the materialist version of evolutionism he previously espoused. In any event, his early work is enormously stamped with the imprint of Leslie White, and it is that work that I want to examine here.

## Specific versus General Evolution

Sahlins's contributions to evolutionism are of both a more abstractly theoretical and a more substantive variety. With respect to the former, Sahlins (1960) contributed an early essay that attempted to reconcile the antagonism between White and Steward concerning the proper scope of evolutionary theories. Sahlins claimed that the dispute between these two thinkers was a misguided and unnecessary one that could easily be resolved by recognizing that evolution, in both the biological and the sociocultural realms, is a dual phenomenon. On the one hand there is what Sahlins called *specific evolution*. This is "descent with modification," and it involves the emergence of particular kinds of new structures, which in sociocultural life are of course new social practices and institutions. On the other hand, there is what Sahlins referred to as *general evolution*. This is the "grand movement" or "overall direction" of evolutionary modifications. Despite being unique, specific evolutionary changes are also associated with an overall movement of sociocultural life from one stage of development to another. Given that Sahlins was closely following in White's footsteps, he identified this overall movement as one involving increased energy capture or, alternatively, a higher form of social integration.

Sahlins has stressed that specific and general evolution are not two different concrete processes, but simply two aspects of the evolutionary process, two different dimensions of the same thing. Thus formulated, his conception has a strong intuitive appeal and would seem to put to rest once and for all the conflict between White and Steward over "universal" versus "multilinear" evolution. Unfortunately, as Marvin Harris (1968) has noted, closer inspection reveals several difficulties with Sahlins's formulation. The most serious of these is his smuggling of the concept of progress into the notion of general evolution. Actually, Sahlins has tried to dissociate his notion of progress from any moral or ethical conception, asserting that "general progress also occurs in culture, and it can be absolutely, objectively, and nonmoralistically ascertained" (1960:27). Yet Sahlins's criteria for measuring progress "objectively" are very suspicious. He suggests that this can be done by rating the energy-capturing capacity of a given society, since thermodynamically "higher" societies have greater flexibility and greater control over their environments (hence greater "all-round adaptability"). In addition, he supplements this thermodynamic criterion with an organizational one by pointing out that more thermodynamically advanced societies have greater specialization and a higher level of integration of their parts. This, too, is said to enhance their "all-round adaptability." But these notions are only stated, never argued, and they recall precisely the kinds of difficulties that were earlier identified in connection with White's notion of progress and Parsons's notion of "increased adaptive capacity." The suspicion cannot be avoided, then, that underlying Sahlins's so-called objective criterion of progress is actually a highly subjective and evaluative one.

Purged of its concept of progress and of its misuse of the concept of adaptation, Sahlins's distinction retains the intuitive appeal suggested earlier. However, it can be improved upon by referring to evolutionary phenomena in a tripartite sense – to parallel, convergent, and divergent evolution. We shall encounter these concepts later in this chapter in discussing the work of Marvin Harris.

### Specific Evolution in Oceania

The problems with Sahlins's distinction aside, it is clear that his own substantive contributions to evolutionism have involved specific rather than general evolution. These contributions have concerned the evolution of social stratification and political organization in Melanesia and Polynesia.

In *Social Stratification in Polynesia* (1958), Sahlins attempted to account for variations in the extent to which the societies of Polynesia were stratified. Some of these societies, like Hawaii, Tonga, and Tahiti, had rather elaborate forms of stratification characterized by sharp differences between social strata in power, wealth, and social status. At the other extreme societies such as Pukapuka and Tokelau exhibited only minimal forms of stratified life, with status and power differences being quite small. Sahlins claimed that these differences were of striking evolutionary significance and were closely related to each society's overall level of economic productivity. Historically, he argued, those societies that were now seen to be more stratified were those that in the past had risen to higher levels of economic productivity. This productivity led them to generate economic surpluses, which became the basis for the formation of stratification.

It is obvious that this study of Polynesian stratification systems applies the comparative method to infer an evolutionary sequence. So does Sahlins's study of political evolution in Oceania. In an article that has now become something of an anthropological classic, Sahlins (1963) has contrasted the nature of political systems in Melanesia with that of Polynesia. In Melanesia, he has noted, the typical political structure is the tribe, a segmental form of political organization in which each local village is politically self-sufficient and autonomous. Villages commonly have informal leaders known as big men, who are men of considerable renown and prestige but who lack true authority or power. Thus their political significance is limited, both in geographical range and in their capacity to command the actions of others. In Polynesia, by contrast, chiefdoms rather than tribes tend to prevail. Chiefdoms unite local villages into a larger whole and are overseen by a chief and cadre of subchiefs with the genuine capacity to command others. Whereas village big men rise to their positions through their own efforts, chiefs are installed in permanent offices. And whereas big men can easily lose their positions through failure to lead effectively, chiefs have a much firmer hold on theirs.

Sahlins's study of evolutionary variations in political evolution in Oceania is mainly typological and is thus limited by its lack of any real attempt to explain this evolutionary process. *Social Stratification in Polynesia*, however, explicitly sets forth an explanatory mechanism, this being growing energy capture and rising economic productivity. In essence, Sahlins has formulated what has been called a *surplus theory* of the evolution of stratification, a theory that stems directly from Childe and White. The difficulties with this theory will become apparent in our discussion of the evolutionary theories of Lenski and Harris. Suffice it to say at this point that such a theory, although it correctly takes note of the relationship between productivity and stratification, appears to misconstrue the causal mechanisms involved. In particular, it gives technology a causal role it does not deserve.

### ELMAN SERVICE'S FUNCTIONALIST EVOLUTIONISM

Contemporary interpreters of evolutionary theories usually assimilate the work of Elman Service to that of Marshall Sahlins because of the famous book that they coedited (*Evolution and Culture*, 1960). But these interpreters have generally failed to appreciate the divergence in the particular ideas of these two evolutionists. Despite its similarities to Sahlins's evolutionary views, Service's thinking contains unique features, and in fact represents the greatest departure from the Childe–White materialist tradition of all the thinkers considered in this chapter. Service is no consistent materialist, and he actually insists upon a kind of evolutionism that rejects any particular prime mover as the mechanism of evolutionary change. Moreover, his thinking is perhaps more permeated by functionalist notions than that of any other member of the second generation of the evolutionary revival.

### Service's Basic Evolutionary Notions

At first glance, Service's evolutionism would appear to be not only of a rigid, unilinear sort, but actually a manifestation of a kind of developmentalism.

Indeed, in offering a definition of sociocultural evolution he says (1971b:12):

Let us retain the term evolution with as many of its originally important connotations as possible. Etymologically, it is from the Latin: *evolutis*, "unrolling." In modern ordinary usage, it is "an unfolding"; "a development." Such a very general conception allows its use by many kinds of evolutionists. The central core of meaning is that of direction or progress along some kind of linear scale.

However, it becomes quickly apparent that Service is anything but true to this conception of evolution, for his evolutionism is notable for its remarkable flexibility. He tells us not only that "there is no inner dynamic of inevitable orthogenetic change" (1971b:11), but that evolutionary theories do not even require parallelism. He suggests that a critical ingredient of any evolutionary theory, and one that has been missing in many, is a focus on the complex interrelations between and among societies. This notion actually becomes the basis for his discussion of the evolutionary significance of the present world economic and political hierarchy of societies. The so-called underdeveloped societies of the Third World are not merely following the historical path of the advanced industrial countries, and indeed cannot do so. As he puts it (1971b:53):

the modern conditions to which any new industrialization must adapt are . . . totally different from those of the original industrialization. . . . The original industrialization was such a dramatic evolutionary breakthrough that European culture quickly established its dominance over most of the non-Western world. This is a normal consequence of significant evolutionary advances, the widening of the sphere of dominance. The dominance remains today except in those parts, notably Russia and China, that have made political revolutions against it. But the technological revolution, the Second Industrialization, is still in the future, seriously handicapped and, paradoxically, curiously advantaged by the presence of the already-industrialized states. It can profit from the modern technological advances made by Western science and from its splendid potentialities only if it can free itself from any dependence on the Western world's complicated economic system. This Western web of dominance is what has created an unprecedented environment for the new industrialization, and this is why the new technological evolution can be called revolution, for it must act *against* the dominance of the Euro-American system in the technoeconomic sphere just as in political affairs.

These assertions not only show the kind of flexible evolutionism that Service advocates, but also converge remarkably with contemporary dependency and world-system theories of Third World underdevelopment, the evolutionary importance of which will be noted in the final chapter. Service's remarks also relate closely to his so-called Law of Evolutionary

Potential, one of his more interesting concepts that will be explored in a moment.

## Service and Political Evolution

It is not these notions, however, that have been the basis for Service's reputation as an evolutionist. On the contrary, this reputation derives from his work on political evolution. His main contribution in this regard is embodied in a slim book written in 1962, *Primitive Social Organization: An Evolutionary Perspective* (2nd edition, 1971a). In this book Service proposed an evolutionary classification of forms of political organization that has become widely employed by anthropologists and been used as a basis for substantial archaeological research. Service postulated four main stages of political evolution: bands, tribes, chiefdoms, and states. Bands are highly characteristic of hunters and gatherers. People live in very small, highly mobile groups that lack any positions of formal authority, and the various bands within an overall culture are not unified or integrated in any way into a larger political whole. Tribes were ushered into existence by the Neolithic Revolution. The basic political unit is the village, which is now a larger and more permanent residential unit than the camp of band society. As in bands, leadership tends to be highly informal and personal, and there are no formal offices or positions through which leaders can exercise genuine domination over others. While there are mechanisms integrating the village into a larger whole, these are not political, and each village is a politically autonomous, largely self-regulating unit. Chiefdoms differ from tribes in that the individual villages lose their autonomy and become integrated into a larger political whole, which has a hierarchical organization and a set of formalized offices held by people who command real power and authority. States carry these centralizing and hierarchical characteristics further and institutionalize the use of force in controlling the mass of the subject population.

*Primitive Social Organization* is more a classificatory work than a truly explanatory one, and it is not particularly easy to see just what kind of explanatory mechanism Service relies on to account for the transition from one evolutionary stage of political order to the next. It would appear, though, that his explanation of political evolution is essentially a functionalist one. This is strongly suggested by his identification of his political stages as *forms of integration.* Moreover, each succeeding form of integration is described in more positive terms than the preceding one. Tribes lack political unification but they do contain what Service calls *pantribal sodalities,* or mechanisms that contribute to social integration, and it seems clear that Service views this development favorably. Likewise, chiefdoms constitute real organizational advances over tribes (1971a:133–4):

> the rise of chiefdoms seems to have been related to a total environmental situation which was selective for specialization in production and redistribution of produce from a controlling center. The resulting organic basis of social integration made possible a more integrated society, and the increased efficiency in production and distribution made possible a denser society. . . .
>   Chiefdoms are *redistributional societies* with a permanent central agency of coordination. . . . [T]he central agency . . . can . . . act to foster and preserve the integration of the society for the sake of integration alone.

With respect to the evolution of the state, Service leaves little doubt about his position. In his major work on this problem, *Origins of the State and Civilization* (1975), Service strongly rejects Marxian and other conflict theories and emphasizes instead the benefits that accrued to society as a whole from the emergence of the state. He stresses three major kinds of benefits he believes were conferred by the state: a more complex network of economic redistribution; a more successful war organization with the potential to increase wealth and enhance "national pride"; and public works, such as monumental architecture and irrigation systems (cf. Service, 1978).

It must not be assumed that Service's functionalist theory of political evolution is as simplistically teleological as Parsonian evolutionism. Unlike Parsons, Service does not assume some inherent developmental tendency rooted in the human mind that is made to do all the explanatory work. And he does make at least some attempt to specify the kinds of economic, political, and environmental conditions that are propitious for the emergence of new forms of political organization. Yet these aspects of his theoretical analysis are weakly developed and take a definite backseat to the functionalist emphasis on societal improvement with evolutionary transformation. And this, along with his obvious hostility to Marxian and conflict theories of political evolution, brings his evolutionism uncomfortably close to the Parsonian version. It need hardly be said that this is a major departure from the Whitean evolutionary tradition.

## The Law of Evolutionary Potential

My negative conclusions regarding Service's treatment of political evolution should not allow us to overlook what is of genuine value in his work. I have already commented favorably on Service's recognition of the importance of intersocietal relations in social evolution, and this recognition dovetails somewhat with another important dimension of his evolutionism. This is his attempt to formulate a provocative evolutionary principle that he has called the Law of Evolutionary Potential.

Service sets forth the Law of Evolutionary Potential as follows (1960:97): "The more specialized and adapted a form in a given evolutionary stage, the smaller is its potential for passing to the next stage." As such, it refers to the discontinuous character of evolutionary change. Those societies that have attained the most advanced levels of evolutionary development are unlikely to be the ones that make the transition to a new evolutionary stage. They tend to stagnate and decline, and thus to be overtaken by other societies at lower evolutionary levels.

Service believes that his law has been anticipated numerous times by other scholars, especially by Veblen with his concepts of "the merits of borrowing" and "the penalty of taking the lead," and by Trotsky with his notion of "the privilege of historic backwardness." Since Veblen and Trotsky are referring to the capacity of a society both to avoid the mistakes and to imitate the virtues of an evolutionarily more advanced one, this presumably is the mechanism through which Service conceives the Law of Evolutionary Potential as operating.

Service suggests that history reveals many instances of the operation of this Law. These include such things as the supercession of older civilizations by newer ones and the rapid industrialization of Russia and Germany even though they were relative latecomers to the industrialization process. Service also suggests that some of the larger contemporary underdeveloped countries that have freed themselves from Western dominance, most especially China, may have enormous evolutionary potential.

Service's Law is provocative and tantalizing and little has seemingly been done with it by evolutionary theorists. It would seem to converge in important ways with some aspects of Immanuel Wallerstein's world-system theory (which I will discuss in chapters 9 and 10 as a kind of evolutionism; cf. Chase–Dunn, 1988) and, with appropriate modification, with Marvin Harris's intensification-depletion model of social evolution (which will be discussed later in this chapter). There may thus be great potential in the Law of Evolutionary Potential.

ROBERT CARNEIRO'S SPENCERIAN EVOLUTIONISM

Robert Carneiro's contributions to contemporary evolutionism can be grouped under three headings: his detailed exegeses of Spencer's evolutionism and his effort to place it in a much more positive light; his conceptual and methodological contributions to evolutionary theorizing; and his development of a powerful theory of political evolution. Since I dealt with the first of these contributions in chapter 2, I shall focus here on the second two.

## Conceptual and Methodological Contributions

Carneiro's conceptual and methodological contributions concern his definition of evolution, his rehabilitation of the concept of unilinear evolution, and his application of scalogram analysis to the construction of evolutionary sequences. Carneiro (1972, 1973b) insists that the very best definition of evolution ever offered was the one developed originally by Herbert Spencer: evolution is change in a direction of increasing societal complexity. He notes that since Spencer's time there has been a tendency among both biological and social evolutionists to define evolution in more general terms, and largely as most any sort of qualitative structural change. He laments this fact, but also notes that in recent years there has been something of a return to the conception of evolution offered by Spencer.

Working with this conception of social evolution, Carneiro has also tried to show that the dismissal of the concept of unilinear evolution, by evolutionists as well as antievolutionists, has been premature. In the first instance, he claims, the nineteenth-century evolutionists did not adhere as rigidly to a conception of unilinearism as is usually thought. They actually claimed no more than that *most* societies go through the same basic stages, not that *all* did so. And such a view, he argues, is perfectly valid and can be empirically supported. Thus Carneiro advocates essentially the notion of weak unilinearism introduced in chapter 2.

Carneiro (1973b) also accepts much of what Steward's concept of multilinear evolution was intended to convey, although without the dubious and unnecessary baggage that Steward attached to it. However, he notes that the notion of multilinear evolution should not be allowed to distract us, as it often has, from seeing the unilinear trends that may also be discerned in divergent evolutionary trajectories. As he puts it, "We must not be stopped short when we encounter multilinearity; we must be ready to look for the less obvious unilinearity that may be concealed within it" (1973b:103).

Carneiro has also made an interesting methodological innovation in the study of cultural evolution. This involves his appropriation of Guttman scalogram analysis for use in constructing evolutionary sequences of the weak unilinear type. In an early article (Carneiro, 1962), he tried to demonstrate the logic and potential fruitfulness of *scale analysis*. The logic of scale analysis is simple enough. It involves taking $x$ number of societies and *y* number of culture traits and arranging them together in a single order starting with the society containing the fewest traits and ending with the society containing the greatest number of traits. The extent to which the resulting order forms a Guttman scale can be determined by calculating a coefficient of reproducibility, an acceptable Guttman scale having a coefficient of 0.90 or better. If a perfect Guttman scale could be produced with a set of societies and culture traits, then the following characteristics would be found (Carneiro, 1962): societies higher on the scale would have all the traits of societies of lower rank, and at least some in addition; if we know a trait to be present in a society, we would know what other traits will be present; if we know what trait is absent from a society, then we will also know what other traits will be absent; if we know the number of traits a society has, we will know which traits these are.

The potential significance of scale analysis should not be hard to discern. Within the limitations obviously imposed by the comparative method that underlies its use, successful scaling of societal characteristics clearly establishes the existence of a sequence that cries out for explanation. The establishment of the sequence in and of itself explains nothing, of course, but it certainly provides a solid basis on which the construction of explanations of process can be built. It would establish a kind of logical ordering of societal characteristics in the sense of determining which traits would tend to be prerequisites for the emergence of other traits. Carneiro has seen the potential fruitfulness of scale analysis for evolutionary theorizing quite clearly (1962:168):

Suppose we were to find, for example, that in the evolution of societies slavery, confederacies, priests, human sacrifice, markets, monarchy, courts of law and the corvée consistently followed each other in that order. The very occurrence of this sequence, once recognized, would serve as a challenge to us to apply our knowledge of process and to formulate an explanation of that regularity. I am convinced, in fact, that one of the handicaps under which students of the evolutionary process have had to labor is that many developmental regularities – the raw materials for their theories and interpretations – still lie undiscovered or unrecognized. Since scale analysis is peculiarly well suited to reveal such developmental regularities, it should turn out to be an extremely useful adjunct to the student of the evolutionary process.

In actual attempts to scale societies and their traits, Carneiro (1968, 1973c) has reported very good success. It is impossible to report the details of his results here, but he has carried out scale analysis with a large number of societies and traits and has produced scales with reproducibility coefficients well beyond the acceptable minimum. He believes this vindicates his concept of a basic unilinearism to cultural evolution, but of course in a weak rather than a strong sense of the term. Moreover, he suggests that such a weak unilinearism can now be somewhat reformulated. As he says, "Instead of saying that societies *tend to go through the same stages*, we say that societies *tend to evolve certain traits in the same order*" (1973c:839; emphasis Carneiro's).

It would appear, then, that Carneiro's methodological innovation has done much to advance a powerful kind of evolutionary argument. For this reason it is somewhat surprising that scale analysis has not been employed more extensively by others. On the other hand there are some problems with scale analysis that need to be brought to light, and these may well account for its failure to be more widely developed. In the first place, there is a narrow conception of social evolution that is implied by scale analysis, viz., *evolution as cumulation*. Scale analysis makes it appear that evolution involves essentially a cumulative sequence of cultural development (a very Whitean notion, incidentally). Culture evolves by *adding* new characteristics to old ones. But this is a misleading notion, for cultural evolution is first and foremost a *transformational* rather than an additive process. In other words, societies do not evolve by simply piling new traits on top of old ones, but by developing new characteristics that drive the old characteristics out. Carneiro does recognize the noncumulative character of evolution when he says that "evolution is not only *cumulative* but also *supplantive*" (1973b:105; emphasis Carneiro's). It is quite clear, though, that he thinks of the supplantive character of evolution as distinctly secondary to its additive character.

This difficulty is compounded by a further one that actually involves a problem with Carneiro's overall conception of evolution: his insistence on evolution as change in a direction of increasing complexity. This conception of evolution is at the heart, of course, of functionalist evolutionary views. Carneiro, though, is no functionalist. Indeed, as I shall attempt to show in the next section, his most important work is a vigorous kind of conflict theory. This makes it all the more remarkable that he insists so firmly upon an increasing-complexity view of evolution.[1]

This tension in Carneiro's work aside, what are the difficulties with the complexity concept? As noted in chapter 6, it is valid to say that increasing complexity is a prominent feature of social evolution. But, as suggested there, it is neither what is most important about evolutionary change nor central to explaining why evolution occurs (in chapter 8 I will attempt to account for growing complexity in a way that makes it a secondary aspect of evolution). Some examples may suffice to explain what I mean. Take an issue to which Carneiro has contributed brilliantly, the evolution of chiefdoms and states. Carneiro conceives of these forms of political organization in a way that makes each more complex than what preceded it. There is no need to quarrel with that, but why regard the level of complexity as central to these forms of political organization? Chiefdoms are more complex than tribes, but they also differ from tribes in that they concentrate power and authority in the hands of a small number of individuals who may use it against the mass of the population. Why not regard this latter characteristic, rather than the complexity one, as the crucial feature? The matter is similar with respect to states. They are more complexly organized than chiefdoms, but they also have something chiefdoms lack, viz., the capacity to use repressive force to overcome most forms of rebellion against them. Again, why not regard this as what is evolutionarily central to them? In my opinion, the burden is on those who claim so much for the dimension of complexity to provide a rationale for its evolutionary importance. I do not think they have been able to do so in terms that are acceptable, and unfortunately Carneiro falls into this same trap.

To take another example, consider a problem with which historical sociologists have been greatly concerned: the transition from feudalism to capitalism. Who would doubt that modern capitalism is a much more complex system of social life than the feudal system that preceded it? Yet why regard this as the significance of the evolutionary transition from the one to the other? I would think that the significance of this transition lies in the emergence of a fundamentally new *mode* of social and economic life, one in which very different principles of economic organization are at work. Certainly the complexity of modern capitalist society cannot be ignored, but the burden is upon those who proclaim such to say why this particular characteristic should be elevated to supreme importance.

Finally, consider a different kind of evolutionary problem: that of explaining the evolution of the subsystems or institutions of societies themselves, a problem that Carneiro identifies as an important one. The sex role arrangements of modern industrial societies, for example, differ substantially from those of earlier agrarian societies, but the notion of complexity would seem to be useless as a basis for comparison. If we look at family arrangements the problem becomes even worse, for it has long been recognized that the family patterns of modern industrial societies are generally much *simpler* than those of preindustrial societies. This kind of argument could be extended considerably, but it should be more than sufficient to make the point.

## Carneiro and Political Evolution

Let us now turn away from the more troublesome aspects of Carneiro's work toward his most important contribution to modern evolutionism: his theory of the evolution of chiefdoms and states. This part of his work has been highly praised, has had lasting significance, and, somewhat ironically, is not altogether consistent with his emphasis on complexity as the *sine qua non* of social evolution. Although he continues to mention the increasing complexity that accompanies chiefdoms and states, this takes a definite backseat to his other theoretical considerations.

Carneiro's theory of political evolution is most forcefully presented in his article "A theory of the origin of the state" (1970; see also Carneiro, 1981a, 1987). Carneiro proposes that the key process leading to the state is an ecological one that he calls *environmental circumscription*. Environmental circumscription exists when societies inhabiting a particular region are confronted with physical barriers to their further geographical expansion. The operation of circumscription can best be understood by looking at a situation in which it does not occur. The Amazon Basin of South America is a major area of uncircumscribed land. The horticultural tribes that have occupied this region of the world have generally remained at a level of political evolution well below that of the state. When confronted by population pressure, it was easy for villages to fission and for one group to move into previously unoccupied land. Thus expansion, rather than evolution, has characterized this region of the world.

But in circumscribed zones the expansion of peoples has definite limits. After a point, expansion is no longer feasible because of such physical barriers as deserts, mountain ranges, or bodies of water, and thus village movement is not a possible solution to the problem of population growth. What occurs instead is warfare over land, and this warfare leads to the formation of more powerful and militaristic political systems. Villages begin conquering other villages and subordinating the conquered. Chiefdoms eventually form, but further population growth and warfare lead to the conquest of some chiefdoms by others, thus eventually producing states. As this evolutionary process continues, large empires may be formed out of the conquest of some states by others.

Carneiro has also added a few wrinkles to this basic argument to give it a broader explanatory scope. He notes that circumscription may sometimes take the form of *social circumscription*. This occurs when the barriers to movement involve the presence of other societies rather than aspects of the physical environment. He also adds the notion of *resource concentration* as an occasional factor in political evolution. An area that is particularly abundant in plant and animal resources tends to attract many people to it and permits substantial population growth. When this growth reaches problematic proportions, movement out of the area may be blocked or at least made difficult by the presence of other groups (i.e., social circumscription is operating). Warfare and political conquest are thus predictable outcomes. Carneiro (1987) suggests that this kind of process has been responsible for the emergence of chiefdoms in uncircumscribed areas of Amazonia.

It is important to note that Carneiro's theory differs significantly from Service's functionalist theory of political evolution. Carneiro stresses that his theory is an entirely coercive one that does not assume that people would give up their political autonomy voluntarily. In his view, except for those at the top, people clearly do not see the formation of more powerful political structures as in their interests, and thus Carneiro himself can hardly see it that way either.

The circumscription theory is one of the most impressive theories of political evolution we have, and it has stood the test of time remarkably well (cf. Graber and Roscoe, 1988). It is surely Carneiro's most important contribution to modern evolutionism, and it shows that he belongs firmly within the materialist tradition of evolutionary theorizing.[2]

GERHARD LENSKI'S TECHNOLOGICAL EVOLUTIONISM

The inclusion of the work of Gerhard Lenski in a chapter on anthropological evolutionism may seem odd, given that Lenski is professionally identified as a sociologist and is recognized by the members of that discipline as one of its leading thinkers. Yet despite Lenski's disciplinary affiliation, his ideas bear the unmistakeable imprint of anthropological influences. Like the other thinkers considered in this chapter, Lenski was directly influenced most prominently by the architects of the mid-twentieth-century evolutionary rivival, White and Childe in particular. As we shall see, his evolutionary conceptions also reflect a sociological emphasis that is markedly similar to some of the ideas of Talcott Parsons and the functionalist evolutionists. This aspect of his thinking, though, appears subordinate to the more anthropological tone deriving from White and Childe.

Lenski's earliest publications ranged over a variety of sociological topics and had nothing at all to do with evolutionary concerns. It was not until the mid-1960s with the publication of his *Power and Privilege* (1966) that he demonstrated any sort of evolutionary perspective. This book, a landmark in sociological theory, was an effort to develop a general theory of social stratification by drawing extensively on ethnographic, historical, and sociological data from a wide range of societies. Lenski produced a classification system of human societies with a strong evolutionary tone, and the theory he developed in conjunction with this classification system has frequently been referred to as an evolutionary one. But the evolutionism of this work is largely implicit, and it would be claiming too much to say that it is based on a well-developed theory of social evolution.

Buoyed by the success of this work, however, Lenski went on to crystallize many of the evolutionary ideas latent in it. With the publication four years later of *Human Societies* (1970), Lenski established himself as a major evolutionary theorist. This book was remarkable, for it was intended both as a general undergraduate textbook and a theoretical treatise, and it has generally been regarded by social scientists as such. It has been revised several times, and a fifth edition (Lenski and Lenski, 1987) is now in print, but Lenski has never significantly altered any of his basic theoretical arguments. Since the original edition is the most theoretically explicit and comprehensive, most of my analysis will be based on it.

### Lenski's Basic Theory

Lenski has been especially insistent on developing an evolutionary theory of human societies that has close parallels with evolutionary theory in biology. Theories of biological evolution, he suggests, must deal with four basic phenomena: organic continuity, innovation, extinction, and evolution. A theory of sociocultural evolution must then identify and try to account for the processes of continuity, innovation, extinction, and evolution as they occur within human societies. Sociocultural continuity is, of course, the maintenance of the basic fabric of a society over time, and it occurs primarily through the socialization process. Sociocultural innovation is the introduction of new social elements through invention, discovery, or diffusion. Sociocultural extinction occurs at two levels, what Lenski calls intrasocietal and intersocietal selection, and these selection processes are claimed to be directly analogous to natural selection. Intrasocietal selection is a process whereby particular elements within societies are selected as a result of the choices and actions of various individuals and groups. Intersocietal selection occurs when some societies come to prevail over others, largely through military means. Finally, we have sociocultural evolution, obviously the most important phenomenon to be accounted for by an evolutionary theory. For Lenski, evolution is that process whereby human societies increase their capacity to mobilize energy and information in adapting to their environments. As we shall see, this definition is pregnant with some extremely important implications.

Lenski notes that there are some significant differences between organic and sociocultural evolution, such as the lack of any organic counterpart to the process of cultural diffusion, or the fact that organic evolution can never occur in the conscious or deliberate manner that sometimes characterizes sociocultural evolution. Yet the parallels between biological and sociocultural evolution are clearly of considerably more interest to Lenski, and so much so that he suggests that *"sociocultural evolution is, in essence, an extension of the process of organic evolution"* (1970:60; emphasis Lenski's). Four basic similarities between the evolutionary process in the two realms are stressed. In the first place, genes have a strict analogue in human populations, these being symbols and symbol systems. Like genes, symbols store and transmit information relevant to the process of adaptation to the environment. Second, human societies are the functional analogue of species. Third, the processes of continuity, innovation, and extinction are basic to both forms of evolution. And finally, sociocultural and organic evolution are both complex processes of long duration that are "characterized by the progressive emergence of organizations which possess ever greater capacities for the mobilization of energy and information" (1970:61).

Lenski has taken pains to dissociate his view of sociocultural evolution with any sort of unilinear evolutionism, and this leads him to make another comparison between sociocultural and organic evolution. Here Lenski closely follows Marshall Sahlins (1960) in asserting that, like organic evolution, sociocultural evolution has both specific and general dimensions. Specific evolution, it will be recalled, is the process whereby societies radiate along many lines. General evolution, on the other hand, is the overall movement of societies along a continuum, which for Lenski is one involving the increasing capture of energy and information. Despite his acceptance of this distinction, though, it is clear that Lenski is mainly interested in the latter evolutionary process, for this is what dominates his writings. Not only is there an overpowering concern with sociocultural progress in his work – indeed, virtually an equating of the concepts of evolution and progress – but again and again we find Lenski referring to "the" evolutionary process.

This kind of emphasis in his work has even led some scholars, other evolutionists included, to suggest that Lenski's theory is a type of developmentalism. Gertrude Dole, for instance, has cited Lenski's statement that "there is an *inner dynamic* within human societies that prevents them from becoming completely stable" (1970:80; cited in Dole, 1973:259; emphasis Dole's). Along similar lines, it can be noted that Lenski has commented that the course of societal evolution is "indicated by its inner characteristics" (1976:555). However, once one places Lenski's phrases "inner dynamic" and "inner characteristics" within their proper contexts it becomes quite clear that he is not referring to any sort of abstract, transcendent process that drives sociocultural evolution from beginning to end. With respect to the phrase "inner dynamic," he simply means that humans are curious creatures with strong exploratory needs, and that these needs inevitably lead them to discoveries, inventions, and innovations that alter sociocultural patterns. In regard to "inner characteristics," it is obvious that all Lenski intends is "that characteristics of a variable, or of a system, at one time have consequences for its characteristics at some later time" (1976:555).

It makes little sense, then, to associate Lenski with the doctrine of developmentalism. In point of fact, his evolutionism is predicated upon an ordinary causal conception of evolutionary change that is stated in the most direct and unambiguous terms. On what kind of causal conception does he rely? As a direct intellectual descendant of Leslie White, Lenski has adopted White's tripartite division of societies into technological, social organizational, and ideological components and has claimed technology as the principal determinant of the other components. Technology is far more likely than the other societal components to be an autogenous source of change, he says, and when technological changes occur they exert profound pressures on the other components to change correspondingly. The nature of these changes in social organization and ideology are many and varied, but Lenski points to five that he regards as especially important. First, technological advance generates a more efficient utilization of the environment and this leads to a growth in population. Second, technological advance allows for more permanent and elaborate settlement patterns. Third, increasing technological capacity allows for a general increase in a society's economic productivity and therewith the possibility of greater economic and political inequalities. Fourth, increasing technological sophistication fosters increased societal specialization and differentiation. Finally, accompanying technological advance is a general increase in the amount of leisure time people have, and this time can be put to use in various noneconomic activities that lead to the elaboration of nonmaterial culture.

Although Lenski has rejected the label "technological determinist," holding that social organization and ideology do play a causal role in sociocultural evolution, the explanatory significance he gives to technology is undeniable. This significance is demonstrated even further by his evolutionary classification system. The system that Lenski settles upon is a modified version of a typology developed by Walter Goldschmidt (1959), who based his own typology upon Morgan's nineteenth-century scheme. Lenski's scheme categorizes societies according to their mode of subsistence technology and recognizes four major types of societies: hunting and gathering, horticultural, agrarian, and industrial.

*Hunting and gathering societies* depend for their existence on the hunting and trapping of wild game and the collection of wild plants and vegetables. They have no agriculture, or have developed it only rudimentarily. Two types of hunting and gathering societies are distinguished. *Simple hunting and gathering societies* had as their best weapon only a wooden spear, but *advanced hunting and gathering societies* have acquired both the spear-thrower and the bow and arrow. *Horticultural societies* derive their subsistence from agriculture or, more precisely, horticulture – the tending of small garden plots with hand tools. Horticultural societies are also divided into simple and advanced types. *Simple horticultural societies* have no metal tools and the simple wooden digging stick is the basic cultivating implement. *Advanced horticultural societies* are those that have acquired metal tools, especially the hoe, for cultivation. *Agrarian societies* also depend upon agricultural methods of making a living, but their members cultivate large fields rather than small garden plots, and it is the possession of the plow that distinguishes these societies from horticultural ones. Again we see a division into simple and advanced subtypes, with *simple agrarian societies* lacking iron tools and weapons and *advanced agrarian societies* possessing them. Finally, Lenski speaks of *industrial societies*, which have evolved to energy and information levels far beyond anything previously seen on earth. Specifically, industrial societies have substituted machine power for human power in the work process.

In addition to these major societal types Lenski identifies several minor types. These include *fishing societies*, nonagricultural societies that specialize in fishing rather than hunting; *herding societies*, or those that specialize in animal tending in dry environments not well suited for agriculture; and *maritime societies*, or those that have specialized in seafaring commercial trade. Finally, Lenski recognizes *industrializing societies*, which are the contemporary underdeveloped societies of the Third World.

### The Functionalist and Progressivist Character of Lenski's Theory

One of the more central aspects of Lenski's evolutionism concerns his emphasis on the progressive character of sociocultural evolution. Indeed, Lenski's definitions of progress and evolution are almost identical. These involve, as we have already seen, the increasing capacity of societies to mobilize energy and information in adapting to their environments. Lenski makes it clear, though, that the conception of progress he advocates is not to be confused with progress in the realm of human happiness or morality (1970:69–70):

Many people challenge the thesis that there has been progress in human history. They insist that it is impossible to show that modern man is happier or more moral than his prehistoric ancestors. This is a serious misunderstanding, however, of what modern evolutionists mean by progress. When evolutionists use this term today they are referring primarily to *technological* advance, and secondarily to certain other very specific and limited forms of organizational and ideological advance that are by-products of technological advance.

If progress consists, then, primarily of technological advance, what does such advance bring in its wake that allows us to say that a more efficient form of societal adaptation has been achieved? In essence we have already answered this question in mentioning what Lenski regards as the most significant consequences of technological change. With technological advance, people need not work as hard or long and thus have more leisure time to devote to activities that promote significant developments in the realm of nonmaterial culture (e.g., art, religion, political administration). Furthermore, the more efficient use of the environment that accompanies technological advance allows population to grow, and this population increase can have positive consequences for further technological advance simply because it increases the number of people available to make inventions or discoveries. Because technological advance increases a society's overall level of economic productivity, especially the size of its economic surplus, the possibility also exists for creating new organizational forms that themselves increase the overall level of societal functioning.

It is with respect to this last point that Lenski reveals himself to have one foot placed squarely in the Parsonian evolutionary camp despite his considerable differences from that camp in other respects (especially in terms of his materialism). In fact, at points we find Lenski seemingly invoking the Parsonian concept of "increased adaptive capacity" in precisely the same way as Parsons. For example, he asserts that "the further a society advances on the evolutionary scale, the greater is its ability to overcome the limitations of its environment" (1970:289). In addition, we find Lenski commenting frequently on the manner in which certain evolutionary changes "overcame historic limitations," or "freed creative forces" long dormant in earlier types of societies. Much like Parsons (but without the teleological and developmentalist bias), we find Lenski pointing to modern industrial societies as "the crowning achievement in man's long struggle to build a better life" (1970:428). And this is not only because of the increases in the standard of living brought about by technological advance, but also for many of the same reasons pointed to by Parsons himself. Lenski emphasizes that modern industrial societies are more structurally differentiated and functionally specialized (and thus presumably more efficient), and they have also overcome many of the ascriptive limitations of traditional social orders. It is also highly worthy of note that in his treatment of the underdeveloped societies of the Third World Lenski's analysis is remarkably close to the analyses of the old-fashioned modernization theorists (as one would expect simply from the identification of such societies as "industrializing").

### A Critique of Lenski's Evolutionism

Lenski's evolutionary theory thus reveals itself to be a kind of hybrid built upon foundations laid by White and Childe on the one hand and Parsons on the other. Unfortunately, it perpetuates many of the dubious assertions, blind alleys, and outright errors of those theories.

One of the more serious difficulties with Lenski's evolutionism concerns its conception of causation. Although Lenski recognizes other causes of evolutionary change, it is clear that technological change is for him the prime mover of sociocultural evolution from simple hunting and gathering bands through contemporary industrial societies. Lenski devotes a great deal of attention to showing empirically the strong associations between modes of subsistence technology and various elements of social organization and ideology, and he is frequently concerned to explain why these particular associations should prevail. Unfortunately, he is never able to demonstrate the actual *causal* role of technological advance in sociocultural evolution, leaping quite innocently from demonstrated correlations to inferred causation. This procedure is highly evident throughout *Human Societies*, but it is found most blatantly in one of his separately published empirical analyses (Heise, Lenski, and Wardwell, 1976). On the basis of a factor analysis of world ethnographic data demonstrating the central importance of technology in the organization of human societies, Lenski concludes that technology is a principal causal agent in human affairs. But this is a methodologically inadmissible conclusion. Factor analysis by itself cannot establish such a theoretical conclusion, but can only show patterns of relationships among variables. Lenski is able to make the theoretical inferences that he does, it would seem, only because he is already convinced of technology's causal importance.

There is little doubt that technology is a crucial aspect of processes of sociocultural evolution. However, it can be shown, I think, that technology is at least as often a result of other evolutionary changes as a cause of them. But this major empirical problem aside, there is a further difficulty with Lenski's emphasis on technology, and that is that no systematic attention is given to explaining technological change itself, other than appealing to the processes of invention and discovery. For Lenski, technology reduces largely to knowledge or information, which grows and expands as a result of human exploration, experimentation, and manipulation. Thus, hunter-gatherers began to adopt agricultural methods of making a living when they finally understood the rudiments of plant and animal domestication. Early horticulturists elaborated these methods by learning about new tools and techniques. They invented metallurgy and hoes and became advanced horticulturists. Eventually they acquired the knowledge of how a plow could be fashioned and draft animals taught to pull it, and they became agrarianists. Ultimately humans learned how to construct machines that could replace human muscle power, and this led to a revolution that allowed people to develop industrial societies. And so the story goes.

I would insist that such an argument really amounts to a nonexplanation of technological change because such change is not deemed to require any special explanation. It is simply assumed that technology automatically grows of its own accord, a conception of technological change that essentially reduces Lenski to a kind of "pseudo-materialist." That is, even though technological changes are said to be at the root of nonmaterial changes, these technological changes themselves are not explained in terms of other kinds of material conditions but in terms of forces that have nothing at all to do with material conditions. Indeed, Lenski's view of technological change is essentially an idealist one that does not differ in principle from the views of technological evolution held over a century ago by Morgan and Tylor.

Lenski's view of technological change and its role in sociocultural evolution is one that might be labeled "Socratic": the society that knows the good chooses the good. Not only is technological change the result of increased knowledge, but this new knowledge is obviously seen as beneficial and is put to use as soon as it is acquired. But it is very difficult to reconcile this view with growing evidence of technological inertia in many preindustrial societies. It has become apparent in recent years that virtually all hunting and gathering societies have already "invented" agriculture, that is, have acquired basic knowledge regarding plant and animal domestication (M. Cohen, 1977). Yet they commonly fail to implement this knowledge and are able to give an explicit rationale for their reluctance to change their subsistence practices. Moreover, there are conditions under which some agricultural populations have been reported to abandon more sophisticated agricultural techniques in favor of simpler ones (Boserup, 1965).

It is clear that Lenski's Socratic view of technological change is inextricably bound up with his progressivist view of sociocultural evolution: new technologies lead to a whole series of improvements in the human condition, such as an improved standard of living, a more secure and reliable food supply, a decrease in the workload, and an increase in the availability of leisure time. However, this old-fashioned view of technological change and its alleged benefits is now known to be seriously in error. Research over the past two decades now strongly suggests that hunter-gatherers work less and enjoy more leisure time than the members of more technologically advanced societies, and that agricultural populations seem to suffer from more nutritional inadequacies than do hunting and gathering populations (for a review of supporting evidence, see Sanderson, 1988:chapter 4). In many respects hunting and gathering populations seem to be far better off in a material sense than the vast majority of the members of agrarian societies.[3] Moreover, when we assess the obvious material benefits accruing to the members of contemporary industrial societies we cannot fail to inquire, as Lenski generally has, into whether these benefits for a minority of the world's population have been gained at the expense of the majority (i.e., the contemporary Third World) (cf. Wallerstein, 1983).

It thus appears that Lenski's conception of sociocultural progress deriving from technological advance cannot be maintained. The problems with his view of progress, though, actually run deeper than that. Lenski insists upon a conception of progress that equates it with increasing efficiency of environmental adaptation, mainly through technological advance but also through organizational and ideological developments, and this conception is said to posit nothing with respect to improvements in human morality or happiness. Yet Lenski's notion of "organizational and ideological advance" suffers from exactly the same difficulties as Parsons's evolutionary concept of differentiation. Many of Lenski's examples of these organizational and ideological "advances" are the very ones stressed by Parsons: money and markets, monotheism, Protestantism, occupational specialization, the modern educational revolution, and many others. Consider also the following especially interesting passage (Lenski, 1970:305):

The emergence of the first fishing societies during the Mesolithic was an important new development. Man had at last devised techniques and tools that enabled him to take advantage of the resources of a radically different kind of environment, one that made possible population growth, more permanent settlements, the formation of multicommunity societies, and increased "leisure." These, in turn, made possible the production of new kinds of goods and services, the accumulation of property, and the elaboration of ritual and ceremony – in short, a significant enrichment of human life.

Apparently for Lenski, commercialism is better than the lack of it, monotheism is better than polytheism or animism, Protestantism is better than Catholicism, specialized occupations are better than unspecialized ones, and mass educational systems are more adaptive than elite ones (or none at all). Moreover, bigger populations are better than smaller ones, permanent settlements are better than nomadic ones, multicommunity societies are better than those with only a single community, the accumulation of property is a good thing, and the rituals and ceremonies of hunter-gatherers are adaptively inferior to the rituals and ceremonies of more technologically advanced societies.

But what evaluatively neutral grounds exist for assuming that any of these evolutionary developments leads to an "increased adaptive capacity?" No more than Parsons, Lenski does not really suggest any, and thus it is extremely difficult to escape the conclusion that his judgments spring from anything except his own ethnocentric preferences. In fact, I think it would be virtually impossible to produce an evaluatively neutral criterion whereby the evolutionary events of which Lenski speaks could be shown to be improvements over what came before them, and a good case could probably be made (depending substantially on one's values, of course) that many of the events constituted significant regressions in the quality of human life.

The Parsonian functionalist heritage in Lenski's evolutionism is also readily apparent in his treatment of the transition to modernity. For Lenski, this transition was essentially that of the shift from agrarian to industrial societies, a shift a number of societies have already made and that others ("industrializing societies") are still struggling to make. The Marxian idea that the transition to the modern world is first and foremost the transition from a specifically European feudal system to a capitalist system – a transition that is the whole context for the emergence of industrialism – is almost completely absent. This viewpoint not only leads to a serious overestimation of the positive aspects of industrial societies ("the crowning achievement in man's struggle to build a better life"), but even more seriously to a failure to understand the reasons for the historic and current plight of what we today call the Third World. Dependency and world-system theories of the contemporary global pattern of development and underdevelopment are given little credence, and a view far more like that of old-fashioned modernization theory is adopted. Pitifully, in what has to qualify as one of Lenski's most serious theoretical distortions, Marx is dismissed as little more than the founder of a modern secular religion.[4]

There are, then, a number of severe flaws in Lenski's theory of sociocultural evolution. Yet despite these flaws, a final evaluation of his contribution to evolutionary theorizing should not be as wholly negative as it might seem I have been suggesting. Although Lenski has incorporated much of the Parsonian functionalist heritage into his evolutionism, he has certainly avoided many of the horrendous difficulties of Parsonian evolutionism, especially its resolute developmentalism and its extreme idealism. Moreover, the problems associated with Lenski's emphasis on technological change are essentially no worse than those contained in the theories of White and Childe, from whom he has borrowed in this regard. It may also be said that Lenski has performed a very valuable service by ambitiously attempting to derive a comprehensive theory from a vast amount of ethnographic, historical, and sociological data. The effort is a highly laudatory one even if the results are less than satisfying. And in the final analysis, of course, Lenski's effort can only be properly judged in comparison with a presumably more adequate theory of sociocultural evolution, a problem to which I now want to turn.

MARVIN HARRIS'S EVOLUTIONARY MATERIALISM

Lenski's theory of sociocultural evolution is perhaps the most comprehensive statement of a rather old-fashioned evolutionism that is now being eclipsed. In the last quarter-century there has been a turning away from the kinds of theoretical assumptions basic to Lenski's theory and a shift toward a kind of evolutionary model that is quite different in several crucial respects. This new model is contained (or implied) at least partially in the works of numerous scholars, but the most articulate and complete statement of it is found in the work of Marvin Harris. Harris has come out of much the same tradition as Lenski, being influenced by White's materialism and, more substantially, by Steward's cultural ecology (Harris was actually a student of Steward). But Harris has also shown the influence of Marx in a way that would have been inconceivable for Lenski, and, although there might appear to be elements of functionalism in Harris's thought, whatever elements are there have nothing whatever in common with Parsonianism. In fact, it would be hard to think of a model of cultural evolution more antithetical to Parsonian evolutionism than Harris's.

In one sense the treatment of Harris as an evolutionary theorist may seem inappropriate, or at least a matter of misplaced emphasis. Harris (1968) has been severely critical of White for emphasizing the evolutionary character of his work rather than its materialist causal foundations, and he has shown great impatience with the debate between White and Steward over the appropriate level of generality of evolutionary formulations. He believes that the crucial question for anthropologists is not how much orderliness and pattern there is to historical change, but what kinds of causes one invokes to explain historical changes of all types, be they general or highly idiosyncratic ones. Moreover, he has asserted that White was quite wrong to characterize Boas as an antievolutionist. Not only did Boas accept a type of evolutionism, Harris asserts, but so did a number of other famous anthropologists who are usually classed as antievolutionists (or at least nonevolutionists), such as Malinowski and Radcliffe–Brown.

As we noted in chapter 3, such comments seem confusing and disconcerting, coming as they do from a thinker famed for his commitment to anthropology as a rigorously scientific and nomothetic endeavor. But as also suggested at that time, this whole issue is really a tempest in a teapot because it is based on a very simple confusion that is easily resolved: that between *evolution* as an empirical process and *evolutionism* as a theoretical model of such an empirical process. Harris can only define Boas, Malinowski, Radcliffe–Brown, and others as having evolutionary outlooks because he defines an evolutionary outlook as one concerned with the process of evolution, and evolution for him is any structural transformation in a sociocultural system. It does not matter, he says, whether this transformation has occurred only once, a handful of times, or hundreds of times.

This definition of evolution is perfectly sensible, but it does not follow that an evolutionary approach is simply one that is concerned with any sort of evolutionary process. According to the definition of an evolutionary theory adopted in chapter 1, the absolutely minimal requirement for such a theory is the assumption of at least some general directional trends in history. From this point of view, Boas (at least the mature Boas) could not have been an evolutionist because he generally denied the existence of such trends and opted for an emphasis on the historically unique. Likewise, Malinowski and Radcliffe–Brown could not legitimately be considered evolutionists because they showed no concern with historical directionality. Ironically, despite his formal protestations about what does and does not count as an evolutionary perspective, Harris is clearly an evolutionist in our terms because of his strong nomothetic concerns. In a manner similar to Sahlins's distinction between general and specific evolution, he has distinguished among parallel, convergent, and divergent evolution, and has insisted that parallel and convergent evolutionary processes are far more common than divergent ones. Parallel evolution involves the movement of societies along similar paths, while convergent evolution involves the movement of initially dissimilar societies toward increasingly similar structural patterns. Divergent evolution is characterized by increasing dissimilarity, and of course involves the production of unique social patterns.

Thus it is highly misleading for Harris to have formally characterized an evolutionary outlook in the way that he has. What I think Harris means to say is that, contrary to White's sterile distinction between evolution and history (and thus between evolutionary and historical analyses), nomothetic theories rooted in general evolutionary principles must also apply to historically unique events. And with such an argument, of course, there can be no disagreement. In fact, despite Harris's strong attention to parallel and convergent evolution, he has also shown himself to be concerned with a large variety of divergent evolutionary phenomena. He has truly achieved a balance between the "universal" evolutionism of White and the "multi-linear" evolutionism of Steward.

Since Harris has insisted, though, that the really crucial question concerns the causes of all types of evolutionary changes, and since his main claim to fame rests on the way he answers this question, we need to examine the basic features of his general theoretical model before we can see how it applies to a range of evolutionary phenomena.

### *Harris and Cultural Materialism*

In numerous publications over some three decades, Harris has developed a comprehensive theoretical strategy to which he has given the name *cultural materialism.* The most explicit and detailed formal expositions of this strategy are to be found in *The Rise of Anthropological Theory* (1968) and *Cultural Materialism: The Struggle for a Science of Culture* (1979). In what may be his earliest formal statement of cultural materialism, Harris refers to the existence of a major theoretical principle that is "the analogue of the Darwinian strategy in the realm of sociocultural phenomena" (1968:4). This is the *principle of techno-environmental and techno-economic determinism,* and it (1968:4):

holds that similar technologies applied to similar environments tend to produce similar arrangements of labor in production and distribution, and that these in turn call forth similar kinds of social groupings, which justify and coordinate their activities by means of similar systems of values and beliefs. Translated into research strategy, the principle of techno-environmental, techno-economic determinism assigns priority to the study of the material conditions of sociocultural life, much as the principle of natural selection assigns priority to the study of differential reproductive success.

From the time of the statement of this guiding theoretical principle until the end of the 1970s, Harris's thinking has undergone a certain amount of development, and so by the time of the publication of *Cultural Materialism* in 1979 we find a slightly different and more fully worked out conception of cultural materialism. Demographic variables, though not previously neglected, have now become a more explicit and important part of the cultural materialist research program. Sociocultural systems are explicitly trichotomized into infrastructural, structural, and superstructural components, a deliberate modification and elaboration of the Marxian distinction between base and superstructure. Infrastructure consists of not only a mode of production, but also of a mode of reproduction. The mode of production includes subsistence strategies, technoenvironmental relationships, ecosystems, and work patterns. The mode of reproduction involves the production of human beings rather than the production of subsistence, and it includes mating patterns, demographic features of populations, modes of nurturing infants, and the technology of birth control and population regulation. The structure consists of what Harris calls domestic and political economy. The domestic economy principally involves age and sex roles and patterns of family organization, whereas the political economy involves modes of ownership of productive resources (essentially, Marxian relations of production), stratification patterns, patterns of political organization, and warfare and military organization. The superstructure includes art, music, ritual, sport, science, myths, symbols, philosophies, religion, and various other ideational phenomena.[5]

Having given us a kind of anatomy of sociocultural systems, Harris proceeds to reformulate his earlier principle of technoenvironmental and technoeconomic determinism as the *principle of infrastructural determinism.*

This principle asserts that the flow of causation in social life runs mainly from the infrastructure to the structure to the superstructure. Less abstractly, this essentially means that the modes of production and reproduction have a kind of logical priority in the satisfaction of human needs and thus come to be established first; that these infrastructural conditions therefore provide the foundation upon which various types of domestic and political economies are erected; and that in turn these forms of domestic and political economy elicit various types of values, ideas, symbols and rituals designed to interpret and reinforce the prevailing domestic and political arrangements. As a principle of evolutionary change, Harris's principle asserts that changes tend to be initiated in the infrastructure and that these necessitate corresponding changes in structure and superstructure.

Why does infrastructure have the causal importance it does? For Harris, this has to do with the logical priority of infrastructural conditions, with the fact that they involve the most vital and fundamental of all human concerns: the production of subsistence and the reproduction of human life itself. As he puts it (1979:57):

Infrastructure . . . is the principal interface between culture and nature, the boundary across which the ecological, chemical, and physical restraints to which human action is subject interact with the principal sociocultural practices aimed at overcoming or modifying those restraints. . . . [P]riority for theory building logically settles upon those sectors under the greatest direct restraints from the givens of nature. To endow the mental superstructure with strategic priority, as the cultural idealists advocate, is a bad bet. Nature is indifferent to whether God is a loving father or a bloodthirsty cannibal. But nature is not indifferent to whether the fallow period in a swidden field is one year or ten. We know that powerful restraints exist on the infrastructural level; hence it is a good bet that these restraints are passed on to the structural and superstructural components.

Harris has also been especially concerned in this later version of his work to defend himself against the charge of "vulgar materialism" hurled at him by such structural Marxists as Maurice Godelier (1972, 1977) and Jonathan Friedman (1974). Cultural materialism, he says, by no means entirely reduces the explanation of structure and superstructure to infrastructural conditions. The principle of infrastructural determinism applies probabilistically rather than in a strict one-to-one manner – to what occurs in the majority of cases and over the long run. Moreover, not only do structure and superstructure sometimes play active causal roles in the determination of social outcomes, but they are never to be viewed as mere epiphenomenal reflexes of the modes of production and reproduction. As Harris has said, "On the contrary, structure and superstructure clearly play vital system-maintaining roles in the negative feedback processes responsible for the conservation of the system" (1979:72).

It is obvious that Harris's cultural materialist strategy has strong affinities with both White's and Steward's evolutionisms and with Marxian historical materialism. Harris's trichotomous division of sociocultural systems and his notion of infrastructural causality strongly recall White's division of sociocultural systems into technology, social organization, and ideology and his technological determinism. However, Harris's trichotomous distinction is considerably more elaborate than White's, and his notion of causation is much less simple, involving as it does a range of material conditions in addition to technology. Technological change is as often a result of other evolutionary changes as a cause of them. The influence of Steward is most apparent in the emphasis on ecological conditions as prime causal forces. Steward's multilinear emphasis is also apparent in the very substantial attention Harris gives to a whole range of divergent evolutionary phenomena.

With respect to historical materialism, the key similarities should be obvious enough, and Harris has explicitly recognized his indebtedness to Marx by claiming that Marx's materialist understanding of causation was his greatest intellectual contribution. But there are also a number of crucial differences between cultural and historical materialism, three of which deserve special note. First, it is clear that Harris's notion of infrastructure is considerably broader than Marx's. Harris's mode of production includes ecological conditions and makes them key causal forces. While Marx did not fail to take note of such conditions and sometimes spoke as if they could be counted as forces of production, he hardly considered them in any systematic way. In addition, Harris's entire concept of a mode of reproduction as a determinant of sociocultural structure and evolution not only has no counterpart in historical materialism, but Marx himself was openly hostile to such a notion. He regarded the Malthusian emphasis on population pressure as a cause of poverty as part of a reactionary ideology and referred to Malthus himself as "a baboon."

Second, Harris has transferred what Marx called the relations of production from the infrastructure to the structure (specifically, the political economy), and by doing so he has attempted to explain variations in these productive relations in terms of various elements of the infrastructure. (Although, as we shall see, somewhat inconsistently Harris frequently speaks of "economic conditions" as prime causal forces in a manner that suggests he sometimes thinks of them as part of the infrastructure.)

Finally, and to many Marxists most significantly, Harris has vehemently rejected the dialectical character of historical materialism. Its very worst feature, he declares, is its emphasis on Hegelian dialectical reasoning. The concept of dialectics is said to be mystical nonsense, and Hegel was a "monkey on Marx's and Engels's back." In the hands of most Marxian dialecticians, the concept of dialectics usually refers to the "negations" or "contradictions" that exist within sociocultural systems and that cause them to change from one state to another. Harris suggests, however, that all societies always contain many features that can be identified by the terms "negation" or "contradiction," and therefore it is crucial to identify which of these negations or contradictions is most important in producing changes within the system. But the concept of dialectics is such a rarefied philosophical abstraction that it is thoroughly incapable of providing the kinds of operational instructions necessary for identifying the most causally important contradictions (hence Harris's characterization of it as "mystical nonsense"). As Harris puts it (1979:153):

The problem for dialectical analysis, as much as for any causal explanatory strategy, is not merely to identify any contradictions (or stresses, malfunctions, deviations, amplifications, etc.) but to identify those which decisively determine the system's future state. It is useless to be told as a generality that some components are more important than others. One needs to know which ones they are, and dialectics will not tell us whether infanticide has been a decisive factor in the evolution of modes of production. It will not resolve the question of whether males exploit females in pre-state societies; whether egalitarian redistributors were the structural base for the development of a ruling class; or whether irrigation agriculture promoted the evolution of oriental despotisms in the Middle East and China.

Moreover (1979:146):

the name cultural materialists give to the process in which there is both discontinuity and continuity – in which a thing is both changed and not changed, is negated but affirmed, is destroyed but preserved – is evolution. To call such changes "dialectical" adds no additional information about evolutionary processes unless one is prepared to state some general principles by which dialectical negations can always be distinguished from other evolutionary "negations" (i.e., "transformations"). No one has ever succeeded in stating these principles.

One additional consideration needs to be explored with respect to Harris's general theoretical principles. This concerns the charge, made by numerous scholars but especially by Godelier (1977) and Friedman (1974), that Harris's cultural materialism is simply another version of functionalism. This charge may seem appropriate when we recognize that many of Harris's explanations of sociocultural phenomena concentrate on their "adaptive" character, their functional rationality for the individuals who create them. Such a charge, however, is misplaced and reflects a failure to understand both the specifics of Harris's arguments and the nature of functionalism itself. It is true, of course, that classically functionalist thinkers like Parsons have made the concept of adaptation central to their evolutionary formulations. But we need to recognize that the manner in which this concept is used in such formulations is strikingly different from the way Harris uses it. For Parsons, what adapts is a sociocultural system as a whole (or some subsystem of it). Harris, however, never analyzes adaptation from the standpoint of a sociocultural system as a whole, but only from the standpoint of the particular individuals who make up such systems. As he has said (1979:60), "The selection processes responsible for the divergent and convergent evolutionary trajectories of sociocultural systems operate mainly on the individual level; individuals follow one rather than another course of action, and as a result the aggregate pattern changes." Harris's whole concept of adaptation is actually informed by a thoroughgoing cost/benefit analysis (1979:61): "Cultural evolution, like biological evolution, has (up to now at least) taken place through opportunistic changes that increase benefits and lower costs to individuals."

This kind of methodological individualism is remote from the reifications of Parsons and the functionalists, and it is precisely the kind of analysis that is needed in order to uncover the kinds of societal conflicts and oppositions for which functionalism is highly unprepared. Indeed, Harris's evolutionary analyses often contain precisely the kind of conflict emphasis that is associated with the Marxian tradition and that is so absent in functionalism. Furthermore, when Harris does appear to be analyzing a sociocultural phenomenon from the point of view of the society as a whole (which really means nothing more than from the point of view of all the people in it), it will be seen that the society in question is a small-scale, egalitarian society notably lacking structured forms of social domination and subordination.[6]

Moreover, in Parsonian functionalist evolutionism evolutionary changes are said to produce increasingly well-adapted societies (indeed, occur *in order to* produce such increases in adaptive efficiency; Lenski's evolutionism is based on a similar notion, but without the teleology). Harris, however, emphatically rejects this functionalist notion of social evolution generating "increased adaptive capacity." Indeed, his analyses of general evolutionary trends often lead him to conclusions that are strikingly at odds with this kind of notion.

### Harris's General Evolutionary Model

While *The Rise of Anthropological Theory* and *Cultural Materialism* contain Harris's most important general theoretical statements, it is to his book *Cannibals and Kings: The Origins of Cultures* (1977) that one must look to find his most important arguments that are explicitly *evolutionary*.

In this book Harris offers a theory of sociocultural evolution that contrasts strikingly with the technologically oriented and progressivist views of Childe, White, and Lenski. As he says, his aim is "to replace the old onwards-and-upwards Victorian view of progress with a more realistic account of cultural evolution" (1977:x). For Harris, the essence of cultural evolution over the past 10,000 years lies in the need for the members of human societies to intensify their modes of economic production against the inevitable depletions and lowered living standards they confront. The intensification of production provides a solution to declining living standards, but it is at best only a partial and temporary solution. Eventually intensification leads to a new wave of depletion and declining standards of living, which in turn necessitates a new wave of intensification that is more vigorous than the previous one. This newer wave of intensification in turn produces yet further depletions, and thus there occurs an ever-continuing, spiraling process that is both self-perpetuating and self-defeating.

Harris conceives of two different types of intensification. The first involves no changes in the technology of subsistence. In this case people work harder and longer and make more vigorous use of the basic resources of their environment within their existing technological framework. This may serve for a time to slow down the process of depletion, but eventually a point is reached at which production can no longer be usefully intensified without changing the technology. Technological change – the development of new tools, techniques, and production methods – then results as the only hope of staving off further depletions and ultimately catastrophic consequences.

What sets off the process of depletion that necessitates these intensifying responses? The answer to this question depends on the particular time and place and the type of society involved. For prestate societies, Harris believes that the main engine of depletion is population growth and subsequent population pressure. Given their limited birth control technologies, prestate populations are unable to prevent their populations from growing. Hunter-gatherers are able to control their populations through such techniques as prolonged nursing of infants (which tends to prevent ovulation) and infanticide, and horticultural and agricultural populations are known to make frequent use of infanticide in addition to less drastic means of birth and population control. But these methods only slow down the rate of growth, and techniques like infanticide impose psychological costs on people that they would otherwise wish to avoid. When population pressures eventually lead to levels of depletion that people find intolerable, they are prompted to develop new technologies that for a time will halt (and perhaps even reverse) the depletion. With a more productive environment, people are motivated to relax the constraints they have been placing on their fertility levels (e.g., reduced frequency of intercourse, infanticide), and thus technological advance leads to an increasing rate of population growth, and this in turn is destined to bring about a new wave of depletion.

With the rise of civilization and the state this entire process is aggravated and made more complicated by the existence of severe forms of exploitation between dominant and subordinate classes, as well as severe forms of intersocietal competition and aggression. With the rise of modern capitalism and industrialism, massive technological intensification and depletion occur primarily as a result of the economic motives of capitalist ruling classes and the economic expectations of the materially acquisitive members of modern industrial societies.

This intensification-depletion-renewed intensification model[7] is applied by Harris to numerous parallel, convergent, and divergent evolutionary phenomena over the past 10,000 years. With the model he attempts to account for such phenomena as the origin of agricultural modes of production, warfare and male supremacist institutions in band and village societies, the rise of economic and political hierarchies out of an earlier condition of equality, the origin of the state, the emergence of monotheistic religions of love and mercy, Aztec ritualistic cannibalism, Hindu cow love and Jewish–Moslem pig hate, the origin of hydraulic civilizations, and the origins of modern capitalism and industrialism. It would seem instructive to look at those particular arguments that seem most convincing and best documented.

Ancient hunter-gatherers, Harris suggests, were surprisingly well nourished and led interesting and fulfilling lives. They worked little and had much leisure time. Under these conditions, they were not motivated to turn to an agricultural mode of production, even though they undoubtedly understood the rudiments of plant and animal domestication and thus could have become agriculturalists if they desired. What finally compelled them to do so beginning some 10,000 years ago, Harris claims, was population pressure in the context of a changing environment. The retreat of the glaciers had converted grasslands to forests, thus leading to the extinction of most of the big game animals on which these hunter-gatherers relied. The declining living standards resulting from these demographic and ecological changes necessitated the implementation of the agricultural knowledge that these hunter-gatherer communities already possessed.

With the transition to early Neolithic communities, controls over population growth were relaxed and population pressures once again became severe in due time. This led horticultural societies to systematic forms of intervillage warfare as a means of producing more favorable ratios between population and the food supply, especially the supply of animal protein. With warfare a prominent feature of social and political life, male supremacist institutions arose. Exaggerating masculinity and denigrating the female sex, Harris claims, were means whereby societies dependent on warfare could train young boys to be highly militant, combat-ready warriors.

The need to intensify production has also had definite consequences for the emergence of economic and political inequalities and social stratification. In many horticultural societies, ambitious economic and political leaders known as big men have arisen, and these individuals have played important roles as intensifers of production and the redistribution of economic surpluses. Such individuals lack the capacity to command others, and thus depend on their voluntary compliance. If production is intensified beyond a certain point, however, the relationship between economic and political leaders and the mass of the population comes to be inverted, and big men are transformed into chiefs – individuals who control the productive process and issue commands to their followers. With intensification carried to still higher levels, the conditions are set for the emergence of societies based on ruling classes and the state, and the earliest states emerged under conditions in which production was intensified and reintensified in circumscribed environments.

Harris believes that the transition from the medieval feudal economy of Western Europe to a capitalist mode of production began largely as a result of the overintensification of the feudal system. Population growth in the late Middle Ages produced declining yields, and marginal lands were increasingly occupied and made cultivable. By the fourteenth century the feudal system had reached an ecological and demographic crisis that paved the way for the merchant class and the towns, which had been growing in importance all along, to begin gaining the upper hand and shift the system along more commercialistic lines. With the rise of capitalism, the stage was set for the development of an industrial form of technology that has now depleted the natural environment to a degree previously unimaginable.[8]

### Harris versus Lenski

Although some scholars have been moved to see the evolutionary theories of Lenski and Harris in a similar vein, the differences between them are especially glaring.[9] Of course, both identify the major outlines of cultural evolution in much the same terms, and therefore both recognize broadly similar directional trends in history. But the way in which these trends are explained and their significance evaluated is entirely different. For Lenski, sociocultural evolution is driven by human imaginativeness and inventiveness. People are motivated to find new technologies because they recognize the limitations of their situation and want to overcome them. When new technological possibilities become understood, they are readily implemented because they are seen to produce a more efficient societal adaptation and thus an improvement in the quality of life. Each successive stage in the development of human technology and society is thus an increase in the overall "adaptive capacity" of societies, a very real form of progress indeed.

Harris will have none of this. Technological change does not occur because of the invention or discovery of new ideas, but because of the new human needs that continually arise from environmental depletions. People intensify their production and advance their technologies to keep things from getting worse, not to attain a better life or to increase their society's "adaptive capacity." But most of the time things actually do get worse, and the record of the past 10,000 years of cultural evolution is in many ways a record of cultural regression – of greater workloads and less leisure time, of declining standards of living that reach their nadir in agrarian civilizations and the contemporary Third World, of increasing economic and political inequalities, of the growth of various forms of oppression and exploitation, and ultimately of the possibility of ecological catastrophe and nuclear annihilation.

Patrick Nolan (1984) has suggested that, despite their major differences, the evolutionary models of Lenski and Harris are reconcilable. But it is very difficult to see how that could be the case. While the two models do share a number of elements, their leading assertions are fundamentally opposed, and therefore I think a choice has to be made between them. For my part, I think that Harris's model is overwhelmingly preferable, and that it provides a much better fit to the archaeological and ethnographic evidence.

### The Strengths and Limitations of Harris's Evolutionary Model

In fact, I would go further in claiming that the evolutionary theory given to us by Harris constitutes the very best of the evolutionisms yet developed by social scientists. It is true to the spirit of the classical evolutionists – the creation of a "science of universal history" – but vastly improves upon their evolutionary schemes, causal assertions, and empirical claims. It incorporates much that is of value in classical Marxist evolutionism while at the same time abandoning that theoretical tradition's most dubious features. Its sensible, hardheaded materialism, along with its resolutely antidevelopmentalist, antiteleological, and antiprogressivist character, make it a vast improvement over the Hegelianized evolutionism of Talcott Parsons and his followers.[10] The most powerful rival of Harris's evolutionism is the materialist evolutionism of Childe, White, Steward (and more latterly of Lenski), the tradition from which Harris himself descends. But even here, as I have tried to show, Harris's evolutionism shows itself to be far superior. Harris's far broader and much more flexible materialist model of causation is clearly preferable to the narrow technological emphasis of Childe, White, and Lenski on the one hand, and the limited ecological perspective of Steward on the other. Harris's evolutionism is also superior to this evolutionary tradition in two other major respects: it thoroughly overcomes its dubious (and often highly confused) progressivist bias,[11] and it continually demontrates how an intelligent evolutionary theory attends equally to divergent and parallel/convergent evolutionary trends.

Yet despite these important strengths, Harris's evolutionism is obviously not without its defects, three of which most immediately come to mind. These involve its confusion of emic/etic modes of analysis with the empirical features of sociocultural systems (see note 5), its conception of the relationship between political economy and the material infrastructure, and its claim to apply its theoretical principles equally to both precapitalist and capitalist societies. Since the first of these problems is not concerned with Harris's evolutionary arguments *per se* (being more an aspect of his general, abstract formulations), I shall discuss only the other two.

One major way in which Harris distances himself from Marxism involves the removal of the Marxian relations of production from the material infrastructure and their placement in the social structure. The advantage of this, Harris argues, is that it allows for the explanation of variation in the relations of production themselves in terms of variations in technological, demographic, and ecological conditions. I believe that Harris is at least partly right to claim that economic and class relationships can be explained in such a way. However, his claim is much too strong, for it is often the case that variations in patterns of economic ownership and class relations determine the nature of productive technology, demographic arrangements, and modes of utilization of the environment. One only has to think, for instance, of such things as the responsiveness of fertility rates to economic incentives or disincentives; the fact that the industrialization of the Western world was carried out under the auspices of a capitalist class; and the extent to which many precapitalist ruling classes were opposed to many technological changes. Actually, Harris is well aware of such facts and often explains them in the way I am suggesting. Moreover, when speaking of the principal causal forces in sociocultural evolution he often includes "economy" along with technology, demography, and ecology. All of this can only mean that there is a serious ambiguity in his causal model: apparently Harris frequently does not mean what he says and does not say what he means. But in matters as crucial as these, the precise statement of causal arguments is absolutely essential.

These ambiguities are closely related to another difficulty: Harris's claim to have developed an explanatory model that has equal applicability to all societies. Such a claim must be regarded with extreme skepticism. There seems to have occurred a major "evolutionary rupture" in the transition from precapitalist societies to modern capitalism, a major reordering of the evolutionary "rules of the game," so to speak. This means that explaining evolutionary events after the rise of capitalism is quite a different matter from explaining them in the precapitalist world. Harris's model seems far more useful in explaining precapitalist evolution. Although it can be fruitfully applied to the evolution of societies in the modern capitalist world, its demographic and ecological emphasis is not especially well suited to explain phenomena in which the role of political economy is overwhelmingly dominant. It is true that Harris does tend to shift his causal emphasis from demography and ecology to political economy when he analyzes modern capitalist societies (cf. Harrls, 1981), and that he is well aware of the forces of economic dominance and dependency in the modern world-system. Yet his model does not have nearly enough of a Wallersteinian world-system emphasis to genuinely uncover the essence of contemporary evolutionary processes.[12]

## NOTES

1  Actually, Carneiro does have one foot squarely placed within the functionalist camp and accepts a number of its basic assumptions. This is not surprising for a thcorist who explicitly views himself as working in the evolutionary tradition of Herbert Spencer. This means that Carneiro's thinking is rooted in two mutually antagonistic theoretical camps. However, I would make two points about this tension in Carneiro's work. First, I would claim that Carneiro's functionalism is a rather watered-down version that largely avoids this theoretical tradition's most unacceptable features. Second, I think that the functionalism that is there is clearly playing second fiddle to a conflict view of social evolution. At least this is the aspect of his work that I find most interesting and worth building on.

2  However, his materialism is a noted departure from the technological determinism of Childe and White and, as we shall see shortly, actually converges with the cultural materialism of Marvin Harris (cf. Carneiro, 1974).

3  In the fourth edition of *Human Societies* (Lenski and Lenski, 1982) Lenski's badly outdated view of hunter-gatherers as poverty-stricken wretches who have to work day in and day out just to eke out a bare subsistence was finally abandoned. In adopting a much more positive view of hunter-gatherers, Lenski was also forced to alter his explanation of the origins of agriculture so as to give a significant role to population pressure. However, he has very cleverly saved his technological argument by linking population growth to earlier (20,000 BP) technological changes in hunter-gatherer societies.

4  Further evidence of Lenski's anti-Marxism is contained in his vigorous objection (Lenski, 1972) to a reviewer's (Muller, 1971) remarkable characterization of *Human Societies* as essentially an unacknowledged exercise in Marxian analysis.

5  For the sake of simplification, and because it is not directly related to Harris's explicitly evolutionary concerns, I shall ignore what I believe is the severe (and highly unnecessary) confusion that Harris creates by mixing together his emic/etic distinctlon with his categories of infrastructure, structure, and superstructure. This is a problem that needs to be carefully addressed in any full-scale evaluation of Harris's work. Suffice it to say here that Harris has confused an epistemological approach to the study of social life (emics vs etics) with the empirical features of

social life (infrastructure, structure, superstructure). This is especially ironic in that Harris himself earlier warned against such confusion (cf. Harris, 1968).

6  It is true that in earlier works Harris sometimes seemed to emphasize a kind of functionalist concern for the "equilibrating" or "self-regulating" character of social systems (note in particular his analysis of Tsembaga Maring ritualized pig slaughter in *Cows, Pigs, Wars, and Witches* [1974]). However, this sort of analysis has all but disappeared from his most recent works. Moreover, there has been a noticeable shift toward an increasingly diachronic mode of analysis as a supplement to earlier synchronic analyses (e.g., note the shift to a diachronic mode of analysis in the treatment of Hindu cow love between *Cows, Pigs, Wars and Witches* and *Cannibals and Kings*).

It should also be noted that in *The Rise of Anthropological Theory* Harris refers to Marx and Engels as practicing a sort of "diachronic causal functionalism," a mode of analysis of which he is fully supportive. In the same work we also find Harris endorsing certain non-Marxian modes of functionalist theorizing. It is abundantly clear, though, that the kind of functionalism Harris has in mind is of a very minimal sort that has little in common with classic Parsonian functionalism with its societal needs, teleology, etc. All Harris is really doing is claiming that it is important to look at how the parts of sociocultural systems are interrelated. Indeed, he continues to use this kind of "functionalism" throughout all of his works in the language of systems theory (positive feedback, negative feedback, etc.).

7  No reasonably alert reader can have failed to notice that this model has a strikingly "dialectical" quality about it, and it is inconceivable that Harris himself has overlooked this. But what is important about the model is not simply that it assumes the existence of "contradictions" or "negations" that create continuous evolutionary modifications. What is important is that Harris has avoided the abstract language of the dialecticians and actually identified the specific "contradictions" he believes to be responsible for fundamental social transformations.

8  See Harris (1979:77–114) for an extensive summary of the scope of application of his cultural materialist approach.

9  See Nolan (1984) for a comparison and contrast of the two theories. Although he does an excellent job of bringing some of the key differences between the theories into sharp relief, Nolan's labels for them – "external selection" (Lenski) and "adaptive change" (Harris) – seem dubious and misleading.

10  I have failed to find even a shred of evidence that Harris subscribes to some sort of teleological or developmentalist conception of sociocultural evolution. Indeed, how could he and still maintain the view that in sociocultural evolution things change more often for the worse than for the better? Furthermore, my discussion of Harris's materialist conception of causality should make it crystal clear that his epistemology is precisely the type of ordinary causal one identified by Mandelbaum as essential for the satisfactory explanation of any observed evolutionary trends.

11  Harris's evolutionism is not only antiprogressivist, but is perhaps the only clearly antiprogressivist evolutionary model ever developed. This does not mean that Harris thinks that things never change for the better. Indeed, he acknowledges that sometimes and in some ways they do. But this is not a simple and automatic result, as it is in many (perhaps most) other evolutionary theories, of the adoption of technoenvironmentally more efficient production methods.

12 It is an understandable (and perhaps inevitable) feature of evolutionary models developed by anthropologists that they are weakest with respect to explaining evolutionary transformations in capitalist and industrial societies. Likewise, models developed by sociologists are usually not very impressive in their attempts to explain preindustrial and precapitalist evolutionary phenomena. The ideal, obviously, would be to develop a more coherent and comprehensive model equally capable of handling precapitalist and capitalist evolution. In chapter 10 I offer some brief suggestions toward this end.

# 8

# Evolutionary Biology and Social Evolutionism

The relationship between social and biological evolutionism has long been a matter of considerable interest to social evolutionists, and there has frequently been a desire to ground social evolutionary theories in concepts and principles that spring from evolutionary biology. As we saw in the last chapter, for example, Gerhard Lenski has attempted to show strong parallels between his evolutionism and basic aspects of biological evolutionism. In addition, Randall Collins's (1988) recent discussion of social evolutionism clearly implies that a good social evolutionary theory should correspond to the situation in evolutionary biology. But is there any such thing as "the situation" in evolutionary biology? Is there some single set of concepts and principles developed by evolutionary biologists to which social evolutionists can refer? Skeptical that the answers to these questions can be given in the affirmative, and skeptical that the concepts and principles of evolutionary biology transfer especially well to the social sciences, I embark upon the present chapter. The aim of the chapter is a careful elucidation of the current state of evolutionary biology and a consideration of the extent to which social scientists can develop better theories of social evolution by drawing upon it. I begin with a discussion of different attempts to apply Darwinist notions directly to social evolution. Then, in what is really the heart of the chapter, I explore debates among evolutionary biologists over three crucial concepts – adaptation, differentiation, and progress – and the relationship of these debates to similar debates among social scientists. An appendix to the chapter considers the implications of the recent biological theory of punctuated equilibria for social evolution.

DARWINISM AND THEORIES OF SOCIAL EVOLUTION

*Social Evolution as Natural Selection*

In recent years several scholars have attempted to apply the Darwinian concept of natural selection directly to social evolution. Undoubtedly the best known of these is Donald Campbell (1965). Campbell distinguishes between two fundamentally different types of social evolutionary theories. On the one hand there are theories that attempt to describe the "fact and course" of sociocultural evolution. The various versions of these theories are, of course, what has been discussed thus far in this book. On the other hand there is a type of theory that is concerned to describe the nature of the *process* of evolution. Such a theory would have applicability to explaining the "fact and course" of sociocultural evolution, but its main aim is to identify the mechanism or mechanisms through which evolutionary events occur. Campbell's theory falls into this latter type.

Campbell suggests that social evolutionists have seldom made use of the Darwinian concepts of variation, selection, and the transmission of selected variants. He believes, however, that these concepts are critical to identifying the character of social evolution. Social evolutionism must therefore be Darwinian, and a proper theory of sociocultural evolution contains three essential components:

1  a conception of sociocultural variations as occurring through a process that is "random," "chancelike," or "blind" (and thus directly analogous to genetic mutation in biology);
2  a criterion specifying that differential survival of sociocultural variants occurs (which is directly analogous to the differential survival of genes and organisms);
3  a mechanism specifying that surviving sociocultural variants propagate and spread throughout a sociocultural system (which, of course, is directly analogous to the mechanism of natural selection in evolutionary biology).

Campbell calls this theory the "variation-and-selective-retention model" and proposes that it is as applicable to the evolution of social life as Darwin's natural selection model is to biological organisms. He believes that it is this model that accounts for sociocultural evolution as a cumulative and progressive process: the natural selection of sociocultural variants produces increasingly complex, well adapted, and thus improved sociocultural forms.

A very similar theory has been produced by John Langton (1979). Like Campbell, Langton insists that sociocultural variations are directly analogous to organic mutations, and thereby random or chancelike. Also like

Campbell, Langton insists that sociocultural evolution is a learning process that leads to progressive improvements in the adaptedness of sociocultural forms. In fact, he attempts to work behaviorist learning theory into his evolutionary theory and claims that the central concept of this theory is the "struggle for reinforcement." This concept is obviously intended as a direct analogue of the Darwinian concept of the "struggle for survival." To illustrate his "behavioral theory of sociocultural evolution," Langton chooses the evolution of the serve in the game of tennis (Langton, 1979:306–7):

Take something as simple as the evolution of the serving motion in the game of tennis: when the game of tennis began, the serve was not a powerful, attacking stroke. It was simply a way of getting the ball in play, and it was accomplished by holding the racket up in front of the body and more or less "patting" the ball forward. American players like Tilden, Kramer, Schroeder, and Gonzales began the practice, however, of cocking the elbow and wrist, thereby permitting the racket head to drop down into a "backscratching" position. From this position, they were able to snap the racket forward with a powerful, accurate whipcord motion. Of course, this innovation had momentous effects on the flight and pace of the ball, and the practice quickly spread. I fail to see why the concepts of variation and selection could not be operationally defined in this case or in the case of behavioral evolution occurring in an institutional or organizational context.

Undoubtedly the most ambitious attempt to apply Darwinism directly to sociocultural evolution is the book-length treatment of Cavalli–Sforza and Feldman (1981). The heart of their theory lies in four basic concepts: sociocultural mutation, selection, transmission, and drift. Unlike Campbell and Langton, Cavalli–Sforza and Feldman claim that sociocultural variations are not directly analogous to organic mutuations: they are often directed and purposive rather than random or blind. They also do more with the concept of transmission, noting several different forms, such as between parent and child (vertical transmission) and between unrelated individuals (horizontal transmission). Moreover, their concept of cultural drift is a new wrinkle, and is given considerable attention as a sociocultural process assumed to be directly analogous to genetic drift. All of these concepts are subjected to sophisticated forms of mathematical modeling, and it is clear that Cavalli–Sforza and Feldman view their theory as having great scientific rigor.

What can we make of these three Darwinian theories of sociocultural evolution? On the more positive side, Robert Carneiro (1985) has shown that the concept of natural selection often makes perfectly good sense as an important aspect of theories of sociocultural evolution. He notes that theories assuming a kind of natural selection process in sociocultural evolution have been fairly common in the last century and a half. Spencer,

Morgan, and Tylor, for instance, all made use of a kind of cultural selectionism, and Spencer actually made a cultural selectionist model central to his evolutionary thinking. And cultural selectionist assumptions are either explicitly or implicitly a part of the thinking of such modern evolutionists as White, Lenski, and Harris. More strikingly, Carneiro claims that selectionism's origins can actually be traced to social thinkers like Malthus, from whom Darwin borrowed in developing his own concept of natural selection. Carneiro concludes that there is no reason in principle why the concept of natural selection cannot be reappropriated by social evolutionists.

However, to suggest that social evolutionary theories can be natural selectionist in principle is not to say that the particular theories we have just reviewed can survive close scrutiny. Indeed, several important concerns leap immediately to mind. One difficulty concerns the claim of Campbell and Langton (but not Cavalli–Sforza and Feldman) that sociocultural variation is a random or blind process. Langton defends this claim with an example of how a biomedical scientist by the name of Semmelweis discovered hygienic techniques capable of preventing childbed fever. Against the claim that Semmelweis's discovery was directed and purposive (Ruse, 1974), Langton argues that (1979:293; emphasis Langton's):

it seems more plausible to argue that Semmelweis's discovery of the relationship between the hygiene of attending physicians and childbed fever did just appear at random. It did not appear simply because it was needed. Need – in this case the desire to remove a very punishing phenomenon from the environment – explains why Semmelweis "spent several years thinking and working hard, proposing and testing hypotheses." *Need explains Seimmelweis's behavior* – his searching, his diligent but blind groping for a way to suppress a deadly disease. *It does not explain what he found.*

This extreme case of special pleading is thoroughly unpersuasive, but even if the point about Semmelweis were to be conceded the claim for randomness cannot be made to stand in general. Some sociocultural variations are doubtless random, but many are obviously brought into existence by the conscious and purposive efforts of individuals. This would be especially true of technological innovations, but the same could be said of innovations in many other dimensions of human social life, such as religious and political institutions. There is, then, a strong disanalogy between the nature of variation at the biological level and its nature in sociocultural life (cf. Hallpike, 1986).

Another difficulty with natural selection theories of social evolution involves the strong progressivist element in these theories, especially those of Campbell and Langton. Campbell and Langton insist that sociocultural evolution is a spiraling learning process, and that newer sociocultural forms are better adapted (and thus improvements over) earlier forms. But this is an extremely contentious claim. As we will see later in this chapter, not only are social scientists seriously divided over the validity of such a claim, but biological evolutionists cannot agree on whether a progressivist claim is valid in regard to the evolution of life forms. Although many evolutionary biologists would consent to the view that later bioforms are better adapted than earlier forms, many other distinguished biologists currently strongly reject this view.

Perhaps the most serious problem with natural selection models of social evolution, though, has to do with their limited character – their concern with process over content. As Carneiro has pointed out (1985:5–6; emphasis Carneiro's):

Natural selection is a *mechanism,* not a *determinant.* It is the process through which whatever determinants . . . are at work . . . exert their respective influences. Hence, to believe in natural selection as the *modus operandi* of cultural evolution does not commit one to any particular theory of cultural causation.

Carneiro thus suggests that natural selection theories of social evolution will always be incomplete. To illustrate this point, let us return to Langton's discussion of changes in the game of tennis. I believe that Langton's discussion of the evolution of the power serve in tennis correctly uses the concept of natural selection to describe what happened (even to the point of identifying it as a process of improvement). But the interesting thing about his discussion involves not so much what he says, but what he doesn't say. Langton never asks, for instance, why the power serve began to emerge at the particular historical time that it did. (Apparently this is because he assumes that the idea of the power serve was a random occurrence.) If we go ahead and ask this question, though, we are quickly led to some interesting facts. One of these is that the evolution of the power serve was an intrinsic part of the expansion of the game of tennis as a serious spectator sport instead of a casual pastime. Furthermore, the expansion of tennis as a spectator sport corresponded historically with an expansion in the social significance of other sports. This is even more characteristic of very recent times. In the last 25 years there has been an explosion of spectator sports in Western societies, the United States in particular. Tennis became a prominent spectator sport after 1968 (when amateurs and professionals were allowed to play in the same tournaments), whereas before this time it was a very minor sport enjoyed mostly by social elites. As this has happened, the game of tennis has evolved in several other important respects as well (such as the emergence of the popularity of the two-handed backhand). The point of all this is to indicate that changes within a particular sport cannot be meaningfully explained on their own terms merely by describing them as operating in accordance with a process of natural selection. What has to be explained is the historical timing of these changes and their imbeddedness in larger changes in sports or in society more generally. That is what a substantial evolutionary theory does, and that is what Langton's natural selection theory completely fails to do.[1]

## Coevolutionary Theories

The concept of fitness employed in the theories of Campbell, Langton, and Cavalli-Sforza and Feldman is a purely *cultural* one. That is, there is no assumption that cultural fitness is necessarily related to biological or reproductive fitness. Cavalli-Sforza and Feldman note that cultural fitness may be related to biological fitness, but only on average, and that there are numerous instances of cultural fitness that actually reduce biological fitness.

In recent years, however, several scholars have attempted to develop theories of social evolution that explicitly incorporate Darwinian conceptions of biological fitness. The earliest of these theories were the sociobiological theories of Tiger and Fox (1971), E. O. Wilson (1975, 1978), Robert Trivers (1971), Pierre van den Berghe (1978, 1979), Richard Alexander (1975), and numerous others. Not all of these theories were biologically reductionist, but even those that were not were committed to explaining sociocultural phenomena in terms of their ultimate contribution to the biological fitness of individuals, especially their reproductive success. These theories have lately entered a new phase specifically concerned with showing how genes and culture interact in producing social evolution. This has led to *theories of gene-culture coevolution* or, more simply, *coevolutionary theories*. To a large extent, such theories seem to be implicitly responding to the criticism that sociobiology is unacceptably biologically reductionist.

The best-known coevolutionary theories are those of Lumsden and Wilson (1981) and Boyd and Richerson (1985). In *Genes, Mind and Culture* (1981) Lumsden and Wilson propose the existence of *epigenetic rules*, which are biological mechanisms that direct the organization of the mind. Some of the epigenetic rules apparently have broad or even universal applicability to the human species, but Lumsden and Wilson also conceive of many of them differing significantly among human populations and subpopulations. The rules present in any population direct the development of that population's set of *culturgens*, or its entire "array of transmissible behaviors, mentifacts, and artifacts" (1981:7). However, Lumsden and Wilson insist that the culturgens do not emerge directly from the epigenetic rules, for "the assembly of the mind . . . is context dependent, with the epigenetic rules feeding on information derived from culture and physical environment" (1981:2). Thus the actual evolution of any particular set of culturgens is the joint product of genes and culture, or of gene-culture coevolution.

Much of *Genes, Mind, and Culture* is spent identifying certain basic epigenetic rules and tracing their impact on widespread forms of human behavior. For instance, Lumsden and Wilson suggest that certain widespread phobias, such as the fear of snakes, are rooted in epigenetic rules. Likewise, they see the universal human aversion to incest as deriving from an epigenetic rule. But Lumsden and Wilson also provide some other suggestions that are more interesting from the point of view of long-term evolutionary change. One of these is what they call an *amplification law*, which holds that relatively small changes in the epigenetic rules can lead to major changes in cultural patterns. An even more interesting suggestion is Lumsden and Wilson's *thousand-year rule*, which holds that major culture-altering genetic changes in human populations can occur within a span of a thousand years. Lumsden and Wilson thus believe that the conventional view that substantial genetic evolution within the human species came to a halt some 30,000 years ago is incorrect. Substantial genetic evolution is still occurring, they say, and still having major consequences for cultural evolution.

Numerous criticisms can be made of this version of coevolutionary theory, but the most obvious and serious is that it is not really a form of coevolutionism at all. Marion Blute (1987) has suggested that it amounts to a kind of "sociobiology in drag," and there is little reason to challenge her assertion. Although Lumsden and Wilson continually assert that the epigenetic rules can act only within a given cultural context, and thus that culture is important in its own right, their entire analysis is overwhelmingly biased toward the biological side. For it turns out that culturgens that are (Lumsden and Wilson, 1981:24):

disfavored by the epigenetic rules will be eliminated more quickly and come to occur in lower frequencies across many societies. The process is expected to continue indefinitely unless the novel culturgens confer higher genetic fitness, in which case the epigenetic rules themselves can be altered by genetic evolution over a period of generations in a direction more permissive to the novel culturgens. . . . But the opposite process can also occur: if new culturgens appear that consistently lower fitness, the epigenetic rules will be tightened.

Moreover (1981:178–9):

One nevertheless might conceive of the possible emergence of institutions and customs so powerful . . . that they grow and proliferate even while contravening the epigenetic rules and lowering genetic fitness. . . . But no, not at all. . . . It is possible to demonstrate that no cultural juggernaut will persist indefinitely under such ill-fitting conditions. . . . If epigenetic rules are contravened, they can be expected to exert a steady pressure until the culture is realigned into a more congenial form. Only by changing the genetic basis of the epigenetic rules or of the more fundamental cognitive core rules themselves could a previously maladaptive culture be preserved indefinitely.

So in the end everything comes down to genetic fitness and is adaptive in the long run. Culture apparently does have an effect that is independent of the epigenetic rules, but this can only be the case initially and in the short run. In the long run, the epigenetic rules and adaptive (i.e., genetically adaptive) cultural patterns win out.

It should be fairly clear, then, that Lumsden and Wilson's coevolutionism is really just a new version of sociobiology that has apparently been introduced in order to answer the claim that sociobiology is an unacceptable form of biological reductionism. But the alterations in the old sociobiology are shallow in the extreme, and thus this version of coevolutionism is vulnerable to many of the same criticisms that have been made against Wilson's early sociobiological efforts (cf. Wilson, 1975, 1978). Lumsden and Wilson are genuine babes in the woods. Their knowledge and understanding of the social sciences and their genuine contributions are embarrassingly thin. Moreover, their whole enterprise is extremely speculative and highly artificial. The elaborate mathematical models they develop look impressive, and their most interesting coevolutionary principles (the amplification law and the thousand-year rule) have an air of great sophistication. But I am afraid the emperor is wearing no clothes. With just a little scrutiny it can be seen that their mathematical models and their coevolutionary principles rest upon an incredibly shaky and highly contrived empirical base.[2]

Boyd and Richerson's (1985) coevolutionism shares much with Lumsden and Wilson's but has the merit of avoiding its extreme biological bias. Boyd and Richerson call their theory a *dual inheritance* theory to emphasize that there are two different systems of inheritance that operate to produce evolutionary consequences. One of these is a biological system in which selection and transmission occur genetically and produce behaviors that are adaptive from the point of view of genetic fitness. The other is a cultural system in which selection and transmission occur through nongenetic mechanisms. This system is intertwined in some ways with human biology, but is also autonomous. Thus it may produce effects having nothing to do with, or even contradicting, genetic fitness. Much of the time the cultural system of inheritance produces consequences that are selected and transmitted for their adaptive value, but various forms of maladaptive behavior can also result.

Boyd and Richerson's dual inheritance theory is actually a complex collection of subtheories, and I will devote myself here only to the more significant of these. Some of the subtheories are grouped under the phenomenon Boyd and Richerson call *biased transmission*. Biased transmission is a process whereby aspects of human behavior are transmitted nongenetically (i.e., culturally or through learning), but in which individuals are predisposed ("biased") to adopt certain cultural variants rather than others. Boyd and Richerson specify three subtypes of biased transmission. *Direct bias* involves people's choosing some cultural variants over others as a result of their own judgments about the features these variants contain. Food taboos and dietary preferences exemplify this type of bias. *Frequency-dependent bias* results when individuals adopt a cultural variant because it is common in the population (or avoid it because it is rare). This form of bias, in other words, involves people's tendency to conform to the opinions and behaviors of others. Finally, *indirect bias* occurs when individuals adopt a cultural variant because it is displayed by other individuals whom they find especially attractive. For example, individuals may copy the opinions and behaviors of others because they are powerful or have high prestige.

Biased transmission is closely intertwined with the *natural selection of cultural variations*. This means "that individuals characterized by alternative cultural variants differ in their probability of surviving and becoming effective models" (1985:173). When natural selection operates on cultural variants it may also produce effects that increase genetic fitness, but often this natural selection process works on cultural variants alone. When the latter occurs, genetic fitness can remain unchanged, or in somes cases actually be lowered.

Dietary preferences are good examples of the former process, because the preferences people develop frequently contribute to their biological survival and reproductive success. Consider, in particular, fava bean consumption in the circum-Mediterranean region. Fava beans are widely cultivated in this part of the world despite the fact that their consumption sometimes causes a severe (and frequently fatal) disease. Individuals who are susceptible to this disease have a gene for a particular enzyme deficiency that frequently occurs in many circum-Mediterranean populations. It turns out that fava bean consumption is highest in those populations with the highest frequencies of this particular gene. Although this may appear counterintuitive, it has been argued (Katz and Schall, 1979) that "fava consumption is [genetically] adaptive in the malaria-prone regions because the bean contains compounds that confer resistance to malaria on individuals not protected by G–6–PD deficiency, and that this advantage compensates for the occurrence of favism in sensitive individuals" (Boyd and Richerson, 1985:178). From this Boyd and Richerson conclude that "natural selection is acting on the cultural trait of fava bean consumption much as it is acting on the G–6–PD locus. Individuals characterized by beliefs that lead them to consume fava beans had a higher probability of surviving to adulthood and becoming cultural parents for the next generation than individuals who did not consume fava beans" (1985:178).

An example of natural selection operating on cultural variation without regard for its consequences for genetic fitness (what Boyd and Richerson call asymmetric selection and transmission) involves the demographic transition. As is well known, a major consequence of industrialization has been a sharp decline in the birth rate. Boyd and Richerson suggest that married couples began having smaller families because large families impeded their efforts at upward mobility, and also because couples with small families who achieve social and economic success can then serve as models to spread these new norms regarding family size throughout the population. We thus have a phenomenon that is selected for its ability to confer cultural success, but that in doing so actually reduces genetic (reproductive) success.

This last point illustrates what is a constant refrain in Boyd and Richerson's analysis: the extent to which their dual inheritance model leads to predictions that are often sharply at variance with the predictions of sociobiology.[3] This strongly separates them from Lumsden and Wilson, of whom they are often highly critical. As such, Boyd and Richerson's model is much more palatable to social evolutionists who reject Lumsden and Wilson's tendency toward biological reductionism. Yet there are several problems with their overall model, the total effect of which casts serious doubt on the usefulness of their contributions.

First, some of their arguments suffer from the same basic problem associated with the natural-selection models of Campbell, Langton, and Cavalli-Sforza and Feldman: a failure to offer explanations that are complete or that generate a high level of intellectual satisfaction. Consider as a major example Boyd and Richerson's discussion of the industrialization and modernization of agrarian societies. They give particular emphasis to changing cognitive styles, claiming that industrial and industrializing societies require individuals who are high on the social-psychological trait of "field independence." Individuals possessing this trait are therefore in a favorable position to achieve success and to serve as models for the trait's spread throughout the population. As Boyd and Richerson put it (1985:180):

These data suggest the following hypothesis to explain the increase in field independence with modernization: (1) A modernizing agricultural society begins with a population scoring low on field independence, but with considerable variation. (2) In the modernizing situation, the field-independent individuals are more likely to do well in school and subsequently to become teachers, business owners, or managers, bureaucrats, and so on. Old elite roles favoring more field-dependent cognitive styles become, at least proportionately, less important. (3) The new field-independent elites transmit their values and skills to some extent . . . to their employees and pupils.

Do Boyd and Richerson mean to say that the shift to more field-independent personalities *causes* modernization? If so, then their theory recalls all those psychological versions of modernization theory, such as that of McClelland (1961), and the severe criticisms to which they have been subjected. But if they do not mean to say this, then we have an extreme instance of question begging. What social evolutionists really want to know is why the shift toward modernization occurs in the first place. It may well be that modernizing societies have more field-independent personalities, but that is an *effect* of modernization, not a cause of it. It thus appears that Boyd and Richerson's analysis on this score contributes little of genuine explanatory significance.

A second somewhat related problem concerns the ultimate form of explanation on which Boyd and Richerson rely. Although they are often highly critical of Lumsden and Wilson's biological reductionism, and although they note that their coevolutionary theory often generates predictions that are at odds with some of the predictions of sociobiology, they seem to fall back on a sociobiological argument nonetheless (cf. Blute, 1987:191; Ingold, 1986:365). Culture is never really free from biology, and the word "biased" in their concept of biased transmission really refers to a biological bias. Thus the modes of behavior that individuals acquire under different environmental and cultural circumstances, including those that end up producing maladaptive biological effects, are those that they are biologically predisposed to acquire.

It may turn out that Boyd and Richerson are at least partially correct about the biological biasing of culturally-acquired behavior, and as already noted their coevolutionary model is a considerably more sophisticated and flexible one than Lumsden and Wilson's. Nevertheless, it is difficult to see how such a model explains very much about the kind of long-term evolutionary phenomena in which social evolutionists are most interested. Boyd and Richerson do not have a model capable of saying anything particularly interesting about, say, the Neolithic Revolution, or the origin of pristine states, or the transition from feudalism to capitalism. And the reason their model cannot shed interesting light on these and numerous other major social transformations is because it is mainly a model of the *constraints* operating on human choices, not a model of the *causes* of those choices. They suggest, for example, that humans are biologically biased toward conformity because of the advantages this confers on conforming individuals, an argument I have no difficulty agreeing with. But their model seems incapable of shedding much light on the causes of the particular kinds of social patterns to which conformity would be oriented. More significantly, since social evolution mainly concerns the alteration of established patterns of conformity, a good model of it would offer a coherent explanation of the conditions under which *nonconformity* is a major social outcome. Boyd and Richerson's model does not do this, at least not in more than an extremely general way.

Or take Boyd and Richerson's discussion of how indirect bias can lead to a runaway process of status emulation. Thorstein Veblen described such a process brilliantly in his classic *Theory of the Leisure Class* (1912), even arguing for a type of biological basis for it. However, even if we agree with Veblen and with Boyd and Richerson that there may well be one, how does this explain much about the character of long-term social transformations? Even if the desire for status could be conclusively shown to be an innate human tendency, it is not a cause of anything but only a constraining condition. To explain social transformations, we must move beyond the level of mere constraints to talk about the range of actual causal conditions that motivate humans to give up one set of patterns for another, and this Boyd and Richerson do not do.

In the final analysis, then, although there is much in Boyd and Richerson that can be accepted, the genuine utility of their coevolutionary model is seriously weakened by its narrowness and shallowness. Their work is scarcely one of the more useful guides to constructing a comprehensive theory of social evolution.

THE CONCEPT OF ADAPTATION IN BIOLOGICAL AND
SOCIAL EVOLUTIONISM

*The Concept of Adaptation in Evolutionary Biology*

Although it is widely recognized that the concept of adaptation is an especially contentious one in the social sciences, social scientists might suppose that the concept has a precise and widely agreed on meaning in evolutionary biology. But only a little exposure to the current literature in evolutionary biology will quickly disabuse the encroaching social scientist of such a notion. In point of fact, evolutionary biologists hotly debate the concept of adaptation and do so in ways that remarkably parallel the debates over the concept that continue to rage among social scientists. For the most part, these debates concern two basic questions: to what extent can the concept of adaptation be employed in orienting explanatory efforts?, and what is the biological unit on which adaptational biological processes (to the extent that they occur) operate? Let us consider each of these in turn.

The concept of adaptation is widely employed by evolutionary biologists, and so much so that the search for adaptive features of biological traits has become something of a preoccupation (Futuyma, 1986). This seemingly uncritical determination to find the adaptive significance of all biological traits has produced a sharp reaction by some evolutionary biologists. One of the first biologists to be concerned about the abuses of the adaptation concept was George Williams. In his now classic *Adaptation and Natural Selection* (1966), Williams warned his fellow biologists that the concept is a particularly onerous one that should be used only when truly necessary. Williams argued that it was being abused by its wholesale and casual use, as well as by the absence of sufficiently rigorous criteria for determining the extent to which biological traits could be called adaptations.

In more recent years usage of the concept has come in for further criticism. The harshest contemporary critics of the concept have undoubtedly been Stephen Jay Gould and Richard Lewontin (Gould and Lewontin, 1984; Lewontin, 1984). Gould and Lewontin do not reject the concept's usefulness and indeed admit that numerous features of organisms have undoubtedly arisen as adaptations. As Lewontin notes, "It is no accident that fish have fins, aquatic mammals have altered their appendages to form finlike flippers, ducks, geese, and seabirds have webbed feet, penguins have paddle-like wings, and even seasnakes, lacking fins, are flattened in cross-section" (1984:247). What they object to is the "vulgarization" of the concept, an outcome they believe to be guided more by ideology than by properties inherent in biological organisms themselves. Indeed, they suggest that the intense commitment to the concept of adaptation (a phenomenon they label the "adaptationist program") is driven by Panglossian concerns, and therefore often amounts to nothing but "telling stories."

In attacking what they perceive as the uncritical and indiscriminate employment of the adaptation concept, Gould and Lewontin are obviously suggesting that many features of organisms arise in nonadaptational ways. They propose a number of ways in which this can occur but devote greatest attention to an alternative evolutionary model emphasizing the concept of *Bauplan*, or the basic body plan of an organism. Organisms exist as basic irreducible wholes, they claim, and any attempt to decompose them into their individual parts, and to claim that it is these parts that individually evolve (as those who follow the adaptationist program do), does violence to the very nature of organisms. Organisms evolve as whole structures, they suggest, and many of their traits exist because they are integrated elements of the whole organism, not because they are adaptations to the external environment. The evolution of any trait is therefore constrained by the *Bauplan* of the organism, a constraint that Gould and Lewontin think "may hold the most powerful rein of all over possible evolutionary pathways" (1984:266).

An important weakness in the position of Gould and Lewontin has been identified by Elliott Sober (1984), a philosopher with a special interest in evolutionary biology. Sober notes that Gould and Lewontin fail to distinguish between adaptation and *adaptedness*, and thus automatically assume that the former implies the latter. Adaptation, for Sober, is a concept that should be used to indicate what an organism does in response to certain selection pressures, and thus an adaptation is a trait that arises from a process of natural selection. Adaptedness, though, is essentially equivalent to fitness and refers to a particular end result of the existence of a certain trait. Thus conceived, adaptation is a concept that refers to the *origin* of a trait, whereas adaptedness refers to the kinds of *consequences* that any trait (whatever its origin) produces. Conflating these two processes produces enormous confusion because, as Sober suggests, paradoxically "a trait can be an adaptation without marking an improvement in adaptedness; conversely, it can enhance its bearer's level of adaptedness without being an adaptation" (1984:196).

Whatever its value for evolutionary biologists, Sober's distinction has crucial implications for debates about the merits of the adaptation concept in theories of social evolution. I shall therefore want to return to this distinction in the next section, when the focus of attention shifts to adaptationism in the social sciences. First, though, we need to consider the debates among evolutionary biologists over the unit of adaptation. The contemporary debates on this issue can basically be traced back to the early 1960s and the proposal of V. C. Wynne-Edwards (1962) that many features of animal behavior result from a process of *group selection*. Wynne–Edwards was particularly interested in the densities of animal populations and suggested that some commonly observed animal behaviors – territoriality, for example – arose because of their capacity to maintain populations at suitable levels of density. These behaviors therefore had to be explained as adaptations at the level of the group as a whole, not at the level of individual organisms.

This notion of group selection has been severely criticized by numerous biologists, but most effectively perhaps by George Williams (1966). Williams is extremely suspicious of the idea, holding that on grounds of both scientific parsimony and available evidence it should rarely if ever be invoked. His view is that adaptation "should be attributed to no higher a level of organization than is demanded by the evidence" (1966:4–5). In essence, Williams believes that adaptations that benefit groups are simply the statistical summation of adaptations occurring at the level of individuals or, more precisely, the genes that constitute individuals. As he tells us (1966:252):

The species is . . . a key taxonomic and evolutionary concept but has no special significance for the study of adaptation. It is not an adapted unit and there are no mechanisms that function for the survival of the species. The only adaptations that clearly exist express themselves in genetically defined individuals and have only one ultimate goal, the maximal perpetuation of the genes responsible for the visible adaptive mechanisms.

Similar conclusions have been reached by William Hamilton (1964) and Richard Dawkins (1976). Hamilton introduced the concept of *inclusive fitness* to explain the puzzle of altruism as an evolutionary trend among many species, in particular the elaborate altruism of the social insects. He proposed that selection operated at the level of the gene and that the maximization of inclusive fitness – the total representation of an organism's genes in a population – selected for altruism toward close relatives, even to the point of the organism's surrendering its own life. Dawkins generalized Hamilton's notion of genic selection by arguing that organisms were nothing but "gene machines": structures designed for the perpetuation of the genes composing them.

In more recent years there has emerged skepticism about genic selection as the *only* level of selection and a reconsideration of the concept of group selection (cf. D. S. Wilson, 1983). Stephen Jay Gould, for instance, has suggested that selection may operate simultaneously at different levels "including genes, demes, species, and clades" (1982:384). Indeed, the notion of "species selection" is an integral part of the punctuationalist challenge to gradualism that Gould and others have been leading (cf. Stanley, 1979).

### *The Debate over Adaptation in Social Evolutionism*

Although a sociologist has no business adjudicating these often complex and technical debates among evolutionary biologists, we can learn much from a recognition of them. Most importantly, we should learn that strong criticism of the concept of adaptation does not imply the need to abandon it. Evolutionary biologists critical of it do not recommend it be given up, only that it be used in a more cautious and discriminating manner. For this reason it is rather surprising to learn that many critics of the sociological version of this concept conclude that the concept's weaknesses render it completely useless. Irving Zeitlin (1973), for instance, views the concept as inextricably tied up with functionalism and its errors and therefore suggests it has no place in social science. Anthony Giddens (1981, 1984) draws a similar conclusion on the basis of a considerably more extensive critique of the adaptation concept. Giddens sets forth three basic objections to the concept and its employment by social scientists. First, he suggests, the concept tends to be used so broadly and vaguely that it produces more confusion than illumination. He complains that it is frequently an extremely diffuse notion that is meant to include all possible influences upon a society and its transformations and that, as such, it is essentially useless. Ironically, he also complains that in some cases the concept is being used too narrowly (1984:234–5):

Where "adaptation" is specified with some degree of precision . . . and where what is adapted to is also clearly delimited, the notion is manifestly inadequate as a general mechanism of social change. If environment means "natural environment," and if "adapting" to it means responding to distinguishable changes in that environment in ways which have this effect of modifying existing organic or social traits, "adaptation" simply is much too narrow to be a credible candidate for such a mechanism. It can be made plausible only by expanding one or both aspects of its meaning – by including other societies (i.e., the "social environment") within the term "environment" and/or by including as "adaptation" more or less any major social process which seems to further the chances of maintaining a society in something like a stable form. Once this has been done, however, the concept becomes so vague that it is useless as a means of explaining anything at all.

Gidden's second objection to the concept involves his association of it with functionalist modes of explanation. He suggests that explanations of social phenomena that rely on the concept of adaptation inevitably end up as nothing but tautologies. For example, the concept of superior adaptive capacity may be invoked to explain why a particular society, or a particular feature of a society, has survived or emerged. But then when we inquire into the reasons why a particular society is said to have superior adaptive capacity, we discover that it is because it or a particular feature of it has survived or emerged. Advocates of the concept of adaptation thus generally fail to provide an acceptable criterion for judging a social phenomenon's adaptive capacity.

Finally, Giddens believes that the concept of adaptation always implies the existence of a universal human desire for mastery of and domination over nature. He believes that evolutionary theories employing the concept of adaptation (virtually all such theories, he suggests) explain basic evolutionary transformations, especially technological ones, as springing from this desire for mastery. But there is no such desire, he claims, because there is abundant evidence that the members of many preindustrial societies often actively resist technological advance or incorporation into more technologically advanced societies. Since the desire for mastery is a culturally specific rather than universal human desire, the evolutionists' concept of mastery cannot be a legitimate basis on which to rest explanations of historical changes.

Giddens's objections to the adaptation concept do have some force. There are indeed dangers in the use of the concept in the social sciences, as there are in its use in biology. In many social–scientific theories, adaptation is often employed much too vaguely and loosely, and, it is clear that it sometimes (perhaps frequently) ends up producing explanations that are purely spurious (because of their circularity). It is also true that the concept has been a central one within functionalism and that there is a close association between "adaptation" and "function." Moreover, Giddens is right to note that many social evolutionists employ the concept of adaptation in a way that does assume a universal human desire for mastery, and I completely agree with him that there is no such desire. However, I think the problems to which Giddens points are not inherent in the adaptation concept itself, but spring from the particular uses to which it has been put by various social scientists, evolutionists included. I therefore believe that Giddens has substantially overstated his case.[4] The concept has risks and has been abused, but it is a good – indeed, I shall argue, necessary – one that we would be foolish to abandon. With this idea in mind, let me focus in particular on how the concept has been used by different social evolutionists with an eye to learning from their mistakes (and their insights as well) and to developing a coherent and usable concept of adaptation.

Of the evolutionary theorists discussed in this book, Talcott Parsons clearly stands out as a thinker whose use of the concept of adaptation is highly vulnerable to Giddens's objections. I have already argued that Parsons's concept of adaptive capacity is so terribly vague that its utility is called severely into question. Parsons tells us that adaptation occurs in regard to the environment, but his notion of environment is so fuzzy that the entire claim seems rather meaningless. Moreover, Parsons's usage of the adaptation concept is obviously permeated by functionalist notions. Parsons is a thoroughgoing "group selectionist," as one would expect from a thinker so hostile to any form of utilitarianism (cf. Haines, 1987). For him, it is a society (or an institutional segment thereof) that does the adapting. It is also clear that Parsons makes no distinction whatsoever between adaptation and adaptedness, the former being completely merged into the latter. In essence, not only do Giddens's criticisms of the adaptation concept apply well to Parsons's evolutionism, but so by implication do Gould and Lewontin's. Parsonian evolutionism is as good an example as one can find of a social evolutionary version of the adaptationist program and the "Panglossian paradigm."

As for the notion of a universal human desire for mastery, this too plays a fundamental role in Parsons's evolutionism. However, this idea is in some respects even more fundamental to materialist versions of evolutionism. It is thus in the technological evolutionism of Childe and White that we find the concept of mastery taking center stage. The title of Childe's first major evolutionary work, *Man Makes Himself,* is by itself telling of his belief in a general human desire for mastery as a guiding force in social evolution. The same idea is present in White's evolutionism, although perhaps more implicitly. White's general evolutionary law makes increasing energy capture basic to evolutionary advance, and he often appears to assume that the movement of societies to higher levels of energy capture results from a generalized human desire for control over nature.[5]

In addition, it seems clear that both Childe and White have merged adaptation and adaptedness. Although both recognize a number of negative consequences of technological and social evolution, both clearly view technological advance as producing net benefits for the members of societies in general. However, as we have already seen, White's failure to distinguish adaptedness from adaptation led him into a major reversal of his theoretical position toward the end of his life. He eventually concluded that the story of cultural evolution was not a story of increasing human adaptedness at all, but rather one of increasing misery, oppression, and exploitation. This led him to conclude that culture itself was not adaptive and thus could not be analyzed as such. But as I noted in chapter 5, this extreme conclusion was by no means called for. White could simply have concluded that cultural traits and patterns arose as adaptations – that is, from the aims of particular individuals to satisfy various of their needs and wants – but that these traits often did not lead to the results originally intended. Or, alternatively, he could have concluded that some traits arose as adaptations and did indeed lead to adaptedness for some individuals and groups, but that the existence of the same traits imposed penalties on (and thus were maladaptive for) other individuals and groups. But White did not conclude either of these things and was led into his extreme reversal of position because of his assumption that the concept of adaptation itself implied adaptedness.

When we turn to students and followers of White, we find much the same emphasis. In his essay on specific and general evolution, Marshall Sahlins claims that general evolution leads to an increase in "all-round adaptability." For Sahlins, the concept of general evolution not only merges adaptation and adaptedness, but also rests on an implicit assumption of a general human desire for mastery.[6] Lenski's evolutionism rests on the same employment of the adaptation concept, but much more explicitly. For Lenski, social evolution is fundamentally rooted in the desire of humans to gain control over their environments, and technological advance is what allows them to do this. Lenski's whole discussion of technological change is strongly biased toward what he perceives as its positive features, and thus technology as a human adaptational means is closely intertwined with the notion of adaptedness. Moreover, in Lenski's evolutionism the unit that is doing the adapting is always a sociocultural system as a whole, and thus Lenski is, like Parsons, a strong "group selectionist." In fact, except for the technological emphasis, it is often difficult to distinguish Lenski's concept of increasing adaptive capacity from Parsons's.

So far the picture of the usage of the adaptation concept among social evolutionists is much as Giddens paints it, but when we turn to Harris's evolutionism the picture changes drastically. Harris is not a group selectionist at all, but clearly an individual selectionist. For him, what does the adapting is the individual human organism, not some reified sociocultural system. Harris thus comes the closest of any major social evolutionist to producing an evolutionary model that is based on the sociological equivalent of genic selection.

Harris also clearly distinguishes between adaptation and adaptedness, though without using the terms as such. In fact, the major evolutionary model that he presents in *Cannibals and Kings* assumes that much of social evolution is a story of decreasing benefits for the majority of persons, even though the evolutionary transformations in question result from the efforts of individuals to satisfy various of their needs and desires. Harris has carefully avoided the trap into which White fell at the end of his career. For example, horticulturists may have a lower standard of living than hunter-gatherers, but the first hunter-gatherers to make the transition to reliance on domesticated species did so because they were attempting to cope with increasing population pressures and ecological depletions. Likewise, most people in societies practicing plow agriculture have a lower standard of living than those in horticultural societies, but the adoption of plows was an adaptation arising from the need to intensify production.

It is also obvious that Harris is scarcely assuming any sort of universal desire for mastery that drives social evolution. In fact, his whole evolutionary model rests on just the opposite notion. If there is a universal human desire that affects the course of human evolution, it is not the desire for mastery but the desire to save time and energy – a "Law of Least Effort" (cf. Zipf, 1965[1949]). Harris sees preindustrial societies as governed by a kind of "technological inertia" that arises from people's recognition that more intensive technologies require greater time and energy inputs. People will generally increase their time and energy expenditure only when they are compelled to do so, either by falling standards of living or by more powerful social groups who have their own reasons for wanting to increase economic productivity. For Harris, then, preindustrial social evolution is anything but a process guided by a drive for mastery. The drive for mastery plays a strong role in contemporary industrial societies, and perhaps in some ancient agrarian states, but this is a culturally specific motive.

## *The Concept of Adaptation: A Systematization*

It is clear, then, that many social evolutionists have used the concept of adaptation in questionable or unacceptable ways. But, contrary to Giddens, these usages do not inhere in the concept itself. Harris has demonstrated that social evolutionists can employ the concept to great effect if they do so judiciously. Let me elaborate on this point by suggesting several basic criteria that should govern the employment of the concept in theories of social evolution:

1   Adaptation refers to the process whereby modes of acting and thinking are adopted because they are perceived as effective ways of meeting various needs and desires. Adaptation is a concept that refers to the origin of a trait, or to its persistence, but not to its consequences for the individuals who adopted it.

2   Adaptation is a process pertaining to individuals, and not to any social unit higher than the individual. (This is the sociological counterpart to genic selection in evolutionary biology.) Groups and societies cannot be adaptational units because they are only abstractions. Only concrete, flesh-and-blood individuals can be adaptational units because only they have needs and wants. Durkheim and Parsons notwithstanding, groups and societies do not have (logically *cannot* have) needs and wants. To think otherwise is to commit the fallacy of reification.[7]

3   Adaptation must be sharply distinguished from adaptedness. Whereas adaptation involves processes whereby individuals originate social traits or patterns, adaptedness concerns the extent to which a trait or pattern benefits the individuals who adopted (or inherited) it. Adaptation often leads to adaptedness, but, paradoxically, frequently leads to consequences that are inadaptive or maladaptive and thus that frustrate rather than serve the aims of individuals. For example, it is well known that peasants in contemporary Third World societies desire large families as a cost-effective means of acquiring numerous farm workers, the aim being to improve (or at least maintain) the peasant family's standard of living. But the aggregate effect of each peasant family's behaving in this fashion is to increase population density and land scarcity, and thus to make peasants worse off in the long run. Or, to take an example from one of Marx's famous theories, capitalists innovate technologically in order to improve (or at least maintain) their competitiveness vis-à-vis other capitalists. But the aggregate effect of this process, Marx says, is to increase the organic composition of capital and reduce the overall rate of profit, thus making capitalists worse off in the long run. As a final example, consider Randall Collins's (1979) theory of educational expansion in American society. According to Collins, people seek education in order to improve their level of economic and social success. But the total effect of everyone's staying in school longer is to inflate educational credentials, thus requiring people to stay in school longer still just to keep even in the struggle for success. Eventually people must attend school for very long periods even to obtain ordinary jobs.

4   Although adaptations do frequently lead to adaptedness, this adaptedness may vary greatly from one set of individuals, and from one time, to another. For instance, adaptations that are adaptive for the members of dominant groups may be maladaptive for the members of subordinate groups. Moreover, a trait that is adaptive for the members of one group at one time may become maladaptive at a later time, and vice

versa. To recognize this is to acknowledge that the concepts of adaptation and adaptedness are not inherently functionalist ones, but may be employed with effectiveness by conflict theorists of various types.

5 In addition to recognizing what unit does the adapting (an individual), it is also necessary to specify what an individual is adapting to. An adaptation may be to either the physical environment, to the existing social environment, or to both. Many adaptations arise in response to existing social arrangements, and these arrangements exert powerful constraints on the nature of the adaptations that are likely to arise. There thus exist the social equivalent of biological *Baupläne*, the recognition of which is crucial for theories of social evolution. Marx understood this clearly when he said, "Men make their own history, but they do not make it just as they please; they do not make it under circumstances chosen by themselves, but under circumstances directly found, given and transmitted from the past. The tradition of all the dead generations weighs like a nightmare on the brain of the living" (1978[1852]:595).

6 Individuals who originate (or perpetuate) adaptations are not necessarily attempting to optimize their situation. As Herbert Simon (1976) has suggested, individuals are often content with merely a satisfactory, rather than an optimal, solution to their problems – that is, they engage in *satisficing* behavior.

7 The concept of adaptation implies no universal tendency toward human mastery that drives social evolution. This drive is generally lacking in preindustrial societies, where a "technological inertia" tends to prevail. The desire to save time and energy is a much better candidate for a universal human drive implicated in evolutionary processes (but as a mechanism preventing rather than promoting evolution).

8 Since there is no transcendent drive for mastery involved in social evolution, new social forms cannot be regarded as higher on some scale of adaptedness than old social forms. New forms are more reasonably regarded as different, not better, adaptations to changing conditions.

9 To the extent that a drive for mastery exists as a (culturally conditioned) motive for action in a particular society, it will tend to serve as a powerful mechanism of adaptation driving social evolution at that particular time and place. In other words, such a drive sets a goal to which the adaptational behaviors of particular individuals and groups are strongly directed. In modern capitalism, for example, capitalists display a drive for mastery that constitutes a major impulse to the expansion and evolution of the capitalist system.

10 The concept of adaptation is primarily *heuristic*. Not all social traits and patterns are adaptations, and thus they must be explained in other terms. But one great virtue of employing the concept of adaptation as a starting point is that "it impels us to do research that will reveal more about

the feature [under consideration]" (Futuyma, 1986:258). This research may eventually show that the feature in question is not an adaptation, but this in itself is an important outcome of beginning with the assumption of adaptation.

I think to specify and clarify the concept in this way, and to recommend its continued use as a key aspect of theories of social evolution, is highly preferable to the drastic recommendation of thinkers like Zeitlin and Giddens that the concept should be abandoned entirely. To retain the concept also has another advantage, although Giddens with his strong antipositivism would not recognize it as such. This advantage is that of contributing to the unity of science, an advantage also gained through the use of the very concept of evolution. Like the concept of evolution, the concept of adaptation has proved itself too fruitful in evolutionary biology, and too fruitful as well in the social sciences, to be abandoned altogether.

BIOLOGICAL AND SOCIAL EVOLUTION AS PROCESSES OF DIFFERENTIATION

The concept of differentiation is another concept that has been a major concern of both biological and social evolutionists. I have already taken a close look at the role this concept has played in various evolutionary theories, particularly those of Parsons and other functionalists. As noted in chapter 6, for Parsons differentiation is both a master process of social evolution and the key to understanding evolutionary transformations. I have been extremely critical of Parsons's use of this concept. I am willing to concede that there has been a general trend toward increasingly differentiated societies throughout human history, but dedifferentiation is also an important social process and many important social transformations have essentially nothing to do with differentiation. Moreover, as I pointed out in my criticisms of Carneiro's emphasis on increasing social complexity in chapter 7, it is by no means clear that differentiation is necessarily any more important than other features of social evolution, and it may well be less important. In short, differentiation has garnered much more attention from social evolutionists than it deserves.

On the other hand, differentiation does seem to be important enough as an evolutionary process to need some sort of systematic explanation. The most widely influential explanation has been that of the functionalists, who argue that increasing differentiation occurs because more structurally and functionally specialized societies are more efficient and better adapted than their less specialized counterparts. Parsons, of course, has produced the most grandiose version of this type of explanation. I have rejected such an explanation, but so far I have not produced an alternative to it. In this section I want to attempt this by looking first at what biologists have had to say about differentiation as an evolutionary process.

## *Differentiation as an Aspect of Biological Evolution*

Increasing complexity is widely regarded by biologists as an important evolutionary process, and it is often explained in terms of its adaptive significance. For example, Jeffrey Wicken claims that (1987:179):

Complexity, even where only weakly functional, provides structural possibilities for new levels of functionality. . . . [T]he axis of increasing complexity provides an important degree of freedom along which organizational coherence can be maintained and functionality developed.

A similar view has been taken by G. Ledyard Stebbins (1969, 1974), a botanist who was a major contributor to the modern synthetic theory of evolution. Stebbins points out that most evolutionary change in the biological world consists of modifications at the same level of organizational complexity, and that the shift from one level of organizational complexity to a higher one is relatively rare. Nevertheless, it has occurred and is said to be a most significant phenomenon. In order to explain this phenomenon, Stebbins formulates a principle that he calls the *principle of the conservation of organization.* This principle holds that "whenever a complex, organized structure or a complex biosynthetic pathway has become an essential adaptive unit of a successful group of organisms, the essential features of this unit are conserved in all of the evolutionary descendants of the group concerned" (1969:124–5). What this really means is that biological evolution places a floor on the degree of complexity that has already been achieved, and this floor creates possibilities for evolution to a higher level of complexity. These possibilities are occasionally realized because of the adaptive significance of more complex structures, that is, more complex structures permit populations of organisms to achieve greater adaptive radiation and evolutionary dominance.

Although Stebbins's explanation of differentiation in biological evolution appears to start out as one appealing to an efficient cause, it ends up looking like a classic teleological one: differentiation occurs because of the superior adaptive possibilities it offers. It is thus interesting that other evolutionary biologists have tried to explain the increasing complexity associated with biological evolution in strictly efficient–cause terms. Most notable in this regard is the work of Saunders and Ho (1976, 1981, 1984). Saunders and

Ho claim that complexity and fitness are independent evolutionary processes and have to be explained differently. Even if it could be shown that biological evolution led to increased fitness (a notion about which they are highly suspicious), they claim that such increasing fitness could not explain increasing complexity. Their alternative to this common sort of explanation is a disarmingly simple one: complexity increases in biological evolution because it is easier to produce than the reverse. As they put it, "The trend toward increased complexity . . . is a consequence of the tendency of a complex system to permit the addition of components more readily than their removal" (1984:136). It appears that Saunders and Ho mean to say that since biological evolution depends on genetic mutation, and since mutations are additions to the genetic store of an organism, then the complexity of organisms can naturally be expected to increase as mutation and evolution occur.[8]

A number of other evolutionary biologists take a position that is opposed to both Stebbins and to Saunders and Ho. These biologists assume that there is really nothing to explain because increasing complexity is not a significant characteristic of biological evolution. J. Wynne McCoy (1977), for example, suggests that, although organisms can be ordered in terms of their complexity, this order often is unrelated to the actual process of evolution. McCoy concedes that evolution does involve increasing complexity to some extent but claims that evolutionary processes that have nothing to do with complexity are at least as important.

George Williams (1966) has also seriously questioned the extent to which increasing complexity is associated with biological evolution. "Is man really more complex structurally than his piscine progenitor of Devonian time?" Williams asks (1966:42). He goes on to assert that, in a comparison of mammals and fishes, a mammal is more complex on some dimensions (such as brain structure), but that a fish is more complex on other dimensions (such as integumentary histology). Moreover, "What the verdict after a complete and objective comparison would be is uncertain" (1966:43).

Richard Levins and Richard Lewontin (1985), writing from a perspective they call "dialectical biology," take a similar view. They claim that the view that evolution is associated with a process of increasing complexity has no empirical basis. They suggest that the concept of complexity can be given different theoretical meanings, and that even if its meaning can be agreed on the difficulties of measuring it and assessing trends regarding it are overwhelming. In the end they reject the utility of the concept of increasing complexity altogether, claiming that it originates not in science but in bourgeois ideology.

*Explaining Social Differentiation*

It is risky for a sociologist to try to reconcile this battle of evolutionary biologists, but I think a reasonably good case can be made for the view that biological evolution over its entire course has involved a certain tendency toward increasing structural complexity (cf. Maynard Smith, 1988). Worms are, after all, more differentiated than protozoans, and humans more differentiated than worms. At least this would appear to be so if we look at the number of body parts, the level of specialization of these parts, and the complexity of the integration of the parts. How then to explain the tendency toward increasing differentiation? In this regard, Saunders and Ho may be onto something when they suggest that increasing complexity occurs in biological evolution because it is easier to produce than the reverse. Can Saunders and Ho's reasoning be applied to social differentiation? They think so (1976:382):

Societies also evolve . . . and the general pattern is the same. . . . [S]o long as changes occur in a relatively piecemeal and uncoordinated fashion, the complexity of a society (as measured by, say, the number of distinct occupations) is likely to increase. The present-day highly complex industrial society is not necessarily fitter or in any sense better than the simple agrarian society from which it evolved and to which some would like it to return, but this return is unlikely to happen other than by some cataclysmic or revolutionary upheaval.

Do societies, then, increase in complexity because it is "easier" for them to do so? In some sense, I think Saunders and Ho's notion helps to explain why some social evolution occurs and that, though their idea is astonishingly simple, it is far preferable to teleological and functionalist explanations. Societies, after all, generally grow in population, and population growth has been proposed by several social evolutionists, Carneiro and Harris being the leading examples, as a prime mover of social evolution. Societies need not become more complex simply because their numbers grow. We know from detailed anthropological studies that when land is sufficiently available, hunter-gatherer and horticultural societies will generally fission as a response to population growth, and that the new bands or villages will essentially be replicas of the old ones. These groups are expanding but not evolving. They begin to evolve when there are barriers to their further expansion, barriers that can be imposed by physical limitations (the lack of any suitable land to occupy) or by other social groups. Under such circumstances, these groups begin to evolve in a direction of greater complexity along a number of social dimensions. And they evolve in this direction because it is "easier," which really means because it is the only realistic option they have.

The process I am describing should sound familiar because it is basic to Carneiro's theory of the origin of chiefdoms and states. As we have seen, Carneiro regards increasing complexity as the most essential aspect of social evolution, and this notion forms part of his theory of political evolution. But Carneiro's actual explanation for the emergence of complex chiefdoms and yet more complex states is not a functionalist or teleological one. As we have seen, it is a conflict theory that views the formation of increasingly complex political structures as being linked most directly to warfare and political conquest, which in turn derive from population pressure within circumscribed physical environments.

Carneiro's theory can be used as a basis for arguing that complex political structures evolve not because they are more fit or adaptive, but because this is the way the process of political evolution works – because it is "easier" or "more logical" for it to work in this way than in any other way. But Carneiro himself is saying something more, and that is that *power* is a crucial aspect of the evolution of political complexity. Carneiro's argument about the evolutionary role of power has been extended to social differentiation more generally by Dietrich Rueschemeyer, and Rueschemeyer's argument takes us far beyond any possible application of Saunders and Ho's simple point.

Rueschemeyer's *Power and the Division of Labor* (1986) is an extended attack on functionalist explanations of social differentiation and an argument for the crucial importance of power in producing more complex social structures. Rueschemeyer's argument is essentially that the form and level of social complexity is largely a function of the interests of powerful individuals and groups. When the aims of powerful individuals and groups are better facilitated by more complex social structures, such structures tend to arise. The complex division of labor associated with industrial capitalist societies, for example, is adjusted to the needs of capitalists for productivity and profit. Likewise, the world-economy of which Wallerstein and others speak is an incredibly complex social system, and one that has resulted from the economic and political power of particular groups in particular nation-states.

While admitting that differentiation is a common aspect of evolutionary change, Rueschemeyer also insists that stagnation and actual dedifferentiation are important evolutionary processes. These too, he suggests, are to be explained primarily in terms of power relations. The technological stagnation so characteristic of many large-scale agrarian states, for example, has resulted primarily from a lack of interest of agrarian ruling elites in technological change. Devolutionary reversals of differentiation, such as the collapse of the Roman Empire, have occurred as a result of drastically changing balances-of-power relations.

It appears, then, that increasing differentiation does not occur because it promotes improvements in the functional efficiency of societies. To the extent that functional improvements occur, they contribute to the aims and interests of powerful social groups and frequently impose penalties and deprivations upon other groups. Whether this process is comparable to what occurs in biological evolution is uncertain. Biological evolution is, after all, rooted in a struggle for survival, and it is the stronger ("more powerful") that survive. Is it generally the case that the more complex organisms are the best suited for survival, and thus that differentiation and fitness are closely related? As we have seen, this kind of explanation is rejected by biologists like Saunders and Ho (who see fitness and differentiation as separate processes requiring different explanations), but favored by others like Stebbins (who sees leaps in complexity as contributing to the capacity of organisms for evolutionary radiation and dominance). Perhaps Stebbins's explanation of increasing biological complexity is really much the same kind of "power theory" in the biological realm as Rueschemeyer's is in the social realm. After all, both are really saying that differentiation and power are closely intertwined (although Rueschemeyer says that power leads to differentiation, whereas Stebbins produces a teleological explanation that says that increased differentiation results from the capacity to acquire superior power [dominance]). Moreover, it may be that the theories of Stebbins and of Saunders and Ho are not completely at odds. Although these theories disagree about the relationship between fitness and complexity, Stebbins's principle of the conservation of organization is seemingly compatible with Saunders and Ho's notion that complexity increases because it is easier to add components than to take them away.

Perhaps, though, all this is idle speculation. What business does a sociologist have entering into complex and technical debates among biologists that he all too imperfectly understands? And is it realistic to think that one can attempt to produce a coherent theory that would simultaneously explain differentiation in two quite different phenomenal realms? My remarks, then, are risky to say the least. But I have been motivated to make them because of my profound dissatisfaction with conventional explanations for evolutionary differentiation in human societies and, by implication, with what appear to be similar explanations for differentiation in the organic realm. I have also been motivated by a conception of the unity of science and by the principle of parsimony, and thus I have thought the risks worth taking. In the end, I think I have made a good case that social differentiation has everything to do with the constraints of human social life itself and with social power, and I suspect that the process of social differentiation is similar in these ways to the process of biological differentiation. I am reasonably confident about the former statement but, alas, much less confident about the latter.

EVOLUTIONARY PROGRESS

Of all the concepts that theories of biological and social evolution share, that of progress is in some ways the most important. At least it is the most fascinating. The question of whether evolutionary transformations are tantamount to some sort of betterment or improvement has been a fundamental one that has preoccupied both biological and social evolutionists for generations. Regarding this problem of progress, I hope to show that three major conclusions are warranted: first, that the leading evolutionists of both types have generally been progressivists; second, that the translation of evolutionary modification into progress has little justification; and finally, that the equation of evolution with progress springs from strongly entrenched cultural beliefs rather than from any objective examination of evolutionary trends themselves.

## The Concept of Progress in Biological Evolutionism

An historical assessment of the fate of the concept of progress among biological evolutionists appropriately begins with Darwin. Was Darwin a progressivist? The traditional answer to this question is that he was not. Ernst Mayr (1982), for example, argues that Darwin objected to any interpretation of evolution that saw it as based on some sort of intrinsic tendency to perfection. Stephen Jay Gould (1977) also views Darwin as opposing any association of progress and biological evolution. He makes much of Darwin's caveat to himself to "never say higher or lower" in regard to organisms, and he believes that Darwin's notion of fitness was a purely local and situational one that could not be used to characterize species over the long term.

In recent years, though, the tide has turned against this traditional interpretation. Elliott Sober claims that Darwin never did totally proscribe the notion of progress, and indeed that he "was very interested in finding a way to characterize progress" (1984:172). He suggests that Darwin's attitude was one of caution, not of rejection. Other interpreters of Darwin have gone further. Robert Richards (1988) claims that Darwin held such a strong belief in progress that he "crafted natural selection as an instrument to manufacture biological progress and moral perfection" (1988:131). In opposition to the traditional view that Darwin and Spencer were miles apart in their thinking about progress, Richards claims that they were actually strikingly similar. To support his interpretation, Richards quotes liberally from various of Darwin's works, especially his early notebooks but also from

*Origin.* Richards is able to produce a large number of passages in which Darwin clearly seems to be arguing for a general process of improvement with the evolution of life forms.

Michael Ruse (1988) takes a similar view, which he openly confesses is a complete reversal of his earlier view of Darwin. Ruse now claims that it is foolish to believe that Darwin was anything but a progressivist, for he adhered to a doctrine of progress just as fervently as did his predecessors and contemporaries. Ruse produces fewer quotes to bolster his case than does Richards, but he places great reliance on the closing lines of *Origin.* Here Darwin says (1964[1859]:490; quoted in Ruse, 1988:103):

Thus, from the war of nature, from famine and death, the most exalted object which we are capable of conceiving, namely, the production of the higher animals, directly follows. There is grandeur in this view of life, with its several powers, having been originally breathed into a few forms or into one; and that, whilst this planet has gone cycling on according to the fixed law of gravity, from so simple a beginning endless forms most beautiful and most wonderful have been, and are being, evolved.

My own reading of *Origin* puts me in complete sympathy with Richards, Ruse, and others who claim Darwin as a progressivist. Darwin may have warned against using the words higher and lower, but he ignored his own advice again and again. These words appear repeatedly throughout *Origin,* and there are numerous passages in which Darwin speaks about the improvement of life forms. In some cases the kind of improvement he has in mind may be of a purely local and situational type, but in other cases it seems clear that he is referring to an improvement of a more general, long-term sort. In addition, he frequently uses the word progress, and on more than one occasion claims that improvement and progress result from the growing complexity and diversification of organisms. In addition to the closing lines of *Origin,* there are many other passages in this book that are extremely telling about Darwin's position. To avoid overburdening the reader, let me quote just three of them here:

in one particular sense the more recent forms must, on my theory, be higher than the more ancient; for each new species is formed by having had some advantage in the struggle for life over other and preceding forms. If under a nearly similar climate, the eocene inhabitants of one quarter of the world were put into competition with the existing inhabitants of the same or some other quarter, the eocene fauna or flora would certainly be beaten and exterminated (1964[1859]:337).

The inhabitants of each successive period in the world's history have beaten their predecessors in the race for life, and are, in so far, higher in the scale of nature; and this may account for that vague yet ill-defined sentiment, felt by many paleontologists, that organisation on the whole has progressed (1964[1859]:345).

And as natural selection works solely by and for the good of each being, all corporeal and mental endowments will tend to progress towards perfection (1964[1859]:489).

On the basis of such statements, it is perfectly reasonable to believe that Darwin was a committed progressivist and that Richards and Ruse are right to align him with the general progressivist tenor of his time.

Upon moving to the next major phase in the development of evolutionary biology – the modern synthetic theory that emerged in the 1930s and 1940s – we find the same picture, for the leading scholars who fashioned this theory were progressivists one and all (cf. Ruse, 1988). It would be hard to find a more fervent progressivist than Julian Huxley (1953, 1962). Huxley sees progress as a general characteristic of the whole course of biological evolution. For him, this progress mainly involves the production of organisms that are more highly specialized and differentiated. More differentiated organisms function more efficiently and have a greater independence of the environment. The greatest improvements in biological evolution have occurred with respect to the nervous system, and these have been carried to their highest level in humans. Huxley sometimes writes as if he thinks that humans have been the aim and goal of evolution.

Stebbins (1969, 1974) has a progressivist view of biological evolution that is similar to Huxley's, though less extreme. Recall that Stebbins views the occasional transition to a higher level of organizational complexity as occurring because of its adaptive possibilities. This is certainly a notion of progress, because more complex and internally diversified organisms are being judged as superior to others in their capacity for dominance and further evolutionary advance.

Another leading architect of the modern synthesis, George Gaylord Simpson (1949), may also be regarded as a progressivist, although of a rather weak sort. Simpson lists several criteria that have been suggested at one time or another as indicators of progress. One of these is Huxley's and Stebbins's notion of complexity. Simpson suggests that this is a poor criterion for marking biological progress because increasing complexity is only crudely correlated with the actual course of evolution. Moreover, "within this broad picture correlation of complication and progress becomes quite irrelevant as regards particular cases. It would be a brave anatomist who would attempt to prove that Recent man is more complicated than a Devonian ostracoderm" (1949:253). Another commonly proposed criterion for progress is that of dominance, but Simpson is suspicious of this as well. The reason is that several different phyla of organisms can be dominant at the same time, each in their own particular sphere. Simpson ends up suggesting that there is only one truly adequate criterion of biological progress: the expansion of life. We can say biological progress has been occurring, he believes, because throughout biological history there has been a general tendency for life to expand and fill up all the livable environments on the earth.

Francisco Ayala (1974) takes a view very similar to Simpson's. Like Simpson, he believes that the most reliable criterion for marking biological progress involves the expansion of life. For Ayala, this means four things: expansion in the number of kinds of organisms; expansion of the total number of individual organisms of all kinds; expansion of the total bulk of living matter; and expansion in the total rate of energy flow. Ayala believes that the expansion of life in these four ways is a good thing because life itself is a good thing; hence more of it is better than less of it. (It should not escape attention that this criterion for progress is the biological equivalent of Childe's and White's criterion for social progress). To his credit, Ayala does not pretend that this criterion of progress is an objective one, and he frankly notes that any criterion anyone could ever produce would have to be based on their particular values.

It is obvious that the belief in biological progress is a common one among evolutionary biologists.[9] Yet even if the majority of evolutionary biologists hold to progress to at least some extent, there are some important dissenting voices. No one has done more to attack the notion that biological evolution has produced progress than George Williams (1966). Williams examines several commonly proposed criteria for progress and finds them all wanting. Williams's discussions of three of these criteria deserve special mention here. In regard to the criterion of increasing complexity, we have already seen that Williams is suspicious that firm statements can be made to the effect that complexity increases in any regular way in biological evolution. A second criterion is the accumulation of genetic information. Williams doubts that evolution has been associated with any systematic increase in the content of genetic information. Rather, what we see is "a history of substitutions and qualitative changes in the germ plasm, not an increase in its total content" (1966:42). Finally, and most importantly, Williams notes that improvement in adaptation is often proposed as a criterion of progress. This criterion, though, flounders in the face of enormous evidence that animal species generally regarded as "lower" or "less advanced" often have exceptional adaptive capacities. These capacities often equal or exceed the adaptive capacities of animals regarded as "higher" or "more advanced." Evolution has involved, Williams claims, largely a substitution of one type of adaptation for another, not some sort of steady accumulation of adaptive capacity.

Levins and Lewontin (1985) have also attacked the concept of biological progress. As they note, no evolutionary trend can be regarded as progressive except in terms of some underlying theory of value. Since there is no way to define and measure progress objectively, biological evolutionists who believe in progress do so simply because of a hidden cultural predisposition.

Gould goes even further in asserting that the concept of biological progress "is a noxious, culturally imbedded, untestable, nonoperational, intractable idea that must be replaced" (1988:319).[10]

## Progressivism and Antiprogressivism in Social Evolutionism

If the prevalence of progressivist views among biological evolutionists seems surprising, the same level of commitment to progressivism among evolutionary social theorists is not news at all. Since we have already looked at the views of leading social evolutionists on the problem of progress, only a brief recapitulation is necessary.

The classical evolutionists were, of course, strong progressivists. They were not the untempered advocates of progress they have commonly been made out to be, but they were firm believers in progress nonetheless. I have in mind mainly Spencer, Morgan, and Tylor, but Marx and Engels were no exceptions. These last two thinkers obviously had a different evaluation of the society in which they lived than did the other three, as well as a very different conception of how it had gotten to be what it was, but the nineteenth-century current of progressivism certainly affected them greatly.

When we turn to the major figures of the evolutionary revival, we again encounter progressivist thinking. Steward formally dissociated the concepts of evolution and progress, and thus it would be difficult to think of him as a progressivist. But Childe and White clearly were, and in much the same manner. Both linked social progress to technological change by arguing that more advanced technologies permitted larger numbers of people to survive. Their Marxist leanings also taught them that technological changes were associated with increases in class struggle and in oppression and exploitation, but their recognition of these outcomes never undermined their formal progressivist views. They seemed to believe that, on balance, social evolution produced overall improvements in the human condition.

The students and followers of Childe and White have generally been progressivists. This is true of the early Sahlins, and especially of Service and Lenski. Service's theory of the origin of the state is a functionalist one that assumes increasing benefits to society as a whole with the rise of the state. Lenski's evolutionism is permeated by a progressivism, and progress for him is linked to both technological advance and increasing social differentiation. Lenski claims that his use of the word progress contains no moral connotations, but in chapter 7 I suggested that he had smuggled in a conception of progress as moral improvement.

The most extreme progressivist among contemporary social evolutionists is clearly Parsons who, of course, links progress to increased social differentiation. Parsons is not only an extreme progressivist, but his conception of progress is closely intertwined with a developmentalism. For him, there exists some sort of inner dynamic to human social life that produces increasingly improved social arrangements.

There seems to be only one major antiprogressivist among contemporary social evolutionists, and that of course is Marvin Harris. As we saw in the last chapter, for Harris much of human history over the past 10,000 years has been a record of regression rather than progress. Moreover, the very nature of the most powerful constraints that operate on human societies has made it difficult for humans in most societies to do much more than struggle vigorously to keep the quality of life from getting worse.

### Progress and its Partisans

What has motivated the majority of evolutionists in both biology and the social sciences to embrace the concept of progress, and sometimes fervently so? And, whatever the origin of this belief, can it be justified?

Taking the second question first, my answer is, no, the belief in progress cannot be justified. On the biological side, some of the arguments presented in defense of progress seem downright silly, others highly dubious. For example, the criterion of progress proposed by Simpson and Ayala – that of the sheer expansion of life itself – is an entirely subjective criterion that is completely meaningless apart from Simpson's and Ayala's values. Simpson and Ayala may themselves delight in the abundance and variety of life, and so may many other persons, but the subjective preferences of particular human beings have no bearing on the value of the expansion of life *as a biological process*. Is the expansion of life a good thing or a bad thing? Some biologists may say that it is a good thing, and therefore want to call it progress, but I would think that the truly significant question would be whether it is a good thing or a bad thing in some sort of objective biological sense (whatever that might mean). Since the answer given by Simpson and Ayala has nothing to do with objective biological considerations, their answer is essentially beside the point.

When we turn to progressivist views that come closer to being based on objective biological considerations, we find views that can be scientifically (rather than axiologically) judged, but these views also seem wanting. Some biologists propose a species' evolutionary dominance as an indication of its progress, others its level of complexity, and some link these together. But, as we have seen, species at several different phylogenetic levels may all be dominant at any given geological time, each in their own ways and their own spheres. Thus, dominance bears no clear relation to evolutionary grade or to any presumed degree of biological progress. Furthermore, although there does seem to be a correspondence between an organism's level of organizational complexity and its position in the phylogenetic scheme, this correspondence is only rough and it is by no means clear that species have greater adaptive capacity precisely because they are more complex.

In the final analysis, I think that Williams has pointed to the fact that most convincingly undermines the idea that biological evolution is generally progressive: ancient and "lower" organisms continue to survive and thrive alongside the more recent and "advanced" ones. New adaptations emerge and are, strictly speaking, advantageous over the ones they replace. But such advantage is local and situational, not general and cumulative. Insects are more numerous than any other kind of animal life on earth, and rats have enormous adaptive capacity, including the kind of adaptive flexibility so prized by many biological progressivists. And what about humans, the crowning achievement of biological progress for Huxley? In what nonaxiological sense do they have greater adaptive capacity than, say, insects, rats, or sharks?

I think that the kind of reasoning Williams applies to biological evolution applies precisely to its sociocultural counterpart (cf. Granovetter, 1979). Horticulture is not a superior adaptation to hunting and gathering in any absolute sense, and many hunter-gatherer societies are known actively to resist becoming horticulturalists (M. Cohen, 1977). Hunting and gathering has numerous advantages over horticulture (cf. Sahlins, 1972:chapter 1), and the shift from hunting and gathering to horticulture has tended to occur only under specific local and situational conditions, such as population pressure and environmental degradation. Moreover, slash-and-burn cultivation is not absolutely less efficient than cultivation with plows and draft animals. It is much more efficient in saving labor costs, which is undoubtedly a major reason why it has persisted in some parts of the world as long as it has, including some regions of Sweden as late as the nineteenth century (Boserup, 1965). Slash-and-burn cultivation *is* inefficient and adaptively inferior when land is scarce. Under these conditions, the transition to plow agriculture may be made because it allows available land to be used more productively (Boserup, 1965). And thus, the adaptive advantage of plow agriculture over slash-and-burn cultivation is also a purely local and situational one. To take one final example, industrial capitalism is not adaptively superior in any absolute sense to any mode of production that has preceded it. It has enormous adaptive significance for the capitalist classes that control it, as well as for the standard of living it can produce for the majority of the citizens who live within it. But it imposes enormous costs, both in terms of the depletion of natural resources and the direct or indirect exploitation, through the world capitalist economy, of much of the world's population. Because of these features, its survival as a form of social life may be very short lived (cf. Wallerstein, 1983, 1984a,b).

This kind of reasoning can be extended indefinitely, but I trust the point is established. The transition from one major stage of social evolution to another is not some sort of steady improvement in the adaptive capacity of societies, as Parsons would have it, nor even a maintenance of the quality of life for a majority of the world's population. As Harris has documented in detail, much of the history of human societies is a history of regression that people have forced upon them by powerful material constraints. It would be difficult to argue that a majority of the world's population is better off today than the average hunter-gatherer was, say, 15,000 years ago. Most people alive today are poor Third World peasants or urban workers, and they are generally worse off than ancient hunter-gatherers with respect to most of the relevant dimensions of human life (cf. Wallerstein, 1983; Sanderson, 1988:chapter 21). The evolutionary changes that human societies have undergone have largely been adaptations, but they have not been adaptive in any absolute or cumulative sense, at least not for most of the participants.[11]

If there is so much reason to be suspicious of progressivist evolutionary views, why have they been so common? Gould (1988) and Levins and Lewontin (1985) have insisted that biological progressivism is rooted in ideology rather than science, specifically in the cultural beliefs in progress so deeply entrenched in Western societies. I think they are entirely correct, and that their argument applies *a fortiori* to the prevalence of progressivist views among social evolutionists. In the heyday of old-fashioned positivism it was thought that science was a realm of existence sealed off from the larger social world in terms of the content of its ideas. Scientists were dispassionate seekers of the truth, and their concepts and theories were derived from processes and activities internal to science itself. In the last two or three decades (mainly since Thomas Kuhn [1962] wrote his famous book on scientific revolutions), we have learned better. We have learned that science is deeply affected by its surrounding social and cultural milieu, and that scientists frequently have nonscientific reasons for accepting and rejecting concepts and theories (cf. Laudan, 1977). The progressivism so characteristic of evolutionary theories in biology and the social sciences is probably one of the best examples available of the intrusion of historically and culturally specific beliefs and values into scientific theorizing. The belief in progress, then, does not spring from any objective analysis of evolutionary trends, but rather involves imposing a cultural mindset on those trends. Progress is not in the data of evolution themselves, but in the eye of the beholder of these data.

CONCLUSIONS

It is doubtful that most social scientists, evolutionists and antievolutionists included, have more than a rough conception of what evolutionary biologists are up to, but I hope to have shown that a careful exploration of biological evolutionism has much to teach us. At the very least, it is comforting to learn that biological evolutionists carry on many of the same debates and controversies that have characterized social evolutionists, and at much the same level of intensity. But more importantly, social evolutionists can gain considerable insight from reading the literature in evolutionary biology. They can learn, for example, that the difficulties associated with the concept of adaptation can be overcome so that it can be employed as a fruitful analytical tool; that theories that make differentiation the *sine qua non* of social evolution cannot easily justify their efforts by any appeal to what evolutionary biologists have said about differentiation as a bioevolutionary process; and that their own desire to extract progress from the evolutionary record is replicated in evolutionary biology, even though this desire is extremely difficult to justify and springs more from extrascientific than from scientific considerations. To my mind, learning these things is worth the effort it takes to comprehend an entirely different discipline.

Yet social evolutionists must tread carefully, and they must resist any temptation to make evolutionary biology a general model for their own work. As we saw early in this chapter, theories of social evolution that start with assumptions drawn from evolutionary biology may be useful, but they are also very limited. Much of social evolution can be characterized as a process of natural selection, but natural selection as a social process is different in some crucial respects from natural selection as a biological process. Genetic mutation, for instance, has no strict equivalence in social life. Nor does genetic drift have any close sociocultural counterpart. Although natural selection models of sociocultural evolution can produce insight, one of their most significant weaknesses is an inability to account for the origins of the innovations that can be spread by natural selection. Thus they leave us dangling with respect to what we most want to know.

The problems generated by employing natural selection models of social evolution become more severe when natural selection is seen as operating simultaneously on biological as well as sociocultural traits. If carried to extremes, we end up with sociobiology in disguise, and thus with all the problems associated with that approach to social life. But even if carried out more moderately, the extent to which such an approach produces truly interesting and valuable insights about the process of sociocultural evolution is very much in doubt. Coevolutionary theories seldom focus on the kinds of long-term social transformations that genuinely interest social evolutionists, and when they do their conclusions seem less than scintillating.

The unity of science requires that social evolutionists take seriously the agendas of biological evolutionists. But we must not forget that social evolutionists have their own agendas, and that these only partially overlap those of their biological counterparts. For example, many evolutionary biologists have noted that the most common bioevolutionary process is cladogenesis, or the adaptive radiation of species at approximately the same phylogenetic level (Sahlins called this specific evolution). Anagenesis (Sahlins's general evolution), the leap of organisms to radically new phylogenetic levels, is a rare occurrence, and therefore most evolutionary biologists spend most of their time studying adaptive radiation rather than general evolutionary trends. But social evolutionists' agenda in this regard is quite different, for it is general rather than specific evolution that has been their predominant concern. Indeed, almost the definition of a social evolutionist is someone who is attempting to identify and explain general directional trends in history. For its entire history, social evolutionism has developed largely independent of evolutionary biology, and I suspect it will continue to do so into the future. The former can benefit from greater knowledge of the latter, but there are definite limitations on the extent of this benefit.

## NOTES

1 The same criticism can be made in principle of the theories of Campbell and Cavalli-Sforza and Feldman. The latter frequently trivialize important phenomena. Their discussion of the demographic transition, for example, concentrates on the processes by which changing fertility behavior is propagated, but they basically ignore the whole problem of what motivates people to change their fertility behavior in the first place.

2 This highly negative conclusion about Lumsden and Wilson should not be taken to imply a complete rejection of the claims of sociobiology. Indeed, I think Lumsden and Wilson are right to suggest a strong biological basis to human cultural phenomena like incest avoidance, and sociobiology may have some contribution to make in identifying biological foundations to other features of human behavior (for elaboration of this point see Sanderson, 1988:chapters 2, 15, and 16). But as a theory of long-term social evolution, neither traditional sociobiology nor its coevolutionary cousin has much to offer.

3 Another major example concerns what Boyd and Richerson call the *runaway process*, which is a possible outcome of indirectly biased transmission. For instance, if people are using high-status individuals as models for their own selection of cultural variants, then a spiraling process of status emulation can result. This process can lead to exaggerated behaviors that are highly maladaptive in the long run. Boyd and Richerson liken this process to the bioevolutionary process of sexual selection, such as is exemplified by the elaborate plumage of peacocks.

4 Another major attack on the concept of adaptation has recently been made by Hallpike (1986), who perpetuates many of the same misconceptions about the concept as Giddens. He claims, for instance, that it is inherently functionalist and that it implies a universal human tendency toward mastery. He also mistakenly believes that the

concept implies an adaptedness of outcome, and that this outcome will tend to be optimal. In contrast to Giddens, however, Hallpike suggests that the concept of adaptation should not be abandoned entirely. Even though it has no application to primitive societies (where the "survival of the mediocre" obtains), it does apply to more advanced ones, because "functional and adaptive efficiency is actually an emergent property of society" (1986:122). Such misconceived views lead Hallpike to the development of a version of evolutionism notable for its functionalist and idealist premises and its remarkable ethnocentrism – a version, in other words, strikingly like Parsonian evolutionism.

On the more positive side, Hallpike does suggest several important criteria for appropriate use of the concept of adaptation, some of which correspond to criteria I will set forth (cf. Hallpike, 1986:97).

5 However, there is some evidence that White may not have always believed this. For example, he does not explain the Neolithic Revolution as resulting from the invention or discovery of the techniques of domestication, but rather from an ecological disequilibrium that compelled hunter-gatherers to change their mode of production. White tells us that pre-Neolithic hunter-gatherers already had acquired knowledge regarding domestication but failed to put this knowledge to use. Thus he could hardly have believed unreservedly in a universal human desire for mastery.

6 Sahlins (1972) has now strongly repudiated this view and takes the position that such repudiation necessitates a rejection of any sort of evolutionism.

7 See James Coleman's (1986) development of a similar point.

8 John Maynard Smith takes a similar view. As he comments, "since the first living things were necessarily simple, it is not surprising that the most complex things alive today are more complex than their first progenitors" (1988:221).

9 Ruse (1988) has traced evolutionary biologists' views about progress right up to the present. He claims that three well-known living evolutionary biologists – E. O. Wilson, Richard Dawkins, and Stephen Jay Gould – are also progressivists. (He obviously sees Gould as a "closet progressivist." I strongly agree with him about Wilson, am inclined to agree about Dawkins, but have substantial doubts with respect to Gould.) Clearly, the belief in progress is a dominant theme in the entire history of evolutionary biology.

10 Antiprogressivist views (or at least views skeptical of progress) are also evident in the essays by Hull, Provine, Ruse, Maynard Smith, and Wiley in Nitecki (1988).

11 I do not mean to imply that the notion of progress has no application whatever to the evolutionary history of human societies. It can be applied in a limited way to some evolutionary developments, such as the expansion of human knowledge, or the creation of possibilities in some societies for at least some individuals to realize their human potential. But such developments cannot be called progressive apart from a specific axiology, and even then they are associated with a range of negative consequences and thus are not an unmixed good.

APPENDIX
THE THEORY OF PUNCTUATED EQUILIBRIA: A MODEL FOR SOCIAL EVOLUTION?

In the last 15 years a fundamental form of rethinking has been going on within evolutionary biology. There have been challenges to some aspects of the currently reigning modern synthetic (or neo-Darwinist) paradigm, especially to its emphasis on biological evolution as a slow and gradual process. This view of "phyletic gradualism," which can be traced back to Darwin, has been attacked by a number of evolutionary biologists, but most prominently by Niles Eldredge and Stephen Jay Gould (1972; Gould and Eldredge, 1977; cf. Stanley, 1979). Eldredge and Gould have attempted to replace the gradualist model with what they call a "punctuated equilibria" model. This model assumes that evolutionary changes have been sudden and rapid rather than gradual and slow. Eldredge and Gould suggest that evolutionary stasis rather than change is what is primarily observed in the fossil record, and that long periods of stasis are interrupted every so often by sudden and rapid transformations in which old taxa are converted into new taxa.

In a recent assessment of social evolutionary theories, Randall Collins (1988) has suggested that the model of punctuated equilibria may be a much better model for social evolution than a gradualist model. As he tells us, "Historically, major changes in societies have often occurred 'catastrophically' rather than gradually. Not only revolutions but even more importantly, wars and conflict in general have played a major part in affecting the form of the state, the economy, religion and culture, the family, and other social institutions" (1988:34).

This claim seems to be either wrong or strongly overstated. In the first place, the theory of punctuated equilibria is far more controversial among evolutionary biologists than Collins appears to realize. The majority of evolutionary biologists either reject it outright, or suggest that it may explain only some aspects of the evolutionary record (cf. Stebbins and Ayala, 1981; Charlesworth et al., 1982; Futuyma, 1986). Those favoring the latter view thus plead for a theoretical pluralism rather than for a shift from gradualism to punctuationalism. It does indeed appear that the punctuationalist theory must be considered with caution. As the prominent evolutionary biologist Douglas Futuyma has noted (1986:404):

The data of the fossil record permit several interpretations. There is some debate, first of all, about whether some sequences display gradualism or stasis with punctuation. . . . That is, the distinction between gradual and punctuated change is not well defined. . . . Geologically 'instantaneous' events, in the eyes of a paleontologist, may take thousands of years – during which considerable change can occur which a population geneticist views as slow and gradual.

If there is this much uncertainty regarding the punctuationalist model among evolutionary biologists themselves, among whom it originated, then extreme caution would seem to be in order in considering its application to social evolution. Collins thinks that most social evolutionary events have been rapid transformations, but it is not clear what his conception of "rapid" is. Perhaps he has in mind the emergence of modern capitalism in Western Europe. But even though the changes characteristic of this evolutionary event have been massive and sudden when compared to most other evolutionary events, it is clear that this was a long transition that took place over hundreds of years. Western Europe was not feudal one year and capitalist the next. In fact, no historian or historical sociologist could possibly date this transition with any precision at all. Moreover, it has become increasingly apparent in recent years that the historical developments that paved the way for the feudal–capitalist transition themselves occurred over hundreds of years. It was once thought that the Middle Ages were a time of fundamental stasis, but we now know that Europe in AD 1400 was different in many fundamental respects from what it was in, say, AD 900. No stasis there, and yet were the of fundamental stasis, but we now know that Europe in 1400 was different in many fundamental respects from what it was in, say, 900. No stasis there, and yet were the changes rapid and sudden? Not by any historical account ever produced.

If we shift back to earlier times, the punctuationalist argument seems even more dubious. The Neolithic Revolution, for example, was, despite the name, anything but revolutionary in a temporal sense. Hunter-gatherers were not hunter-gatherers one year (or one decade, one century, or perhaps even one millennium) and agriculturalists the next. Archaeologists have now established that the transition to agriculture was a very long, slow, and gradual process. It was actually one in which hunter-gatherers experimented with various forms of domestication, then began to employ domesticates to supplement their foraging activities, and then gradually shifted the balance of their subsistence activities away from foraging to reliance on domesticated plant and animal species (cf. Harris, 1977, 1988; M. Cohen, 1977; Wenke, 1980). If ever there was a gradual social evolutionary process, this was it.

Let me make it clear, though, that I am not claiming that the punctuationalist model has no applicability to social evolution. Collins is partially right. The French Revolution, for instance, was a catastrophic event, as was the Bolshevik Revolution. My claim, rather, is that many important social evolutionary phenomena are indeed well described by a gradualist model, and thus that a theoretical pluralism on the question of the pace of evolutionary change is the most justified position. In any event, questions about the pace of change are better settled empirically by the concrete examination of particular cases, not by the *a priori* endorsement of one theory over another.

# 9

# Contemporary Antievolutionism

Evolutionary theories of human society are not fashionable among social scientists in the late twentieth century. Although major evolutionary theories continue to be developed, the voices of the antievolutionists are louder and stronger and are heard with more approval. At least this is the situation in sociology, where evolutionism is often assumed to be associated with repudiated doctrines of developmentalism and functionalism. In anthropology the intellectual climate is more receptive to evolutionism, though even there antievolutionary currents are strong (cf. Johnson and Earle, 1987:vii), and former evolutionists like Sahlins have come forth to confess their sins.

Three of the leading antievolutionists of the late twentieth century are Robert Nisbet (1969), Maurice Mandelbaum (1971), and Anthony Giddens (1981, 1984), many of whose objections to evolutionism we have already encountered. Close study of their work, and of that of other antievolutionary social scientists, suggests eight major criticisms that are currently advanced against social evolutionism. These criticisms and their principal advocates may be listed approximately as follows:

1 Evolutionary theories depend upon a developmentalist explanatory logic, a conception of causation that is illegitimate (Nisbet, Mandelbaum, Giddens).
2 Evolutionary theories have an endogenous bias in that they frequently fail to give proper attention to the role of external influences, such as cultural diffusion or war, in producing the changes that societies undergo (Nisbet, Mandelbaum).
3 Evolutionary theories are ahistorical and rely on an illegitimate methodological procedure known as the comparative method (Nisbet, Mandelbaum).
4 Evolutionary theories have a strong tendency to merge progression with progress, and thus convert statements about evolutionary stages of development into normative statements implying a betterment or improvement in societal functioning and the quality of social life (Giddens, R. Collins [1988]).
5 Evolutionary theories depend on a specious concept of adaptation (I. Zeitlin [1973], Giddens, C. R. Hallpike [1986]).

6  Evolutionary theories give no place to human agency, and thus conceive of history as taking place "without a subject" and "behind the backs" of its participants (Giddens).
7  Evolutionary theories engage in the fallacy of homological compression, which is the tendency to imagine a direct correspondence between stages of social evolution and stages in the development of the human personality (Giddens).
8  Evolutionary theories assert a directionality to historical change that does not exist (Nisbet, Mandelbaum, A. Smith [1973]).

This chapter systematically explores the nature of these criticisms and shows that they are either misconceived or highly exaggerated. Enough has already been said about the first, fourth, and fifth criticisms, so I will concentrate on the others. (The second and third criticisms have also been discussed previously, but a brief recapitulation and extension of my arguments may be helpful.)[1]

EVOLUTIONISM AND EXTERNAL INFLUENCES

In chapter 3 we encountered the claim of Boas and his followers that the classical evolutionists ignored the facts of diffusion, which in the words of Lowie "played havoc with any evolutionary scheme." As we noted, Leslie White demolished this claim with respect to the evolutionary theories of Morgan and Tylor (and by implication with respect to evolutionary theories in general). The classical evolutionists were not only well aware of the facts of diffusion, but had an explicit conception of how these facts could be squared with an evolutionary perspective. Diffusion was a highly selective process, they said, and societies accepted or rejected elements of other cultures according to their own needs and cultural outlooks. A society may be able, for example, to take from another what it would otherwise be forced to develop on its own.

Contemporary antievolutionists like Nisbet and Giddens are latter-day Boases who are convinced that all versions of evolutionism are committed to a doctrine of endogenism: a view that all essential change comes from within a society itself. Nisbet goes on to claim, against evolutionism, that "significant change is overwhelmingly the result of . . . factors inseparable from external events and intrusions" (1969:180). But like the Boasians earlier in this century, Nisbet and Giddens have set up a false dichotomy. It may well be the case that the most objectionable forms of contemporary evolutionism, such as Parsonian evolutionism, are largely endogenist. (Given the developmentalist structure of Parsonian evolutionism, what else would be expected?) It may even be the case that other less objectionable versions of contemporary evolutionism incline toward endogenism. But all of these more suitable versions of evolutionism give considerable weight to various kinds of external factors in evolutionary change. White and Lenski, for instance, explicitly recognize the role of external factors again and again. And in those versions of evolutionism that I have assessed as the very best (the theories of Carneiro and Harris), the role of external factors is considerable. In fact, Carneiro's theory of the origin of the state gives external factors major consideration. Carneiro does not conceive of social evolution as a process that goes on purely or mainly within a society as a self-contained evolving whole. On the contrary, political evolution is critically dependent upon intersocietal contact, mainly in the form of warfare and political conquest. If ever a theory was not an endogenous theory, Carneiro's is it. Yet this theory is evolutionary in all crucial senses of the term.

The claim, then, that evolutionary theories are flawed because they are endogenous theories will not hold up to careful examination. There is no inherent connection between an evolutionary perspective and an endogenist one.[2]

EVOLUTIONISM AND THE COMPARATIVE METHOD

Another objection to evolutionary theories that has continued to be raised is also one that was made famous by the Boasians. This is the claim that evolutionary theories rest upon an illegitimate methodological device, the comparative method. Boas himself made this claim, and it was widely repeated by his students. This methodological objection is a key element in Nisbet's rejection of evolutionary theories. Nisbet objects to the comparative method for the same basic reason the Boasians did: the belief that taxonomic schemes constructed out of cross-sectional data cannot legitimately be made to yield conclusions about actual historical change or process. As he puts it (1969:196–7):

Where in this series of asserted developmental steps is the process of change? The answer is plain. There is no change; only a succession of conditions . . . drawn from all possible periods of history and all possible areas of the earth, and then arranged in a series bearing as much relationship as possible to the actual historical series in the West but synchronized also with the logico-spatial series that inevitably yields the widest variation. What we have, in fact, in the so-called developmental series is a finely-graded, logically continuous series of "stills" as in a movie film. It is the eye – or rather, in this instance, the disposition to believe – that creates the illusion of actual development, growth, or change.

The answer to this objection was given in chapter 3 and need only be briefly recapitulated. True enough, the comparative method, which is indeed widespread among social evolutionists, depends upon a willingness to assume that a particular classification system that is not in itself historical corresponds well to what actually happened historically. But the employment of the method is justified on a number of counts. First, the same type of method has been widely used in the physical and biological sciences, and under conditions in which precisely the same degree of inference is required. Since it has produced intellectually satisfying and justifiable results in those sciences, there is no compelling reason why its application in the social sciences should be banned. Second, use of the method is often necessary because the actual observation of historical change over long periods of time is usually difficult, and in many instances impossible. Failure to use the method means that social evolutionists will be condemned to ignore huge quantities of ethnographic data, and will also be forced to try to explain world-historical social changes using the limited amounts of truly historical data available to them. Third, the inferences that are required in employing the method can be justified to the extent that evolutionary classification schemes constructed from cross-sectional data correspond well to independently derived schemes that are themselves historical – schemes produced by archaeologists and historians.[3] Fourth, caution is obviously called for in use of the comparative method, and any good method can be abused. But the level of caution recommended by the Boasians and contemporary antievolutionists like Nisbet is obviously inimical to intellectual progress in any field.

In conclusion, as I claimed in chapter 3, the comparative method is in principle sound and can appropriately be used by social evolutionists so long as certain considerations are made. The comparative method is a substitute for what would be a better method – the historical method – but is essential when the availability of historical data is limited.

## EVOLUTIONISM AND HUMAN AGENCY

An important objection to social evolutionary theories we have not considered thus far involves how such theories conceive the role of human subjects in historical change. Giddens has suggested that evolutionism is an extreme form of objectivism that gives no role whatever to humans as agents of history. Evolutionary theories see history as "subjectless" – as occurring "behind the backs" of its participants.

One of Giddens's most important contributions to recent social theory is his attempt to give the concept of human agency a central role. He faults social theories like functionalism and structuralism for having no concept of agency and for assuming that social systems have their own logic, one that the human participants therein can neither understand nor influence. Individuals are knowledgeable actors who act in the world in ways that shape it, and social theory must not only take this into account, but must make it a crucial assumption. Theories like phenomenology and ethnomethodology do so, he says, but in a much too extreme fashion. They end up committing the opposite error, that of seeing social life as the product of unconstrained human intentions. What both functionalism and structuralism on the one hand, and phenomenology and ethnomethodology on the other, fail to recognize is the "duality of structure": that social life is the outcome of the simultaneous operation of intention and constraint, which are recursively implicated in each other. Giddens, of course, has been attempting to develop a form of social theory – structuration theory – that explicitly gives the duality of structure center stage.

As we have seen, Giddens puts evolutionism into the same objectivist category as functionalism and structuralism, and faults it thereby. I think that Giddens is right for some versions of evolutionism. However, there is nothing inherent in evolutionism that makes it a form of objectivism, and I wish to argue that the very best versions of evolutionism are actually built on a notion of the duality of structure, although not in the very same way that Giddens conceives of this concept.

The evolutionary theories of Parsons and Leslie White may be taken as exemplifications of the most extreme objectivist forms of evolutionism. The entire corpus of Parsons's social theory rests upon a horrendously reified social system in which individual actors are but "carriers" or "bearers" of the properties of the system. This reified view of social life is thoroughly present, of course, in his evolutionism. It is societies that differentiate, adapt, and have identities of themselves. If ever an evolutionism was an extreme objectivism, Parsonian evolutionism is it.

In a sense much the same can be said of White's materialist version of evolutionism. As in the case of Parsons, White's evolutionism is really just a part of his more general social theory, and that social theory is resolutely objectivist and determinist. In many of the essays collected in *The Science of Culture* (1949b), White is at pains to show that culture has a logic of its own that determines the thoughts and beliefs of the individual participants in it. White's determinism, and its connection to his evolutionism, is nowhere more apparent than in his essay "Man's control over civilization: an anthropocentric illusion," the mere title of which tells you virtually all you need to know to understand his position. In this essay he says the following (1949b:358).

Man is wholly at the mercy of external forces, astronomic and geologic. . . .

And so it is with culture. Belief in our omnipotence has, as Durkheim says, always been a source of weakness to us. But we are now discovering the true nature of culture and we can in time reconcile ourselves to this extra-somatic order as we have to the astronomic, geologic, and meteorologic orders.

For White, then, humans are anything but knowledgeable agents whose actions create the world in which they live.

Since it would be tedious to carry out a detailed exegesis of all the major versions of social evolutionism on this matter, suffice it to say that most social evolutionary theories have probably tended toward this objectivist position, although in most cases not in such an extreme way. Yet there is one major version of evolutionism that, despite widespread assertions to the contrary, does not do so. This is Harris's evolutionary materialism. I believe that this version of evolutionism is completely consistent with Giddens's dictum that "human history is created by intentional activities but is not an intended project" (1984:27).

At first blush Harris's evolutionism appears to be a hard form of objectivism and determinism, and indeed it is usually thought of as such. After all, in *Cannibals and Kings* Harris tells us that, "In my opinion, free will and moral choice have had virtually no significant effect upon the directions taken thus far by evolving systems of social life" (1977:xii). But a careful look at Harris's main arguments will show that he is no objectivist who sees humans as mere "bearers" of cultural patterns that have their own autonomous logic. Consider, for instance, the fact that Harris is an individual rather than a group selectionist, a point emphasized in chapter 7. Sociocultural patterns emerge and are transformed according to choices made by individuals, and these choices, Harris believes, are made largely according to rational cost-benefit considerations. Yet these choices are not "free," because they are constrained by the nature of humans as biopsychological organisms and by the material conditions of human existence. What we end up with looks to me startlingly like a version of Giddens's duality of structure in which the extremes of voluntarism and determinism are simultaneously avoided. Indeed, as Harris declares (1979:60):

It is essential to the task of constructing cultural materialist theories that one be able to establish a link between the behavioral choices made by definite individuals and the aggregate responses of sociocultural systems. One must be able to show why one kind of behavioral option is more likely than another not in terms of abstract pushes, pulls, pressures, and other metaphysical "forces," but in terms of concrete biopsychological principles pertinent to the behavior of the individuals participating in the system.

In claiming that Harris's evolutionism is built upon a conception of the duality of structure, I do not mean to suggest that it is so in a way that would satisfy Giddens. Indeed, Harris's knowledgeable human agents who act in the world would not be nearly knowledgeable enough for Giddens. As critics of Giddens have often pointed out, his human agents have a surprising amount of freedom for a theorist who wants to avoid slanting social theory too far to the subjectivist side (cf. Callinicos, 1985.) My point is simply that Harris's evolutionism is in principle the kind of social theory that Giddens's claims we need (and I strongly agree with Giddens that we need such a theory). This being the case, evolutionism *per se* cannot be faulted as inherently prone to unacceptably objectivist and determinist forms of theorizing. Giddens has once again committed a version of the fallacy of composition – of assuming that what is true of some of the parts must be true of the whole.

### EVOLUTIONISM AND HUMAN PSYCHOLOGY

There is another criticism of evolutionary theories that I have encountered only in Giddens, although I suspect it is more widely shared by antievolutionists. This is the problem that Giddens refers to as *homological compression*, by which he means the tendency "to imagine that there is a homology between the stages of social evolution and the development of the individual personality" (1984:239). More specifically, it is often (1984:239–40):

supposed that small, oral cultures are distinguished by forms of cognition, affectivity or conduct found only at the relatively early stages of the development of the individual in more evolved societies. The level of complexity of societal organization, for instance, may be supposed to be mirrored by that of personality development.

Giddens admits that the tendency toward homological compression does not necessarily stem directly from evolutionism itself. However, since it is often associated with it, it is therefore a "danger" to which evolutionism is especially subject. Is Giddens correct? He certainly seems to be for at least some of the classical evolutionists, Spencer in particular, although it is extremely difficult to imagine such a difficulty being associated with the work of Marx and Engels. Among earlier social thinkers, the problem of homological compression is actually most strongly associated with the work of Lucien Lévy-Bruhl (1923), who is not generally thought of as a formulator of evolutionary theories (which is not to say that he was not some sort of evolutionist in his outlook). But Lévy-Bruhl's basic notion – that people in societies at simple levels of technology and social organization are characterized by "prelogical" forms of thinking – has been severely criticized and largely abandoned by modern social scientists, evolutionary theorists included. To some extent the problem of homological compression is found in Habermas's evolutionism, where Piaget's and Kohlberg's cognitive–developmental psychologies are used to develop a set of evolutionary stages. The problem is also found in Kohlberg's work itself. In some of his most recent work (Kohlberg, 1981), he has not only suggested that stages of moral thinking and of social evolution are closely related, but has actually implied that the shift to a new stage of moral thinking is a necessary basis for the transition to a later stage of social evolution. It might also be argued that Parsonian evolutionism has this kind of tendency, given Parsons's extreme ethnocentrism, idealism, and progressivism, but if so it is much less obvious.

But apart from these instances, I think it would be extremely difficult to locate a tendency toward homological compression in the other contemporary evolutionists we have explored in this book. It is certainly not found in the works of the students and followers of Childe, White, and Steward, and it is extremely dubious that it can be located in Childe, White, and Steward themselves. In fact, I am reasonably confident that all of these thinkers would strongly repudiate any connection between stages of social evolution and stages of the development of the individual personality. In the final analysis, then, the danger to which Giddens refers, while not nonexistent, is scarcely one to provoke much anxiety.

### EVOLUTIONISM AND DIRECTIONALITY

As noted in chapter 1, a crucial element of an evolutionary theory is the postulation of a certain degree of directionality to historical change. This is roughly equivalent to saying that evolutionary theories are those that discern and attempt to explain patterns of historical change that are common to a large number of societies. And it is a trump card in the suit of antievolutionists that history reveals no patterns of change, or at least no patterns of sufficient generality to justify the claims of social evolutionists. Robert Nisbet, for instance, claims that "long-run directionality tends to be in the beholder's eye, not in the materials themselves" (1969:284).

Nisbet is a latter-day historical particularist, and it is this particularism that is the guiding element in his onslaught against social evolutionism. Is long-run directionality merely in the eye of the beholder? Gerhard Lenski (1976) is incredulous at such a suggestion. He tries to turn the tables on Nisbet by suggesting that what we find in history depends largely on what we are looking for, and that if we are already convinced that something is not there then we will certainly not be able to find it. Regarding the presence or absence of long-term historical trends he writes the following (1976:554):

Even if one limits one's study to European history, the presence of long-term trends is clearly evident – trends that have endured for 500 years or more: growth in numbers, growth especially of urban populations, increasing division of labor, increasing monetization of the economy, growth of trade and commerce, shift in employment from primary to secondary to tertiary industries, increased production of goods and services, growth in the power of the state, and increased bureaucratization, to name but a few of the more obvious. Perhaps it should be added that these trends are by no means trivial matters. On the contrary, they constitute the foundation of what can only be described as a revolution in the conditions of human life.

If we shift our focus to precapitalist and preindustrial historical trends, then we find several major instances of parallel evolution. The Neolithic Revolution occurred independently in at least five different regions of the world at approximately the same time in human history, and this after some three million years in which humans lived as hunters and gatherers. This was an evolutionary trend of momentous significance (cf. Cohen, 1977), and its consequences for the societies that emerged from it were remarkably similar. Another great evolutionary trend was the origin of the state, which occurred several thousand years later in essentially the same regions that were the original centers of the transition to Neolithic communities. The parallels that can be identified in this process are truly remarkable (cf. Adams, 1966) and surely give the lie to the notion that long-run trends are merely in the eye of the beholder. The third great transformation in human history is the one that Lenski was referring to above: the transition from feudalism to capitalism. As the world-system and dependency theorists remind us, this transition has produced very uneven consequences in different regions of the world, but the expansion and evolution of the capitalist world-economy has certainly marked a directional trend if there ever was one. And in many ways this directional trend has continued many of the trends of the precapitalist and preindustrial era: expanding populations, growth of trade and commerce, concentration and centralization of political power, increase in social and economic inequalities, and so on.

If the notion of directionality is taken to refer to some sort of single master trend that alone summarizes all of human history, then it immediately loses its usefulness.[4] Lenski himself attempts to identify such a trend, which he refers to as growth in the store of information humans have available to them. And Parsons finds a single master trend in increasing differentiation.[5] But the notion of such a trend is too general, too abstract, to have much value. In using the notion of directionality, we must be on guard against the tendency toward a kind of simplistic unilinearism. This is a very real tendency to which the classical evolutionists were certainly subject, and toward which modern evolutionists like White, Lenski, and (especially) Parsons are also inclined. It has been said many times before, but it bears repeating that we must constantly be alert to the distinction between general and specific evolution or, in Harris's terminology, parallel, convergent, and divergent evolution. No one has done more in this regard than Harris himself, whose evolutionary studies give important weight to all these types of evolution.

I have no illusions, however, that these last remarks will satisfy committed historical particularists like Nisbet. With Lenski, I believe that such thinkers find no patterns in history because they don't want to find them. In this regard, consider the recent work of Michael Mann. In the first volume of his projected three-volume *The Sources of Social Power* (1986), Mann claims that an evolutionary view of world history has validity up through the Neolithic Revolution, but after that general social evolution comes to an end. From this point on, Mann becomes an avowed historical particularist in his analysis of world-historical social transformations. In analyzing the rise of civilization and the state, for example, he claims that, since there were "only" six instances in which such a social transformation occurred independently, this process cannot be represented in evolutionary terms. What a truly remarkable assertion this is. "Only" six instances?! To most anthropologists and archaeologists, six independent instances is of startling significance and can only be understood in evolutionary terms. Mann's refusal to see it that way – one wonders how many independent instances he would require in order to declare the transition to civilization and the state an evolutionary phenomenon – only seems to make sense if we assume that he has started out with particularist assumptions and is intent on proving them in the end.

But in closing this chapter let me say something in favor of the particularists. While I do not share their overall view of history, I do not wish to bar particularistic historical studies themselves from the court of evolutionism, broadly conceived. Social evolution involves transformations of markedly different levels of generality. In this regard, Harris calls our attention to (1968:645):

a continuum involving degrees of abstraction away from the description of specific cases.

At one end of this continuum there is the evolutionary transformation which is characterized by or known through one case. For example, one might want to consider the development of a four-caste apartheid system (Africans, Europeans, Coloreds, and Asians) as an evolutionary product peculiar to South Africa. . . .

On a slightly higher level of generality, we may note the evolutionary products characteristic of several societies within a single culture area. The peculiar Australian specialty involving eight marriage sections is an evolutionary product of the transformation of two- and four-section systems. . . .

Finally, there are the universal evolutionary products such as the nuclear family incest taboo or the belief in animism.

All of these categories can be expanded or contracted indefinitely in accordance with the amount of ethnographic detail which is required before we are willing to grant that two instances are the "same" or different. . . . By ignoring millions of trivial differences, in order to emphasize a few significant similarities, we arrive at such theoretically vital notions as egalitarian societies, state organization, feudalism, capitalism, or oriental despotism. Conversely, with a sufficiently intense historical-particularist mandate, we may prove to our satisfaction that the state of affairs in eleventh century France had no parallel anywhere else in Europe, much less in Japan or West Africa. The . . . failure . . . to grasp the epistemological issues which underly our judgments concerning evolutionarily significant similarities and differences goes a long way toward explaining the prolongation of . . . controversy beyond useful limits.

As Harris is suggesting, it is fruitless to argue that unique social transformations should not be called social evolution, and thus that evolutionists should not study them. What distinguishes an evolutionary perspective is not its refusal to recognize and appreciate the historically unique. Rather, it is its refusal to believe that the historically unique is of greater intellectual significance than the historically general. Evolutionists do not use their concern with the general to deny the particular. Particularists, however, *do* use the particular to deny the general, and it is this – not the existence or importance of the particular *per se* – that constitutes the rub for social evolutionists.[6]

NOTES

1 Nisbet's *Social Change and History* (1969), the best-known of the contemporary onslaughts against evolutionism, also contains numerous other criticisms of evolutionary theories. Nisbet asserts, for instance, that fixity is more common than change and thus that evolutionary theories start from the wrong assumption about what needs explaining; that evolutionary theories are inextricably linked to a metaphor of organismic growth; and that all evolutionary theories are essentially alike. These criticisms and others have been effectively answered by Lenski (1976), and they are so far wide of the mark that I do not wish to take up space to pursue them here. (Nisbet's most absurd suggestion is that evolutionary theories must be rejected because they cannot explain historical events like the New York Giants' winning the National League pennant in 1951. It is truly scandalous that anyone would think this could possibly constitute a valid objection to social evolutionism.) Although Nisbet is a scholar of the first rank, much of *Social Change and History* is a good example of sloppy thinking in the extreme.

2 Actually, the terms internal and external with respect to this whole debate are rather misleading, and proof once again that a false dichotomy has been created. As Christopher Chase-Dunn (personal communication) has suggested, the critical question is "internal or external *to what?*" Since the very best evolutionary theories talk about evolving systems at a variety of different levels (i.e., individuals, groups, societies, constellations of societies), the whole notion of "internal versus external factors" becomes rather meaningless.

3 This is in fact generally the case. The great expansion of archaeology in recent decades has not only vindicated the use of the comparative method, but has actually rendered it less essential. As Lenski (1976) points out, much evolutionary theorizing now rests on a firm bedrock of prehistorical data.

4 Even to the extent that we can identify overall trends in human history, the concept of directionality need not be limited in its application to such general trends. The concept can be used in a more restricted way to refer to processes that occur within particular phases of the entire flow of history. In this sense one might more intelligently speak of "directionalities" rather than "directionality." But to do so does not vitiate a claim to be practicing evolutionism.

An excellent example of what I have in mind is the work of Immanuel Wallerstein (1974, 1980, 1989). Wallerstein is engaged in an evolutionary analysis of one phase of history: the emergence and expansion of modern capitalism since the sixteenth century. He has no particular interest in the flow of history before this time, and there is no evidence that he views the evolution of capitalism as the continuation of evolutionary trends in operation for centuries or millennia before its rise (in fact, there is considerable evidence that he sees capitalism as a phenomenon that evolves in its own unique way). But Wallerstein's analysis is evolutionary because he is engaged in tracing the overall directionality of the capitalist world-system as a whole.

What is the nature of this directionality? Wallerstein (1984a) tells us that there are three main trends involved: increasing mechanization of production, increasing commodification of the factors of production, and increasing contractualization of economic relationships. These trends are part of a "deepening" of capitalist development that derives from the accumulationist motivations of capitalist entre-preneurs.

The evolution of the world-economy is said to have proceeded thus far through four basic stages. The first stage (approximately 1450–1640) involved the emergence of capitalism from the crisis of feudalism and its initial expansion to cover significant portions of the globe. The second stage (roughly 1640–1750) was a stage of the "consolidation" of the world-system. The third stage (about 1750–1917) marked the eruption of industrial capitalism and was a period of renewed expansion of the world-economy, which by the end of this period covered essentially the entire globe. .The fourth (final?) stage began with the Russian Revolution, and is a stage of the "consolidation" of industrial capitalism.

It is obvious that Wallerstein has embraced what might be called Marx's "evolutionary eschatology" (see especially Wallerstein, 1984b). Like Marx, Wall-erstein is convinced that capitalism is essentially evil, that it is rife with contradictions that will tear it apart in the end, and that when it collapses it will lead to something more humane. But for Wallerstein all of this occurs on a world, rather than a national, scale. The gap between core and periphery continues to widen, and this spawns "antisystemic movements" that increasingly threaten the continued viability of the system. Within the next 100–150 years capitalism will be replaced by, most likely, a socialist world-government. Marx thus turns out in the end to have been basically right. It is just that he had his units of analysis mixed up, and so he failed to gauge accurately the timing of the transition from capitalism to socialism.

It will no doubt be startling to many to think of Wallerstein as an evolutionist. His painstakingly detailed focus on the historically concrete, and his continual condemnation of modernization theory, seem to suggest something quite different. And hasn't Wallerstein repeatedly cited the basic argument of Nisbet's *Social Change and History* with strong approval? But people have been thrown off the track about Wallerstein for at least two fundamental reasons. First, they falsely assume an incompatibility between a focus on historical concreteness and an evolutionary perspective (see note 5). Second, Wallerstein's opposition to modernization theory (as well as to rigid versions of Marxist evolutionism) bespeaks an antagonism only to one particular version of evolutionism, not to evolutionism *per se*. It is an opposition to rigid unilinear versions of evolutionism that make individual societies or nation-states the unit that is doing the evolving. As he has said, "What thus distinguishes the developmentalist and the world-system perspective is not . . . evolutionism versus something else (*since both are essentially evolutionary*)" (1979:54; emphasis added).

5  Ironically, despite his vehement antievolutionism, Anthony Giddens has also identified such a trend. In his *A Contemporary Critique of Historical Materialism* (1981), Giddens tries to capture the flow of human history in terms of a notion of increasing *time–space distanciation*. Time–space distanciation involves the "stretching" of social institutions through time and space. This means, in essence, that societies with high time–space distanciation are spread over larger geographical areas and have developed greater capacities for concentrating power and storing information.

Giddens distinguishes three basic forms of human society in terms of their level of time–space distanciation. Tribal societies are non-class-divided societies regulated by kinship and the power of tradition. Class-divided societies are typified by the agrarian civilizations. In them social class divisions exist, but class is not the central organizational principle of the society. Class societies, which have existed only since the advent of modern capitalism, have class divisions, and these divisions are the central organizing feature of the society.

As we move from tribal to class-divided to class societies, the level of time–space distanciation increases. Giddens insists, however, that the relationship between these types of society is not an evolutionary one. Rather, the societies relate in terms of what he calls time–space edges. The societies do not represent a temporal progression throughout history, for all coexist at the same time. Class-divided societies did not replace tribal ones entirely, nor have class societies entirely displaced class-divided societies.

As for the movement from one type of society to another, Giddens says that this has occurred through what he refers to as episodic transitions, which are "processes of social change which have a definite direction and form, analysed through comparative research, in which a major transition takes place whereby one type of society is transformed into another" (1981:82). While this definition sounds amazingly like one for the word "evolution," Giddens insists that no evolutionary notion is implied. There is nothing inevitable about such transitions, he says, and they have no transhistorical causes; therefore they are different from the kinds of changes implied by evolutionists.

Frankly, it is very difficult to see how Giddens has improved on what he has identified as some of the major weaknesses of evolutionism, or indeed how he has been able to avoid an evolutionary perspective at all (cf. Wright, 1983:24–34). Despite Giddens's disclaimers – which largely reflect a distorted view of what an evolutionary theory is – his theory of time–space distanciation is evolutionary. In fact, it is difficult to resist the conclusion that what Giddens has essentially done is invent a novel and pretentious language to redescribe processes long familiar to many social evolutionists.

6 This is a good point at which to stress that, contrary to what many historical sociologists apparently believe, there is no inherent incompatibility between so-called historical sociology and an evolutionary perspective. (Historical sociologists often see the difference as involving a focus on concrete historical situations or events versus a focus on ahistorical abstraction using some sort of comparative methodology.) Indeed, they are overlapping and mutually reinforcing at the very least and, as we have seen in the case of Wallerstein (note 3), sometimes one and the same thing. As additional examples, consider two major works in historical sociology, Barrington Moore's *Social Origins of Dictatorship and Democracy* (1966) and Perry Anderson's famous pair of books, *Passages from Antiquity to Feudalism* (1974a) and *Lineages of the Absolutist State* (1974b). These works can be interpreted as being, at the very least, good examples of a kind of Stewardian multilinear evolutionism. They may even implicitly contain a more general commitment to an evolutionary perspective (see, for Moore, D. Smith [1984:313]; and, for Anderson, Fulbrook and Skocpol [1984:197-202]). Thus it is incorrect (or at least an exaggeration) to say that an evolutionary analysis does not involve careful study of concrete historical cases.

# 10

# Toward a Comprehensive Theory of Sociocultural Evolution

A principal aim of this book has been to expose the considerable mythology that exists in regard to social evolutionism and in consequence to show that certain versions of evolutionary theory are intellectually defensible. There are certain types of evolutionism that should be abandoned, as well as dubious elements within some of the more acceptable evolutionary theories, but world history can still be – indeed, should be – understood in evolutionary terms.

But, as the expression goes, the proof of the pudding is in the eating. If an evolutionary interpretation of world history is defensible, then the reader has every right to expect me to develop such an interpretation in detail and to set forth the empirical evidence needed for such a defense. Such an undertaking, however, cannot be adequately carried out in the space allotted here; another volume will be required. Nevertheless, I can try to sketch the general outlines of such an interpretation and indicate the kinds of social phenomena that it most critically needs to be able to explain.

A formalized, propositional theory of sociocultural evolution adequate as a general theoretical guide to world history should:

1 recognize general directional trends in world history, while at the same time acknowledging the importance of many forms of historical uniqueness and divergence;
2 eschew any sort of developmentalist explanatory principle, i.e., refuse to explain directional trends in world history as the result of some sort of unfolding of a predetermined pattern from beginning to end; a good evolutionary theory is antidevelopmentalist and antiteleological;
3 adopt a multidimensional materialist conception of explanation emphasizing the causal priority of demographic, ecological, technological, and economic factors (while at the same time allowing for a certain amount of "superstructural feedback"); moreover, it would explicitly recognize that which of these factors (or which

combination of factors) is most causally significant varies from one historical period and type of social transformation to another;

4 start with the assumption that evolutionary events are adaptations, while at the same time recognizing that these adaptations may not lead to any absolute improvement in adaptedness (and in fact may be associated with decreases in overall absolute adaptedness); it therefore eschews any identification of evolutionary transformation with social progress;

5 make the individual, rather than some abstract social system, the unit of adaptation and thus assume that evolutionary events are somehow rooted in the cost–benefit calculations of individuals caught up in particular circumstances;

6 see evolutionary events as the product of human agency, while recognizing that much of what happens in these events is different from, or even contradictory to, human intentions; in other words, a good evolutionary theory takes seriously Giddens's notion of the duality of structure in social life;

7 eschew any strict endogenism with respect to the "location" of evolutionary events; sociocultural evolution occurs not only within societies, but also within whole networks or "world-systems" of societies, and it is often impossible to understand evolution within a single society without situating that society within its larger "world-systemic" context; this is especially true in the modern capitalist world, but it is also true to a considerable extent in many precapitalist social systems;

8 assume that both "gradualist" and "punctuationalist" forms of change characterize the social evolutionary record; the pace of change varies from one historical situation to another, and is a matter for empirical study;

9 eschew any overly close identification of sociocultural evolution with biological evolution; while the two forms of evolution have much in common, and thus while social evolutionists can learn from biological evolutionists, theories of social evolution must be formulated and evaluated largely on their own terms.

In my *Macrosociology: An Introduction to Human Societies* (1988), I have developed a rudimentary version of the above and applied it to many types of historical transformation in world history: the evolution of subsistence technologies, modes of political economy and class stratification, ethnic stratification, gender stratification, family and kinship, educational systems, religion, and science. This book therefore serves as a sort of preliminary effort to show the fruitfulness of one particular version of evolutionism. Yet this is nothing more than a bare beginning. *Macrosociology* is mainly a textbook for undergraduates and thus cannot be conceived as providing any sort of real empirical test of an evolutionary theory. It is far too sketchy and its empirical analyses are designed largely for illustrative rather than evaluative purposes. It will take another very different volume to do the job properly.

What would such a volume address? To my mind, there have been three fundamental evolutionary transformations in human history, and a good theory of sociocultural evolution would have to apply well to them all. First there is the Neolithic Revolution, which archaeologists now tell us occurred independently in at least five major regions of the world: the Middle East, China, Southeast Asia, Mesoamerica, and Peru. This is one of the great instances of parallel evolution in world history, and explaining why it occurred independently in several places at much the same time (beginning about 10,000 years ago in the Old World), and after several million years during which humans subsisted by hunting and gathering, is obviously a great challenge for an evolutionary theory. The dominant explanation today focuses on the role of population pressure. The most famous version of such an explanation is that of Mark Cohen (1977), but there are other theories that give population pressure a strong role (cf. Binford, 1968; Flannery, 1973; Harner, 1970; Harris, 1977). However, such an interpretation has not gone unchallenged (cf. Cowgill, 1975; Bronson, 1972; B. White, 1982). I believe a population pressure argument can be defended, but this requires a detailed explication of the logic of such an argument (which requires a certain acquaintance with demographic archaeology) and an identification of the flaws in the objections of the critics.

The second great historical transformation in world history is the rise of civilization and the state, another great instance of parallel evolution that began in the Old World roughly 5,000 to 6,000 years ago. It is now generally understood that civilization and the state arose independently in at least six regions of the world, and these regions are largely the same ones that underwent the transition to agriculture several thousand years earlier: Egypt, Mesopotamia, China, India, Mesoamerica, and Peru. At the present time there is enormous debate about how to explain this great transition. The most important theories are Service's (1975) functionalist argument, Fried's (1967) Marxist interpretation, and Carneiro's (1970, 1987) circumscription theory, but there are others (cf. Claessen and Skalnik, 1978; Claessen, van de Velde, and Smith, 1985), and the whole issue has been muddied by a strong tendency to consider Wittfogel's (1957) famous hydraulic theory a theory of the origin of the state (rather than a theory of the origin of a particular type of state). So there is a great deal of work to be done in order to articulate and defend a materialist interpretation of the transition to civilization and the state.

The third great historical transformation is what Marxists call "the transition from feudalism to capitalism." There are two problems here. First there is the problem of explaining the transition itself, a problem on which a great deal of work has been done in recent years (without, however, any significant theoretical consensus being produced). Materialist theories of the transition come in several versions and emphasize class struggle (Dobb, 1963), the revival of trade (Sweezy, 1976[1950]), demographic and ecological crisis (Postan, 1972; Wilkinson, 1973; North and Thomas, 1973; P. Anderson, 1974a; Le Roy Ladurie, 1974; Harris, 1977), or a combination of these (Wallerstein, 1974). Weber's (1958[1905]) Protestant ethic thesis is still very much with us, and in recent years we have seen the emergence of contrasting neo-Weberian arguments emphasizing eclectic combinations of politics, bureaucracy, Christianity, and "rationality" (Collins, 1980; Chirot, 1985; Hall, 1985; Mann, 1986). But this list is hardly exhaustive (cf. Holton, 1985), and that should give some idea of the size of the task of sorting these theories out. I believe a materialist explanation that stresses the interaction of class struggle and the ecological crisis of the feudal mode of production is the most workable, but so far I have only articulated and defended this in the sketchiest way (cf. Sanderson, 1988:129–33; a more elaborate treatment that also implicates the role of the revival of long-distance trade is found in Sanderson, in press). A much more detailed and convincing defense remains to be erected.[1]

In addition to the transition problem, there is the whole problem of the evolution of the capitalist world-system itself. Wallerstein is still in the process of completing his detailed historical study of the evolution of this system from 1450 to the present (three volumes having appeared to date [Wallerstein, 1974, 1980, 1989], bringing us up to the 1840s). It is inconceivable that a single volume could attempt to perform anything like an adequate test of this model for the roughly five hundred years of its alleged applicability. But more limited tests might be attempted. One might, for example, take a few core, peripheral, and semiperipheral societies and trace the historical changes in their world-system position over a certain period of time (say 50–100 years). Or one might compare better-off underdeveloped countries (say Latin American semiperipheral countries like Brazil or Mexico) to some of the poorest of the underdeveloped countries (say some of the truly peripheral societies of Africa). This might also afford an opportunity to look at how the interaction of world-system variables and internal societal characteristics produces particular outcomes. For example, Lenski and Nolan (1984) have argued that the greater economic development of contemporary Latin America is rooted primarily in historically greater technological advance – that the Latin American countries started their developmental efforts on an agrarian base whereas contemporary African nations have been erected principally on a horticultural technology. One need not endorse this particular point to realize that many internal material conditions are doubtless at work in influencing the specificities of economic development in any particular nation within the world-system.

The enthusiasm for Wallerstein's world-system model has led some scholars to take the bold step of attempting to apply it to precapitalist societies. Thus the idea has arisen that there are "precapitalist world-systems" analogous to the capitalist world-system (Schneider, 1977; Ekholm, 1980, 1981; Ekholm and Friedman, 1982; Rowlands, Larsen, and

Kristiansen, 1987; Abu-Lughod, 1988, 1989; Chase-Dunn, in press). So far little work has been devoted to considering the evolutionary dynamics of these systems (an important exception is Chase-Dunn, 1988), but this may well be a very important matter for further study. Wallerstein has theorized a particular kind of evolutionary trajectory to the capitalist world-economy that he believes derives from the basic accumulationist logic of the system. It seems clear that he conceives this trajectory to be unique to capitalism, and thus it appears sensible to say that there has been a major "evolutionary rupture" in world history since the sixteenth century. If there were precapitalist world-systems, what kind of "evolutionary logic" did they contain? Or perhaps there were several different kinds of precapitalist world-systems, as Chase-Dunn (in press) has recently suggested. Then the problem becomes the more complicated one of teasing out what may be several precapitalist "evolutionary logics" (cf. Sanderson, in press).

All of this is highly provisional and rather speculative, but it seems especially important in light of what has long been a knotty problem for social evolutionism: the "stagnation" in the era of world history dominated by agrarian civilizations (approximately 5000 BP to AD 1500). Of course the term stagnation here is relative; a good deal of change went on during this time, but there seems to have been no real movement to a qualitatively new stage of socioeconomic life. That was not to occur until the rise of capitalism. What explains this stagnation? Lenski (1970) and Rueschemeyer (1986) have attributed it to the lack of interest in (or actual antagonism to) technological change on the part of ruling classes, who already had well-developed mechanisms for the extraction of huge quantities of wealth. This seems to explain much, but are there other important factors at work as well, especially factors that relate to precapitalist core-periphery hierarchies? At this writing it is not at all clear what the answer is, but the problem certainly is an important one demanding further consideration.

There are, of course, many more phenomena to which a coherent evolutionary theory should apply. I have limited myself here to some of the most important transformations in the areas of subsistence technology and political economy because they have been of crucial concern to historically minded social scientists, and also because they present a formidable challenge in their own right. Should this challenge be met, new ones can always be defined.

### NOTE

1 Another dimension of the feudalism-to-capitalism transition problem involves the case of Japan. The European transition is usually regarded as a unique occurrence, but Perry Anderson (1974b) has suggested some interesting parallels between Japan and Western Europe. He regards both civilizations as having passed through several

centuries of a feudal epoch, and he seems to be suggesting a certain "evolutionary logic" within feudalism for it to turn toward capitalism. Anderson's views on this matter are highly controversial, but I suspect that a more detailed comparative analysis of Western Europe and Japan might bear considerable fruit (this point is elaborated in Sanderson, in press).

# References

Abu-Lughod, Janet. 1988. "The shape of the world system in the thirteenth century." *Studies in Comparative International Development* 22(4):3–24.
——. 1989. *Before European Hegemony: The World-System AD 1250–1350*. New York: Oxford University Press.
Adams, Robert McC. 1966. *The Evolution of Urban Society: Early Mesopotamia and Prehispanic Mexico*. Chicago: Aldine.
Alexander, Jeffrey C. 1983. *Theoretical Logic in Sociology, Volume 4. The Modern Reconstruction of Classical Thought: Talcott Parsons*. Berkeley: University of California Press.
Alexander, Richard D. 1975. "The search for a general theory of behavior." *Behavioral Science* 20:77–100.
Anderson, Perry. 1974a. *Passages from Antiquity to Feudalism*. London: New Left Books.
——. 1974b. *Lineages of the Absolutist State*. London: New Left Books.
Appelbaum, Richard P. 1970. *Theories of Social Change*. Chicago: Markham.
Ayala, Francisco J. 1974. "The concept of biological progress." In Francisco José Ayala and Theodosius Dobzhansky (eds), *Studies in the Philosophy of Biology*. Berkeley: University of California Press.
Barnes, Harry Elmer. 1960. "Foreword: my personal friendship for Leslie White." In Gertrude E. Dole and Robert L. Carneiro (eds), *Essays in the Science of Culture in Honor of Leslie A. White*. New York: Crowell.
Bell, Daniel. 1973. *The Coming of Post-Industrial Society*. New York: Basic Books.
Bellah, Robert N. 1964. "Religious evolution." *American Sociological Review* 29:358–74.
Binford, Lewis R. 1968. "Post-Pleistocene adaptations." In S. R. Binford and L. R. Binford (eds), *New Perspectives in Archaeology*. Chicago: Aldine.
Blute, Marion. 1987. "Biologists on sociocultural evolution: a critical analysis." *Sociological Theory* 5:185–93.

Boas, Franz. 1932. "The aims of anthropological research." *Science* 76:605–13.

——. 1940a. "The limitations of the comparative method of anthropology." In Franz Boas, *Race, Language, and Culture.* New York: Macmillan. (Originally published 1896.)

——. 1940b. "The methods of ethnology." In Franz Boas, *Race, Language, and Culture.* New York: Macmillan. (Originally published 1920.)

——. 1940c. "The aims of anthropological research." In Franz Boas, *Race, Language, and Culture.* New York: Macmillan. (Originally published 1932.)

Boserup, Ester. 1965. *The Conditions of Agricultural Growth.* Chicago: Aldine.

Boyd, Robert, and Peter J. Richerson. 1985. *Culture and the Evolutionary Process.* Chicago: University of Chicago Press.

Bronson, Bennett. 1972. "Farm labor and the evolution of food production." In Brian Spooner (ed.), *Population Growth: Anthropological Implications.* Cambridge, Mass.: MIT Press.

Burrow, J. W. 1966. *Evolution and Society: A Study in Victorian Social Theory.* Cambridge: Cambridge University Press.

Callinicos, Alex. 1985. "Anthony Giddens: a contemporary critique." *Theory and Society* 14:133–66.

Campbell, Donald T. 1965. "Variation and selective retention in socio-cultural evolution." In Herbert R. Barringer, George I. Blanksten and Raymond W. Mack (eds), *Social Change in Developing Areas: A Reinterpretation of Evolutionary Theory.* Cambridge, Mass.: Schenkman.

Carneiro, Robert L. 1962. "Scale analysis as an instrument for the study of cultural evolution." *Southwestern Journal of Anthropology* 18:149–69.

——. 1967. "Editor's introduction." In Herbert Spencer, *The Evolution of Society.* Edited by Robert L. Carneiro. Chicago: University of Chicago Press.

——. 1968. "Ascertaining, testing, and interpreting sequences of cultural development." *Southwestern Journal of Anthropology* 24:354–74.

——. 1970. "A theory of the origin of the state." *Science* 169:733–8.

——. 1972. "The devolution of evolution." *Social Biology* 19:248–58.

——. 1973a. "Classical evolution." In Raoul Naroll and Frada Naroll (eds), *Main Currents in Cultural Anthropology.* Englewood Cliffs, NJ: Prentice-Hall.

——. 1973b. "The four faces of evolution." In John J. Honigmann (ed.), *Handbook of Social and Cultural Anthropology.* Chicago: Rand McNally.

——. 1973c. "Scale analysis, evolutionary sequences, and the rating of cultures." In Raoul Naroll and Ronald Cohen (eds), *Handbook of Method in Cultural Anthropology.* New York: Columbia University Press.

——. 1974. "A reappraisal of the roles of technology and organization in the origin of civilization." *American Antiquity* 39:179–86.

——. 1981a. "The chiefdom: precursor of the state." In Grant D. Jones and

Robert R. Kautz (eds), *The Transition to Statehood in the New World*. New York: Cambridge University Press.

———. 1981b. "Herbert Spencer as an anthropologist." *The Journal of Libertarian Studies* 5:153–210.

———. 1982. "Successive reequilibrations as the mechanism of cultural evolution." In William C. Schieve and Peter M. Allen (eds), *Self-Organization and Dissipative Structures*. Austin: University of Texas Press.

———. 1985. "The role of natural selection in the evolution of culture." Unpublished manuscript. New York: American Museum of Natural History.

———. 1987. "Further reflections on resource concentration and its role in the rise of the state." In Linda Manzanilla (ed.), *Studies in the Neolithic and Urban Revolutions*. Oxford: British Archaeological Reports, International Series, No. 349.

Cavalli-Sforza, L. L., and M. W. Feldman. 1981. *Cultural Transmission and Evolution: A Quantitative Approach*. Princeton: Princeton University Press.

Charlesworth, Brian, Russell Lande, and Montgomery Slatkin. 1982. "A neo-Darwinian commentary on macroevolution." *Evolution* 36:474–98.

Chase-Dunn, Christopher. 1988. "Comparing world-systems: toward a theory of semiperipheral development." *Comparative Civilizations Review* 19:29–66.

———. In press. *Rise and Demise: The Transformation of World-Systems*. Boulder, Colo.: Westview Press.

Childe, V. Gordon. 1925. *The Dawn of European Civilization*. London: Kegan Paul.

———. 1936. *Man Makes Himself*. London: Watts & Co.

———. 1951. *Social Evolution*. London: Watts & Co.

———. 1954. *What Happened in History*. Harmondsworth: Penguin Books. (First edition 1942.)

Chirot, Daniel. 1985. "The rise of the West." *American Sociological Review* 50:181–95.

Claessen, Henri J. M., and Peter Skalnik (eds). 1978. *The Early State*. The Hague: Mouton.

Claessen, Henri J. M., Pieter van de Velde, and M. Estellie Smith (eds). 1985. *Development and Decline: The Evolution of Sociopolitical Organization*. South Hadley, Mass.: Bergin & Garvey.

Clark, Grahame. 1976. "Prehistory since Childe." *Institute of Archaeology Bulletin* 13:1–21.

Cohen, G. A. 1978. *Karl Marx's Theory of History: A Defence*. Princeton: Princeton University Press.

Cohen, Mark Nathan. 1977. *The Food Crisis in Prehistory*. New Haven: Yale University Press.

Coleman, James S. 1986. "Social theory, social research, and a theory of action." *American Journal of Sociology* 91:1309–35.

Collins, Randall. 1979. *The Credential Society: An Historical Sociology of Education and Stratification.* New York: Academic Press.

——. 1980. "Weber's last theory of capitalism: a systematization." *American Sociological Review* 45:925–42.

——. 1986. *Weberian Sociological Theory.* New York: Cambridge University Press.

——. 1988. *Theoretical Sociology.* San Diego: Harcourt Brace Jovanovich.

Cowgill, George L. 1975. "On causes and consequences of ancient and modern population changes." *American Anthropologist* 77:505–25.

Darwin, Charles. 1964. *On the Origin of Species.* A Facsimile of the First Edition. Introduction by Ernst Mayr. Cambridge: Harvard University Press. (Originally published 1859.)

Dawkins, Richard. 1976. *The Selfish Gene.* New York:. Oxford University Press.

Dobb, Maurice. 1963. *Studies in the Development of Capitalism.* Revised edition. New York: International Publishers.

Dole, Gertrude E. 1973. "Foundations of contemporary evolutionism." In Raoul Naroll and Frada Naroll (eds), *Main Currents in Cultural Anthropology.* Englewood Cliffs, NJ: Prentice–Hall

Dole, Gertrude E., and Robert L. Carneiro (eds). 1960. *Essays in the Science of Culture in Honor of Leslie A. White.* New York: Crowell.

Durkheim, Emile. 1933. *The Division of Labor in Society.* Glencoe, Ill.: Free Press. (Originally published 1893.)

Eisenstadt, S. N. 1963. *The Political Systems of Empires.* New York: Free Press.

——. 1964. "Social change, differentiation and evolution." *American Sociological Review* 29:375–86.

——. 1966. *Modernization: Protest and Change.* Englewood Cliffs, NJ: Prentice–Hall.

——. 1973. *Tradition, Change, and Modernity.* New York: Wiley.

—— (ed.). 1968. *The Protestant Ethic and Modernization.* New York: Basic Books.

Ekholm, Kajsa. 1980. "On the limitations of civilization: the structure and dynamics of global systems." *Dialectical Anthropology* 5:155–66.

——. 1981. "On the structure and dynamics of global systems." In J. S. Kahn and J. R. Llobera (eds), *The Anthropology of Precapitalist Societies.* London: Macmillan.

——, and Jonathan Friedman. 1982. " 'Capital' imperialism and exploitation in ancient world-systems." *Review* 4:87–109.

Eldredge, Niles, and Stephen Jay Gould. 1972. "Punctuated equilibria: an alternative to phyletic gradualism." In Thomas J. M. Schopf (ed.), *Models in Paleobiology.* San Francisco: Freeman, Cooper.

Elster, Jon. 1985. *Making Sense of Marx*. Cambridge: Cambridge University Press.

Engels, Frederick. 1935. *Ludwig Feuerbach and the Outcome of Classical German Philosophy*. New York: International Publishers. (Originally published 1888.)

———. 1939. *Herr Eugen Duhring's Revolution in Science (Anti-Duhring)*. Third edition. New York: International Publishers. (Originally published 1894; first edition 1878.)

———. 1970. *The Origin of the Family, Private Property and the State*. New York: International Publishers. (Originally published 1884.)

Flannery, Kent V. 1973. "The origins of agriculture." *Annual Review of Anthropology* 2:271–310.

Freeman, Derek. 1974. "The evolutionary theories of Charles Darwin and Herbert Spencer." *Current Anthropology* 15:211–37.

Fried, Morton H. 1967. *The Evolution of Political Society*. New York: Random House.

Friedman, Jonathan. 1974. "Marxism, structuralism and vulgar materialism." *Man* 9:444–69.

———. 1982. "Catastrophe and continuity in social evolution." In Colin Renfrew, Michael J. Rowlands, and Barbara Abbott Segraves (eds), *Theory and Explanation in Archaeology*. New York: Academic Press.

Fulbrook, Mary, and Theda Skocpol. 1984. "Destined pathways: the historical sociology of Perry Anderson." In Theda Skocpol (ed.), *Vision and Method in Historical Sociology*. New York: Cambridge University Press.

Futuyma, Douglas J. 1986. *Evolutionary Biology*. Second edition. Sunderland, Mass.: Sinauer.

Gathercole, Peter. 1971. "Patterns in prehistory: an examination of the later thinking of V. Gordon Childe." *World Archaeology* 3:225–32.

Giddens, Anthony. 1981. *A Contemporary Critique of Historical Materialism*. Berkeley: University of California Press.

———. 1984. *The Constitution of Society*. Berkeley: University of California Press.

Godelier, Maurice. 1972. *Rationality and Irrationality in Economics*. New York: Monthly Review Press.

———. 1977. *Perspectives in Marxist Anthropology*. Cambridge: Cambridge University Press.

Goldenweiser, Alexander. 1937. *Anthropology*. New York: F. S. Crofts.

Goldschmidt, Walter. 1959. *Man's Way: A Preface to the Understanding of Human Society*. New York: Holt.

Goldstein, Leon J. 1967. "Theory in anthropology: developmental or causal?" In Llewellyn Gross (ed.), *Sociological Theory: Inquiries and Paradigms*. New York: Harper & Row.

Gould, Stephen Jay. 1977. *Ever Since Darwin*. New York: Norton.

——. 1982. "Darwinism and the expansion of evolutionary theory." *Science* 216:380–7.

——. 1988. "On replacing the idea of progress with an operational notion of directionality." In Matthew H. Nitecki (ed.), *Evolutionary Progress*. Chicago: University of Chicago Press.

——, and Niles Eldredge. 1977. "Punctuated equilibria: the tempo and mode of evolution reconsidered." *Paleobiology* 3:115–51.

Gould, Stephen Jay, and Richard C. Lewontin. 1984. "The spandrels of San Marco and the Panglossian paradigm: a critique of the adaptationist programme." In Elliott Sober (ed.), *Conceptual Issues in Evolutionary Biology*. Cambridge, Mass.: MIT Press.

Graber, Robert B., and Paul B. Roscoe. 1988. "Introduction: circumscription and the evolution of society." *American Behavioral Scientist* 31:405–15.

Granovetter, Mark. 1979. "The idea of 'advancement' in theories of social evolution and development." *American Journal of Sociology* 85:489–515.

Habermas, Jürgen. 1979. *Communication and the Evolution of Society*. Translated by Thomas McCarthy. Boston: Beacon Press.

——. 1984. *The Theory of Communicative Action*. Volume 1. Translated by Thomas McCarthy. Boston: Beacon Press.

Haines, Valerie A. 1987. "Biology and social theory: Parsons's evolutionary theme." *Sociology* 21:19–39.

——. 1988. "Is Spencer's theory an evolutionary theory?" *American Journal of Sociology* 93:1200–1223.

Hall, John A. 1985. *Powers and Liberties: The Causes and Consequences of the Rise of the West*. Berkeley: University of California Press.

Hamilton, William D. 1964. "The genetical evolution of social behavior." *Journal of Theoretical Biology* 7:1–52.

Hallpike, C. R. 1986. *The Principles of Social Evolution*. Oxford: Clarendon Press.

Harner, Michael J. 1970. "Population pressure and the social evolution of agriculturalists." *Southwestern Journal of Anthropology* 26:67–86.

Harris, Marvin. 1968. *The Rise of Anthropological Theory*. New York: Crowell.

——. 1974. *Cows, Pigs, Wars, and Witches: The Riddles of Culture*. New York: Random House.

——. 1977. *Cannibals and Kings: The Origins of Cultures*. New York: Random House.

——. 1979. *Cultural Materialism: The Struggle for a Science of Culture*. New York: Random House.

——. 1981. *America Now: The Anthropology of a Changing Culture*. New York: Simon and Schuster.

——. 1988. *Culture, People, Nature: An Introduction to General Anthropology*. Fifth edition. New York: Harper & Row.

Hegel, Georg Wilhelm Friedrich. 1953. *Reason in History: A General Introduction to the Philosophy of History*. Translated with an introduction by Robert S. Hartman. Indianapolis: Bobbs–Merrill (Library of Liberal Arts). (Originally published 1837.)

———. 1956. *The Philosophy of History*. Translated by J. Sibree. New York: Dover. (Originally published 1899.)

Heise, David, Gerhard Lenski, and John Wardwell. 1976. "Further notes on technology and the moral order." *Social Forces* 55:316–37.

Heyer, Paul. 1982. *Nature, Human Nature, and Society: Marx, Darwin, Biology, and the Human Sciences*. Westport, Conn: Greenwood Press.

Hirst, Paul Q. 1976. *Social Evolution and Sociological Categories*. London: Allen & Unwin.

Hobhouse, L. T., G. C. Wheeler, and M. Ginsberg. 1965. *The Material Culture and Social Institutions of the Simpler Peoples*. London: Routledge & Kegan Paul. (Originally published 1915.)

Hobsbawm, E. J. 1964. "Introduction." In Karl Marx, *Pre-Capitalist Economic Formations*. New York: International Publishers.

Holton, Robert J. 1985. *The Transition from Feudalism to Capitalism*. New York: St Martin's Press.

Hoselitz, Bert F. 1960. *Sociological Aspects of Economic Growth*. New York: Free Press.

Hull, David L. 1988. "Progress in ideas of progress." In Matthew H. Nitecki (ed.), *Evolutionary Progress*. Chicago: University of Chicago Press.

Huxley, Julian. 1953. *Evolution in Action*. New York: Harper & Bros.

———. 1962. "Higher and lower organisation in evolution." *Journal of the Royal College of Surgeons of Edinburgh* 7:163–79.

Ingold, Tim. 1986. *Evolution and Social Life*. Cambridge: Cambridge University Press.

Johnson, Allen W., and Timothy Earle. 1987. *The Evolution of Human Societies: From Foraging Group to Agrarian State*. Stanford: Stanford University Press.

Kaplan, David, and Robert A. Manners. 1972. *Culture Theory*. Englewood Cliffs, NJ: Prentice–Hall.

Katz, S. H., and J. Schall. 1979. "Fava bean consumption and biocultural evolution." *Medical Anthropology* 3:459–76.

Keller, Albert Galloway. 1915. *Societal Evolution*. New York: Macmillan.

Kohlberg, Lawrence. 1981. *The Philosophy of Moral Development*. New York: Harper & Row.

Krader, Lawrence. 1977. "Still more on Marx, Engels, and Morgan." *Current Anthropology* 18:333–5.

Kuhn, Thomas S. 1962. *The Structure of Scientific Revolutions*. Chicago: University of Chicago Press.

Langton, John. 1979. "Darwinism and the behavioral theory of sociocultural evolution: an analysis." *American Journal of Sociology* 85:288–309.

Laudan, Larry. 1977. *Progress and Its Problems: Towards a Theory of Scientific Growth.* Berkeley: University of California Press.

Leacock, Eleanor Burke. 1963. "Editor's introduction." In Lewis Henry Morgan, *Ancient Society.* Gloucester, Mass.: Peter Smith.

Lenski, Gerhard. 1966. *Power and Privilege: A Theory of Social Stratification.* New York: McGraw-Hill.

——. 1970. *Human Societies: A Macrolevel Introduction to Sociology.* New York: McGraw-Hill.

——. 1972. "Comment on Muller's review." *Contemporary Sociology* 1:306.

——. 1976. "History and social change." *American Journal of Sociology* 82:548–64.

——, and Jean Lenski. 1982. *Human Societies: An Introduction to Macrosociology.* Fourth edition. New York: McGraw-Hill.

——, 1987. *Human Societies: An Introduction to Macrosociology.* Fifth edition. New York: McGraw-Hill.

Lenski, Gerhard, and Patrick D. Nolan. 1984. "Trajectories of development: a test of ecological–evolutionary theory." *Social Forces* 63:1–23.

Le Roy Ladurie, Emmanuel. 1974. *The Peasants of Languedoc.* Champaign: University of Illinois Press.

Levins, Richard, and Richard C. Lewontin. 1985. *The Dialectical Biologist.* Cambridge: Harvard University Press.

Lévy-Bruhl, Lucien. 1923. *Primitive Mentality.* Translated by Lilian A. Clare. London: George Allen & Unwin.

Lewontin, Richard C. 1984. "Adaptation." In Elliott Sober (ed.), *Conceptual Issues in Evolutionary Biology.* Cambridge, Mass.: MIT Press.

Lloyd, Christopher. 1986. *Explanation in Social History.* Oxford: Basil Blackwell.

Lowie, Robert H. 1937. *The History of Ethnological Theory.* New York: Holt, Rinehart and Winston.

Luhmann, Niklas. 1982. *The Differentiation of Society.* Translated by Stephen Holmes and Charles Larmore. New York: Columbia University Press.

Lumsden, Charles J., and Edward O. Wilson. 1981. *Genes, Mind, and Culture: The Coevolutionary Process.* Cambridge: Harvard University Press.

Mandelbaum, Maurice. 1971. *History, Man, and Reason: A Study in Nineteenth-Century Thought.* Baltimore: Johns Hopkins University Press.

Mann, Michael. 1986. *The Sources of Social Power, Volume 1: A History of Power from the Beginning to AD 1760.* Cambridge: Cambridge University Press.

Marx, Karl. 1972. *The Ethnological Notebooks of Karl Marx.* Edited by Lawrence Krader. Assen: Van Gorcum. (Originally written 1879–82.)

——. 1973. *Grundrisse: Foundations of the Critique of Political Economy.*

Translated by Martin Nicolaus. New York: Random House (Vintage). (Originally written 1857–8.)

——. 1978. "The eighteenth brumaire of Louis Bonaparte." In Robert C. Tucker (ed.), *The Marx–Engels Reader*. Second edition. New York: Norton. (Originally published 1852.)

——. 1979. "Letter to Engels." In Saul K. Padover (ed.), *The Letters of Karl Marx*. Englewood Cliffs, NJ: Prentice-Hall. (Originally written June 18, 1862.)

——, and Frederick Engels. 1964. *The German Ideology*. Moscow: Progress Publishers. (Originally written 1845–6.)

Maxwell, Nicholas. 1974a. "The rationality of scientific discovery part I: the traditional rationality problem." *Philosophy of Science* 41:123–53.

——. 1974b. "The rationality of scientific discovery part II: an aim oriented theory of scientific discovery." *Philosophy of Science* 41:247–95.

Maynard Smith, John. 1988. "Evolutionary progress and levels of selection." In Matthew H. Nitecki (ed.), *Evolutionary Progress*. Chicago: University of Chicago Press.

Mayr, Ernst. 1982. *The Growth of Biological Thought*. Cambridge: Harvard University Press.

McClelland, David C. 1961. *The Achieving Society*. Princeton: Van Nostrand.

McCoy, J. Wynne. 1977. "Complexity in organic evolution." *Journal of Theoretical Biology* 68:457–8.

McNairn, Barbara. 1980. *The Method and Theory of V. Gordon Childe*. Edinburgh: Edinburgh University Press.

Miller, Richard W. 1981. "Productive forces and the forces of change: a review of Gerald A. Cohen, *Karl Marx's Theory of History: A Defense*." *Philosophical Review* 90:91–117.

——. 1984. *Analyzing Marx: Morality, Power and History*. Princeton: Princeton University Press.

Moore, Barrington Jr. 1966. *Social Origins of Dictatorship and Democracy: Lord and Peasant in the Making of the Modern World*. Boston: Beacon Press.

Morgan, Lewis Henry. 1974. *Ancient Society, or Researches in the Lines of Human Progress from Savagery through Barbarism to Civilization*. Gloucester, Mass.: Peter Smith. (Originally published 1877.)

Muller, Gert H. 1971. "Review of Gerhard Lenski, *Human Societies: A Macrolevel Introduction to Sociology*." *American Sociological Review* 36:1119–20

Murphy, Robert F., and Julian H. Steward. 1956. "Tappers and trappers: parallel processes in acculturation." *Economic Development and Culture Change* 4:335–55.

Nisbet, Robert A. 1969. *Social Change and History: Aspects of the Western Theory of Development*. New York: Oxford University Press.

Nolan, Patrick D. 1984. "External selection and adaptive change: alternative models of sociocultural evolution." In Randall Collins (ed.), *Sociological Theory 1984*. San Francisco: Jossey-Bass.

North, Douglass C., and Robert Paul Thomas. 1973. *The Rise of the Western World: A New Economic History*. New York: Cambridge University Press.

Olding, A. 1978. "A defence of evolutionary laws." *British Journal for the Philosophy of Science* 29:131–43.

Opler, Morris E. 1964. "Cause, process, and dynamics in the evolutionism of E. B. Tylor." *Southwestern Journal of Anthropology* 20:123–44.

——. 1965 "Cultural dynamics and evolutionary theory." In Herbert R. Barringer, George I. Blanksten, and Raymond W. Mack (eds), *Social Change in Developing Areas: A Reinterpretation of Evolutionary Theory*. Cambridge, Mass.: Schenkman.

Parsons, Talcott. 1937. *The Structure of Social Action*. New York: McGraw-Hill.

——. 1951. *The Social System*. New York: Free Press.

——. 1964. "Evolutionary universals in society." *American Sociological Review* 29:339–57.

——. 1966. *Societies: Evolutionary and Comparative Perspectives*. Englewood Cliffs, NJ: Prentice–Hall.

——. 1971. *The System of Modern Societies*. Englewood Cliffs, NJ: Prentice-Hall.

——, and Neil J. Smelser. 1956. *Economy and Society*. Glencoe, Ill.: Free Press.

Peace, William J. 1988. "Vere Gordon Childe and American anthropology." *Journal of Anthropological Research* 44:417–33.

Peel, J. D. Y. 1971. *Herbert Spencer: The Evolution of a Sociologist*. New York: Basic Books.

Popper, Karl R. 1957. *The Poverty of Historicism*. Boston: Beacon Press.

Postan, Michael M. 1972. *The Medieval Economy and Society*. Berkeley: University of California Press.

Provine, William B. 1988. "Progress in evolution and meaning of life." In Matthew H. Nitecki (ed.), *Evolutionary Progress*. Chicago: University of Chicago Press.

Richards, Robert J. 1988. "The moral foundations of the idea of evolutionary progress: Darwin, Spencer, and the neo-Darwinians." In Matthew H. Nitecki (ed.), *Evolutionary Progress*. Chicago: University of Chicago Press.

Rigby, S. H. 1987. *Marxism and History: A Critical Introduction*. New York: St Martin's Press.

Rowlands, Michael, Mogens Larsen, and Kristian Kristiansen (eds). 1987. *Centre and Periphery in the Ancient World*. Cambridge: Cambridge University Press.

Rueschemeyer, Dietrich. 1986. *Power and the Division of Labor.* Stanford: Stanford University Press.

Ruse, Michael. 1974. "Cultural evolution." *Theory and Decision* 5:413–40.

——. 1988. "Molecules to men: evolutionary biology and thoughts of progress." In Matthew H. Nitecki (ed.), *Evolutionary Progress.* Chicago: University of Chicago Press.

Sahlins, Marshall D. 1958. *Social Stratification in Polynesia.* Seattle: University of Washington Press.

——. 1960. "Evolution: specific and general." In Marshall D. Sahlins and Elman R. Service (eds), *Evolution and Culture.* Ann Arbor: University of Michigan Press.

——. 1963. "Poor man, rich man, big man, chief: political types in Melanesia and Polynesia." *Comparative Studies in Society and History* 5:285–303.

——. 1972. *Stone Age Economics.* Chicago: Aldine.

——. 1976. *Culture and Practical Reason.* Chicago: University of Chicago Press.

——, and Elman R. Service (eds). 1960. *Evolution and Culture.* Ann Arbor: University of Michigan Press.

Sanderson, Stephen K. 1987. "Electicism and its alternatives." In John Wilson (ed.), *Current Perspectives in Social Theory,* Volume 8. Greenwich, Conn.: JAI Press.

——. 1988. *Macrosociology: An Introduction to Human Societies.* New York: Harper & Row.

——. In press. "The evolution of societies and world-systems." In Christopher Chase-Dunn and Thomas D. Hall (eds), *Core/Periphery Relations in the Precapitalist Worlds.* Boulder, Colo.: Westview Press.

Saunders, Peter T., and Mae-Wan Ho. 1976. "On the increase in complexity in evolution." *Journal of Theoretical Biology* 63:375–84.

——. 1981. "On the increase in complexity in evolution II: the relativity of complexity and the principle of minimum increase." *Journal of Theoretical Biology* 90:515–30.

——. 1984. "The complexity of organisms." In J. W. Pollard (ed.), *Evolutionary Theory: Paths into the Future.* New York: Wiley.

Schneider, Jane. 1977. "Was there a precapitalist world-system?" *Peasant Studies* 6:20–9.

Service, Elman R. 1960. "The law of evolutionary potential." In Marshall D. Sahlins and Elman R. Service (eds), *Evolution and Culture.* Ann Arbor: University of Michigan Press.

——. 1962. *Primitive Social Organization: An Evolutionary Perspective.* New York: Random House.

——. 1971a. *Primitive Social Organization: An Evolutionary Perspective.* Second edition. New York: Random House.

——. 1971b. *Cultural Evolutionism: Theory in Practice.* New York: Holt, Rinehart and Winston.

——. 1975. *Origins of the State and Civilization: The Process of Cultural Evolution.* New York: Norton.

——. 1978 "Classical and modern theories of the origins of government." In Ronald Cohen and Elman R. Service (eds), *Origins of the State.* Philadelphia: Institute for the Study of Human Issues.

——. 1981. "The mind of Lewis H. Morgan." *Current Anthropology* 22:25–43.

Shaw, William H. 1984. "Marx and Morgan." *History and Theory* 23:215–28.

Simon, Herbert A. 1976. *Administrative Behavior.* Third edition. New York: Free Press.

Simpson, George Gaylord. 1949. *The Meaning of Evolution.* New Haven: Yale University Press.

Smelser, Neil J. 1959. *Social Change in the Industrial Revolution.* Chicago: University of Chicago Press.

——. 1968. *Essays in Sociological Explanation.* Englewood Cliffs, NJ: Prentice-Hall.

Smith, Anthony D. 1973. *The Concept of Social Change: A Critique of the Functionalist Theory of Social Change.* London: Routledge & Kegan Paul.

Smith, Dennis. 1984. "Discovering facts and values: the historical sociology of Barrington Moore." In Theda Skocpol (ed.), *Vision and Method in Historical Sociology.* New York: Cambridge University Press.

Sober, Elliott. 1984. *The Nature of Selection: Evolutionary Theory in Philosophical Focus.* Cambridge, Mass.: MIT Press.

Spencer, Herbert. 1873–1934. *Descriptive Sociology.* 15 volumes. New York: D. Appleton.

——. 1899. *The Principles of Sociology.* Volume 2. New York: D. Appleton.

——. 1900. *The Principles of Sociology.* Volume 3. New York: D. Appleton.

——. 1937. *First Principles.* Sixth edition. London: Watts & Co.

——. 1972. *Herbert Spencer on Social Evolution.* Edited by J. D. Y. Peel. Chicago: University of Chicago Press.

Stanley, Steven M. 1979. *Macroevolution: Pattern and Process.* San Francisco: Freeman.

Stebbins, G. Ledyard. 1969. *The Basis of Progressive Evolution.* Chapel Hill: University of North Carolina Press.

——. 1974. "Adaptive shifts and evolutionary novelty: a compositionist approach." In Francisco José Ayala and Theodosius Dobzhansky (eds), *Studies in the Philosophy of Biology.* Berkeley: University of California Press.

——, and Francisco J. Ayala. 1981. "Is a new evolutionary synthesis necessary?" *Science* 213:967–71.

Steward, Julian H. 1949. "Cultural causality and law: a trial formulation of the development of early civilizations." *American Anthropologist* 51:1–27.

———. 1955. *Theory of Culture Change: The Methodology of Multilinear Evolution.* Urbana: University of Illinois Press.

———. 1977. "Cultural evolution." In Julian H. Steward, *Evolution and Ecology: Essays on Social Transformation.* Edited by Jane C. Steward and Robert F. Murphy. Urbana: University of Illinois Press. (Originally published 1956.)

Sumner, William Graham, and Albert Galloway Keller. 1927. *The Science of Society.* 4 volumes. New Haven: Yale University Press.

Sweezy, Paul. 1976. "A critique." In Rodney Hilton (ed.), *The Transition from Feudalism to Capitalism.* London: New Left Books. (Originally published 1950.)

Terray, Emmanuel. 1972. *Marxism and "Primitive" Societies.* New York: Monthly Review Press.

Thomas, Nicholas. 1982. "Childe, Marxism, and archaeology." *Dialectical Anthropology* 6:245–52.

Tiger, Lionel, and Robin Fox. 1971. *The Imperial Animal.* New York: Holt, Rinehart and Winston.

Tilly, Charles. 1984. *Big Structures, Large Processes, Huge Comparisons.* New York: Russell Sage Foundation.

Toulmin, Stephen. 1972. *Human Understanding.* Volume I. Princeton: Princeton University Press.

Trigger, Bruce G. 1980. *Gordon Childe: Revolutions in Archaeology.* London: Thames & Hudson.

Trivers, Robert L. 1971. "The evolution of reciprocal altruism." *Quarterly Review of Biology* 46(4):35–57.

Tylor, Edward Burnett. 1871. *Primitive Culture: Researches into the Development of Mythology, Philosophy, Religion, Language, Art, and Custom.* 2 volumes. London: John Murray.

———. 1878. *Researches into the Early History of Mankind.* New York: Holt.

———. 1889. "On a method of investigating the development of institutions; applied to laws of marriage and descent." *Journal of the Anthropological Institute* 18:245–69.

———. 1916. *Anthropology: An Introduction to the Study of Man and Civilization.* New York: D. Appleton. (First edition 1881.)

———. 1924. *Primitive Culture: Researches into the Development of Mythology, Philosophy, Religion, Language, Art, and Custom.* Seventh edition. New York: Brentano's. (First edition 1871.)

van den Berghe, Pierre L. 1978. *Man in Society: A Biosocial View.* Second edition. New York: Elsevier.

———. 1979. *Human Family Systems: An Evolutionary View.* New York: Elsevier.

Veblen, Thorstein. 1912. *The Theory of the Leisure Class*. New York: Macmillan.

Voget, Fred W. 1975. *A History of Ethnology*. New York: Holt, Rinehart and Winston.

Wallerstein, Immanuel. 1974. *The Modern World-System: Capitalist Agriculture and the Origins of the European World-Economy in the Sixteenth Century*. New York: Academic Press.

———. 1976. "Modernization: requiescat in pace." In Lewis A. Coser and Otto N. Larsen (eds), *The Uses of Controversy in Sociology*. New York: Free Press.

———. 1979. "The present state of the debate on world inequality." In Immanuel Wallerstein, *The Capitalist World-Economy*. New York: Cambridge University Press.

———. 1980. *The Modern World-System II: Mercantilism and the Consolidation of The European World-Economy, 1600–1750*. New York: Academic Press.

———. 1983. *Historical Capitalism*. London: Verso Editions.

———. 1984a. "Patterns and prospectives of the capitalist world-economy." In Immanuel Wallerstein, *The Politics of the World-Economy*. New York: Cambridge University Press.

———. 1984b. "The quality of life in different social systems: the model and the reality." In Immanuel Wallerstein, *The Politics of the World-Economy*. New York: Cambridge University Press.

———. 1989. *The Modern World-System III: The Second Era of Great Expansion of the Capitalist World-Economy, 1730–1840s*. San Diego: Academic Press.

Weber, Max. 1958. *The Protestant Ethic and the Spirit of Capitalism*. New York: Charles Scribner's Sons. (Originally published 1905.)

Wenke, Robert J. 1980. *Patterns in Prehistory: Mankind's First Three Million Years*. New York: Oxford University Press.

White, Benjamin. 1982. "Child labour and population growth in rural Asia." *Development and Change* 13:587–610.

White, Leslie A. 1943. "Energy and the evolution of culture." *American Anthropologist* 45:335–56.

———. 1945a. "'Diffusion vs Evolution': an anti-evolutionist fallacy." *American Anthropologist* 47:339–56.

———. 1945b. "History, evolutionism, and functionalism: three types of interpretation of culture." *Southwestern Journal of Anthropology* 1:221–48.

———. 1947a. "Evolutionism in cultural anthropology: a rejoinder." *American Anthropologist* 49:400–13.

———. 1947b. "Evolutionary stages, progress, and the evaluation of cultures." *Southwestern Journal of Anthropology* 3:165–92.

———. 1948. "Lewis Henry Morgan: pioneer in the theory of social evolution." In Harry Elmer Barnes (ed.), *An Introduction to the History of Sociology.* Chicago: University of Chicago Press.

——. 1949a. "Ethnological theory." In R. W. Sellars, V. J. McGill, and Marvin Farber (eds), *Philosophy for the Future.* New York: Macmillan.

——. 1949b. *The Science of Culture.* New York: Grove Press.

——. 1959. *The Evolution of Culture.* New York: McGraw-Hill.

——. 1975. *The Concept of Cultural Systems: A Key to Understanding Tribes and Nations.* New York: Columbia University Press.

Wicken, Jeffrey S. 1987. *Evolution, Thermodynamics, and Information.* New York: Oxford University Press.

Wiley, E. O. 1988. "Entropy, evolution and progress." In Matthew H. Nitecki (ed.), *Evolutionary Progress.* Chicago: University of Chicago Press.

Wilkinson, Richard G. 1973. *Poverty and Progress: An Ecological Perspective on Economic Development.* New York: Praeger.

Williams, George C. 1966. *Adaptation and Natural Selection: A Critique of Some Current Evolutionary Thought.* Princeton: Princeton University Press.

Wilson, D. S. 1983. "The group selection controversy: history and current status." *Annual Review of Ecology and Systematics* 14:159–87.

Wilson, Edward O. 1975. *Sociobiology. The Modern Synthesis.* Cambridge: Harvard University Press.

——. 1978. *On Human Nature.* Cambridge: Harvard University Press.

Wittfogel, Karl. 1957. *Oriental Despotism.* New Haven: Yale University Press.

Wright, Erik Olin. 1983. "Giddens's critique of Marxism." *New Left Review* 138:11–35.

Wynn-Edwards, V. C. 1962. *Animal Dispersion in Relation to Social Behaviour.* Edinburgh: Oliver & Boyd.

Young, Robert M. 1969. "Malthus and the evolutionists: the common context of biological and social theory." *Past and Present* 43:109–45.

Zeitlin, Irving M. 1973. *Rethinking Sociology: A Critique of Contemporary Theory.* Englewood Cliffs, NJ: Prentice-Hall.

Zipf, George Kingsley. 1965. *Human Behavior and the Principle of Least Effort.* New York: Hafner. (Originally published 1949.)

# Index